Project Management for Information Systems

SECOND EDITION

Edited by

Don Yeates
Group Director, Train

and

James Cadle
Independent consultant in IT a

FINANCIAL TIMES
Prentice Hall

An imprint of Pearson Education

Harlow, England · London · New York · Reading, Massachusetts · San Francisco · Toronto · Don Mills, Ontario · Sydney
Tokyo · Singapore · nsterdam · Munich · Paris · Milan

Pearson Education Limited
Edinburgh Gate
Harlow
Essex CM20 2JE
England

and Associated Companies throughout the world

Visit us on the World Wide Web at:
http://www.pearsoneduc.com

_____

First published in Great Britain in 1991
Second edition 1996

© Pearson Professional Limited 1996

The right of Don Yeates and James Cadle to be identified as
authors of this work has been asserted by them in accordance
with the Copyright, Designs and Patents Act 1988.

ISBN 0 273 62019 3

British Library Cataloguing in Publication Data
A CIP catalogue record for this book can be obtained from the British Library

10 9 8 7 6
04 03 02 01 00

Printed and bound in Great Britain by Redwood Books, Trowbridge, Wiltshire

The Publishers' policy is to use paper manufactured from sustainable forests.

CONTENTS

000 618 83 79 0010

PREFACE

This completely new edition of *Project Management for Information Systems* is intended for everyone who would like to see systems projects implemented on time, within budget and to quality. While this probably means every user of a computer-based system and every member of an IS department or services company, this would be to expect a very wide readership. Specifically, then, the book will be useful to:

- *Practising systems analysts who find themselves responsible for managing systems projects.* Newcomers to this activity will find much that will be of help to them; we hope also that older hands will find some new ideas that help them to tackle the job with renewed vigour.

- *Students of information systems and project management.* Not everything can be learnt from books. Oscar Wilde said that 'experience is the name everyone gives to their mistakes', and throughout the book we have included advice based on experience learnt the hard way.

- *Part-time developers.* Many people are drawn into the development of application systems and have no need to understand all the duties of the project leader. Selected reading can, however, help you in understanding how your activities fit into the whole scheme and will, we hope lead to better project management.

You will see from the acknowledgments that everyone who has contributed to this book works for or is associated with Sema Group's Training Department. They have given freely of their hard-won project experience and distilled much of the essence of their craft.

This new edition is more comprehensive than its predecessor. Bearing in mind the project leader's duty to manage the team, the task and the individual, we have not only dealt with the team and the individual, but have included more about the task.

Inevitably, not everything can be covered in this book, but we hope readers will find that what has been included helps them to understand a little more about systems project management.

We'd like to thank Kathleen McCullagh of Sema Group, Kara Regan, John Cushion and Elizabeth Tarrant of Financial Times Management for their help in the production of the finished book.

James Cadle
Don Yeates
Covent Garden, London, 1996

ACKNOWLEDGEMENTS

This book is the work of many hands. We have been able to draw on the skills and experience of our colleagues, without whose help this book would not be in your hands now. Our long-suffering and hardworking fellow contributors, to whom we offer our grateful thanks include:

Dick Barton, an Associate Trainer for Sema Group with 12 years' experience of developing projects and project management training. He also consults in human resource management and organisation development.

Alan Paul, a project manager with over 15 years' experience of systems development and project management in the public sector, including the formulation and management of IS strategies.

Debbie Paul, a consultant and trainer in SSADM project development and a member of the Information Systems Examinations Board Certificate Board for SSADM and of the International SSADM Users Group Technical Committee. Debbie is an Associate Trainer to Sema Group.

John Koenigsberger, the Quality Manager of Sema Group's Mobile Telecommunications division, has 25 years' experience of project development management and quality in the UK and overseas. John is also a consultant to the International Management Centre at Buckingham.

David Archer, an Associate Trainer for Sema Group, is a consultant in change management, helping organisations to deal with the changes resulting from the implementation of new systems.

Jill Freinberg, a Trainer with Sema Group specialising in human resources issues, psychometrics and the changes that result from the implementation of new systems.

Chris Donaldson, a Trainer with Sema Group specialising in consulting, psychometrics and project management subjects, with over 15 years' experience in information systems and training.

Patrick Manning, Managing Director of Galileo Consulting, is a consultant specialising in the commercial aspects of project management.

Finally, **James Cadle** is an Associate Trainer with Sema Group and an independent consultant in project management with over 15 years' experience of project management in the public and private sectors; and **Don Yeates** is the Group Director responsible for training in Sema Group, formerly the Chairman of the Information Systems Examinations Board and the editor of the original edition of *Project Management for Information Systems*.

THE ISEB CERTIFICATE

The Information Systems Examinations Board's Certificate in Project Management for Information Systems is the leading qualification for project managers in the information systems industry. This book, while covering a wider range of topics, addresses all parts of the ISEB syllabus. The following information is reproduced from the syllabus by kind permission of the ISEB. The minimum number of hours for each of the eight sections of the course is indicated as guidance, on the assumption that the course is 80 hours' duration. The case study/project is expected to take some 30 per cent of the training time.

1 **Overview** (7% or 5.5 hours)   To give an introduction to the total process of project management. This includes: Strategy (business and project strategy and objectives; initial strategy for the project; technical content and decisions; business and cultural implications); Planning (the need for planning; standards; quality management; the need to record/document; aspects of project management; the management of the plan; the use of software tools); Organisation (project life cycle; project organisation and structure; roles and responsibilities; project management within programme/multi-project environment); Risk (assessment; management; business implications). (*See Chapters 2, 3, 4 and 5 in this book.*)

2 **Managing plans** (15% or 12 hours)   To provide a means to establish control and to monitor the progress of the project. This includes: Plans (types of plans; the scope of the plan; constructing a plan; tools and techniques available to construct plans; revising/updating plans; contingency; cost benefit justification); Estimating (tools available; techniques; metrics; monitoring productivity; revisions; modifications); Acceptance of the plan (presentation; approval; commitment; risk elements; problem areas); Control (monitoring techniques; impact analysis; revisions; exception planning; tolerance); Project reviews (control points; stage assessment; project closure; post-implementation reviews). (*See Chapters 6, 7 and 10 in this book.*)

3 **Managing people** (15% or 12 hours)   To enable project managers to identify, organise, motivate and schedule staff to meet the objectives and project plans within time, cost and quality constraints.   This includes: Skills (identification and profiling of skills needed: estimating and planning a project, monitoring and controlling, consultancy, perception, interpersonal, quality assurance; skills assessment; training and development of skills; negotiation); Organisation (setting up and maintaining project teams; allocating resources; team organisation and control; team building: components, leadership styles and influencing; arranging, running and managing meetings; presentations and reports); Human resource management (human relations; motivation and incentives; team management; communication in all aspects: within team, to team members and from them to team leaders, with clients; conflict management); Technical management (productivity and performance: indicators, reviews, evaluating improvements in effectiveness, understanding and acting on changing competences; scheduling and monitoring; risk management; contracted services: selection, invitation to tender, contract/permanent, fixed price, time and material, contract, legal agreements, consultants; quality assurance). (*See Chapters 18, 19, 20 and 21 in this book.*)

4 **Managing other resources** (8% or 6.5 hours)   To enable project managers to identify, plan, schedule and monitor all other resources required in the project. This includes: Resources required (identifying all non-people resources; identifying resources available; scheduling the availability and use of the resources; risk assessment; cost profile/cash flow); Additional resources (identifying additional resources; justification); Contracted-out services (selection, invitation to tender, etc; contracts, legal agreements, etc; management of contracted-out services); Resource management (monitoring plans; revising plans, etc; assessing alternatives; corrective action). (*See Chapters 8 and 17 in this book.*)

5 **Managing the development and delivery of project products** (25% or 20 hours)   To provide the means of establishing and maintaining control of the products of a project and to provide the product base lines from which change control can be exercised. This includes: Identify all products (business products: deliverables; working products: intermediates; component products: breakdowns, explosions; project products: e.g. plans; quality products: quality/audit trail); Describe/define/specify all products (purpose, use, source, destination; used on, used in, used for, used by; parent/child relationship); Agree quality attributes and criteria, all products (what product will do; how this will be tested/checked; is result pass/fail or graded? Who will do tests? Who signs-off criteria? Who accepts product(s)?); Assign all products for development (ownership; product responsibility; quality control responsibility; quality assurance responsibility); Configuration management (identification of configuration items; methods, librarian, systems; tools, packages); Control during production (monitor progress; reviews; remedial action if necessary); Control after production (quality control/assurance process; baselining after passing quality control; control of re-work; approval(s) for subsequent use/release; application of change control to completed product); Delivery of products (internal transfer: within project, during development, including Intermediates; external deliveries: user products, user manuals, Ops/maintenance products; sign-offs/acceptances). (*See Chapters 6, 9, 10 and 12 in this book.*)

6 **Managing project documentation** (5% or 4 hours)   To provide the means of recording project plans, decisions and progress. This includes: Need for documentation; Use of documentation; Procedures for updating documentation; Documentation roles and responsibilities of each team member (roles of team members – internal, external, Project Manager; Stage Manager, Configuration Management Librarian); Types of documentation (project standards and procedures; project initiation document; organisation documents; plans; progress reports; exception reports; control documents; activity checklist; daily log sheets; quality review forms; correspondence; event diary); Types of file (management files; technical files; quality files). (*See Chapter 11 in this book.*)

7 **Managing quality** (15% or 12 hours)   To provide the means to establish the quality environment and to control the project against agreed standards. This includes: Quality management systems (quality manual; quality policy; quality organisation; review of QMS; certification; quality metrics); Quality standards (external, e.g. BS 5750, ISO 9001, AQAP1, AQAP13; internal: company standards and procedures; project standards); Quality plans (responsibilities: individual, professional; deliverables; reviews); Quality assurance (exceptions; techniques; audits); Quality control (control points, responsibilities, levels). (*See Chapter 12 in this book.*)

8 **Managing change** (10% or 8 hours)   To provide the means to consider and assess proposed changes and to control approved changes. This includes: Inevitability of change (need to plan for; create and design flexibility); Configuration management (see section 5); Possible sources of change (business environment; user requirements; user plans; time requirements; costs: organisation's budget, exchange rates, pricing structures; suppliers: responses, performance, continued operation; government: policy, legislation, fiscal policy; technical: environment, new software products, new hardware, previously ruled out/now feasible); Formal framework to consider and control change (identify all possible sources as above; establish procedure to: impose a discipline, document change requests, maintain control, assess costs and time impacts, avoid post-contractual impacts); Steps in framework (need to challenge proposed change – can it be avoided? can it be minimised? can its effect be minimised?; need to challenge urgency – can the change be deferred? if so, ensure compatibility of present stage with known future; identify all to be affected by the change; assess and quantify impact of change: in scope, in its effect, hardware and software additions rendered idle, supplier, costs, benefits, scheduling; action following impact analysis); After approval (notify all affected areas of project; distribute adequate documentation/withdraw outdated documentation; monitor progress with change; assess actual as against expected impact). (*See Chapters 1, 5 and 16 in this book.*)

For further information, contact the ISEB, 7 Mansfield Mews, London W1M 9FJ.
Tel: 0171 637 2040. Fax: 0171 631 1049.

CHAPTER 1

Managing change

1.1 INTRODUCTION

All new IT systems bring a range of associated changes with them. These may be changes to business processes and procedures, new roles and responsibilities, organisational restructuring, new equipment or facilities, or new skills to learn. All of these involve people, and it is the people within any organisation who are the key to the success of any IT implementation. No matter how well-designed the new system and how well-planned the implementation, without proper consideration of the 'people issues' your project will fail. Managing change is all about dealing with the people issues, and about involving people at every stage in the project to help ensure it realises the full business benefits. Information systems are only tools to enable people to take better decisions, so getting the commitment of the people who will use the system is central to the success of your project.

Managing change means being proactive in identifying and planning for the changes that need to take place within the business to support the new system. Many post-implementation problems are caused by users not having been adequately prepared for the change – for example, a lack of training or communication, or failure to get support and commitment to the changes from key users. These problems can be avoided by planning a change programme at the start of the project and running the programme throughout the life of the project and for some time beyond it.

Organising the project so that there is a user project manager with a responsibility for managing the change can be a great help in enabling these people issues to be tackled.

Key considerations for a change programme are:

- Plan the change programme in the same way as you plan the development and implementation of the system itself – these processes are integral and not separate.

- Ensure that the change programme includes communication and training, but also considers the impact of the change on the users: the timing and methods used to implement the system should be planned to make the transition as easy as possible for the user.

- Phase the introduction of change to ensure that people are not bombarded with too many changes at once, and allow for periods of consolidation to enable people to become comfortable and confident with new responsibilities, processes or environments.

- Involve users in planning and implementing the change programme because they understand the issues in the user community: this will help to ensure that those in the business are in control of the change, and are managing it, rather than being helpless bystanders to something that is imposed on them.

This chapter explores some of these issues in more detail, and gives some practical advice on how to plan and run your change programme.

1.2 ORGANISATIONAL CHANGE

Business change is all around us and the pace is ever increasing. The time to market for new products is decreasing year on year, privatisation has brought radical change to public institutions, and increased globalisation in many sectors has brought the challenge of managing across national boundaries and cultures. Organisational change is now commonplace and given this you might be tempted to suppose that some universally applicable rules would have emerged to guide you when planning a new IT project within a changing business environment. However on closer examination the main lesson seems to be that there is not one easy prescription for managing change – there are many complex influences on the way people react to change and in any given project their behaviour isn't easy to predict. Fortunately there are some patterns that can be found buried in the mystery of organisational change.

The first thing to look for is the business context for your project – what is really driving the investment of all this time and effort in delivering new IT systems? There is further discussion about this in the next chapter, but it is enough for now to note that there are four broad reasons for organisations to invest in large-scale corporate IT development programmes:

- Business survival.
- Improved efficiency.
- Potential competitive advantage.
- External forces, such as legislative change, privatisation, merger and so on.

The business context will have a major influence on your tactics for taking people with you throughout the project lifecycle, and on how you prioritise the efforts of your project team. Let's examine each of the four different reasons.

Business survival   In this context, time is often the key success factor. To hit deadlines you may need to compromise on the specification, marginalise people who resist the change and focus on delivering the essential functionality to those users who are key to the business. Production automation systems and workflow systems often fit this category.

Improved efficiency

In some situations the increase in operational efficiency may come from the design of the system itself – through decreased processing time, for example – but these situations are rare. In most cases it is people making better management decisions based on the information provided by the systems that results in increased efficiency. In this context you have to take people with you and to be sure that they know what a *better* decision is, are able to access and interpret the data which informs that decision, and are motivated to take it. MIS systems and office systems are often the products of this sort of business context.

Competitive advantage

The key here is to encourage innovation and new ideas throughout the project lifecycle. If the way forward were clear at the start of the project then probably most of the competition would have thought of it too and so there wouldn't be much advantage in producing it. Rapid prototyping and end user solutions are tactics that often have value in this context.

External factors

Here, where the specification is not under your own control, you need to be ever mindful of the external stakeholders who have to be satisfied by what you are doing. Involvement is a key process here to ensure that all of the key players, internal and external, are taken along every step of the way. You need to avoid unhappy surprises at the implementation stage but be ready with contingency plans for when the ground rules change under you. It is not enough to comply with the letter of the law but rather to continually test that all parties have a common understanding of what is required. It is unlikely in these circumstances that firm requirements specifications will be available and it is therefore essential that users and computer people move together flexibly towards the target system. Risk profiling techniques are particularly useful tools here. Risk is covered in more detail in Chapter 13.

Once you have established the business context for your work, the next priority is to be clear about the pace and the scale of the change that is required for a successful completion of the project. Simply, this means looking at how many people are affected, how radically they have to change their attitudes and behaviours, and how long you have to bring about this change. Again the answers to these questions will point to very different tactics for managing the people side of the project. Programmes that have to deliver radical changes in short time-scales usually require changes to staffing either through hiring and firing or the acquisition of new organisations that contain the needed skills. If time-scales are longer, but the changes are still large and far reaching then you can look at fundamentally re-engineering business processes to deliver the potential of the new systems and have the time to develop existing staff to run the processes.

If the scale of change is incremental or only affects small numbers of people then tactics borrowed from the total quality management (TQM) world are often appropriate (*see* Fig 1.1). Quality circles or focus groups can both increase buy-in and also generate ideas for process improvements. They can be used

Type of change	Short-term (3–9 months)	Long-term (1 year +)
Radical	Restructuring and redeployment of staff	Business Process Re-engineering
Incremental	Process automation and refinement	TQM, innovation schemes

Fig 1.1 Time and change matrix

throughout the design and development phases and, particularly after implementation, to manage the requests for enhancements to the original functionality. However, our experience shows that it can take more than two years to set up these mechanisms, embed them into the culture and really generate returns on this basis.

Having looked at some large-scale strategic issues which you need to bear in mind when planning the project, the next section focuses on the personal issues. What does it feel like to an individual user who may be part of the target audience for your system, and what might be their reactions to the project?

1.2.1 Resistance to change

How did you feel when you last experienced a major change, for example when you moved house, changed your job or got married? Stressed? Unsure of the future? Worried about how you'll cope? Unprepared? Confident? Organised? Ready for anything? Your personal reaction to any change dictates whether you'll be receptive or resistant to it. The changes resulting from information systems projects often meet resistance because the project managers haven't anticipated the personal reactions to change they might meet from the people affected by a new system.

The Chinese ideogram for change is actually made up from two symbols – one which represents danger, the other opportunity. And that is one of the paradoxes of change – any new situation contains within it some danger, some loss, but also the potential for new opportunities. Daryl Conner and others have done work in developing questionnaires to classify people as D-type or O-type, Danger people or Opportunity people. Not surprisingly most project leaders and business managers are O-type, they have got to their current position by seizing on new opportunities. But the majority of users who are targets for a new system are probably D-type people, and they may well see threat in the change and seek to find ways of resisting it.

Resistance to change can be active or passive. If it's active, the resistance is explicit and obvious. For example, when a dairy introduced a new computer system designed to improve the way milkmen recorded their deliveries, some milkmen put diesel fuel into the milk to sabotage the project. The most obvious way some other workers express resistance to a new project is to go on strike. Passive resistance to change is harder to recognise but can have effects just as devastating on IS projects as active resistance. People involved in the project might agree to functional specifications and then argue later that the system is not what they wanted. Staff sit in meetings, agree solutions and then insist that their interpretation of the proposals was different from yours. Alternatively, they agree with proposed project plans and then sabotage them more subtly. For example, a manager in a building society agreed to provide an individual to become a trainer for a new insurance system, then changed that person four times during the project. Each time, the new person had to be trained in the skills needed to become a trainer, the training approach and the new insurance system – this had time and cost implications that affected the whole project. You can get some insight into the likely forms of resistance by conducting a change readiness assessment with your users at the start of the project.

Before you work out how to deal with resistance to change, you need to understand the pattern of ups and downs that characterises behaviour during the lifecycle of an information systems project. The change curve in Fig 1.2 shows early enthusiasm for change gradually falling off as problems surface, and then accumulating strength again as people lift themselves out of the 'dip'. The point is that, whatever the type of change brought about by your project, you will have to drive individuals and groups along this curve. In planning for this, the first thing to realise is that:

being right is not enough.

The quality of the design of the solution may affect the final level of performance but the time taken to get there and the depth of the dip in performance in the transition will depend on how well you deal with the people issues. Let's look at the phases of change in more detail.

Denial

At the start of an IS project, people may feel challenged and apprehensive about the new system, but confident they can apply current skills to a new situation. They deny the need to change.

Resistance

Then, as people gain more information about the system, they may feel a loss of self-esteem because the job is broader than they expected; a loss of confidence in their ability to perform against the demands being made. They might exhibit signs of stress, such as working longer hours and being indecisive.

Exploration

Gradually, people confront their difficulties by talking them through with colleagues or by trial and error and their self-confidence grows.

Confidence

Over time, people become more responsive, decisive and assertive. They take responsibility for and pride in the exploitation of the benefits that the system can bring.

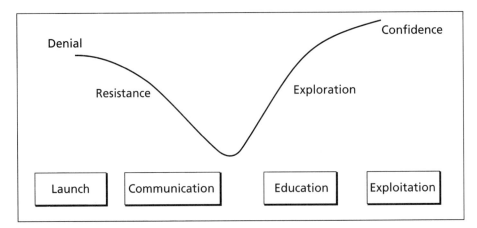

Fig 1.2   The phases of change

1.3   ORGANISATIONAL CULTURE

The impact of the change curve on your project and the tactics you can employ to drive people along it depend on the culture of the organisation in which you are working.

There is more discussion about organisational culture in later chapters, but here we'll use a model of different organisational cultures based on the work of Charles Handy and Roger Harrison, which classifies organisations according to the degree of centralisation and the degree of formality in the way things are done. This is shown in Fig 1.3.

To help to remember them they are characterised with the names of Greek Gods. You may be able to identify organisations that operate in these ways. When you run up against them you'll find the following suggestions helpful in dealing with them.

Zeus or power culture   Here, obtaining and demonstrating sponsorship is the key. Everyone looks to those with the power to supply the answers and sanction actions. Proprietor-owned businesses often fall into this category. But in larger organisations any department with a charismatic leader can develop a power

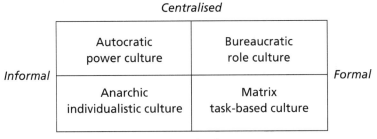

Fig 1.3   Organisational cultures (after Handy and Harrison)

culture. Unless you get the explicit backing of the people in power you may find that you get low participation at user workshops and review sessions where you want a cross-section of users to express their own opinions. You also need to be aware that, whatever formal sign-off route you have agreed, no significant products will really be approved until the person at the top has said 'yes'.

Apollo or role culture

Here the culture is formal and centralised. Everyone has a role, a job description and a formal relationship with others in related roles. Public sector organisations and large financial institutions are often bureaucratic role cultures. The watchword here is to play by the rules but also to be aware that there is probably a parallel informal set of relationships that people use to 'get around the system' and to 'get things done'. If you can identify this and tap into some key contacts you can often get access to information and opinions much more quickly than by going through the formal channels. But remember that when it comes to spending money or other decisions which need to be defensible later you need to have covered the formal systems as well.

Athena or task-based culture

Here tasks are devolved to the lowest practical level but there is still a formal framework for reporting and decision making. Organisations like this are used to forming taskforces and problem-solving teams. Modern manufacturing companies often fall into this category. In many ways it is the easiest culture in which to run a project as many of the traditional disciplines of project management such as planning and control and team responsibility are embodied in a task-based culture. The main source of difficulty here is that user staff may want to get too involved in the running of the project, to question all the internal working arrangements of the project and to be engaged throughout the lifecycle rather than just providing input or review at a specific stage.

Dionysus or individualistic culture

Here the organisation is so informal and decentralised that people often don't like to think of it as an organisation at all. In general, professional organisations often best fit this category. Lawyers may talk of their 'practice' or 'chambers' and designers talk about their 'studio'; people working in a Dionysus culture may say things like – 'we all think of ourselves as more of a family here'. In a culture such as this, everyone has a distinct voice and all opinions deserve to be aired. This type of organisation can be a very challenging place in which to run an IT project. The watchwords are to use the formal mechanisms, such as the baselining of specifications and plans, sparingly. But when you do, make a big show of it. Make it very clear to all concerned why you, as the project manager, need to go through this process in order to do your job properly, and try to win their respect as a fellow professional. Also spell out the consequences of going back on a decision once agreed and highlight any forthcoming decision dates well in advance.

One final word of warning when it comes to organisational cultures. You need to recognise that the culture of an IT department does not always reflect the culture of the rest of the organisation. Working mainly within the confines of the IT department can lead you to misleading assumptions about the wider culture. Get out and spend some time sitting and working in user departments. As an effective project manager you need to be looking in both directions and managing to bridge the cultures to deliver effective systems.

1.4 THE PROJECT MANAGER AND CHANGE

Most information systems are a tool for people to use to support them in their job – therefore to successfully implement the change you have to ensure that people are using the system effectively and efficiently. Just because the system is available doesn't mean that people will use it. Therefore, a change programme that combines training, awareness, communication and business process design activities is crucial to the success of an information systems project. Armed with a knowledge of the business context for the project and an understanding of the organisational culture you are working within, you can design and manage a change programme which takes the users with you and ensures the project as a whole delivers what the business needs.

There are four overlapping stages in a such change programme:

● Launching the project.
● Winning hearts and minds.
● Skilling the end-users.
● After go-live.

1.5 LAUNCHING THE PROJECT

As soon as the project is launched, find a sponsor from the business who will act as the change manager; they will need to be credible and influential rather than senior. You need to work in partnership with this sponsor because you need them to visibly sign up to decisions and take a leading role in bringing about the change. You also need to raise their aspirations so they become a radical champion for the project. Manage their expectations of the technical difficulties, as well as the people difficulties, in implementing the new system so they don't become disillusioned when the going gets tough.

You'll need help from other people as well, so try to identify champions and change agents throughout the organisation and get commitment for their involvement from their line managers. This group will need training and support to develop new skills to carry out change programme tasks. For example, you might need to train people to become system trainers or run user acceptance tests. Remember, though, that delegation of tasks does not

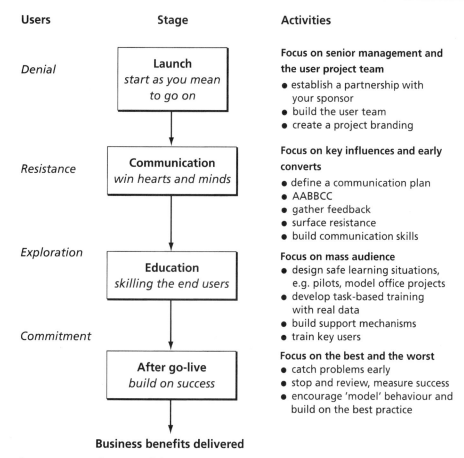

Users	Stage	Activities

Users

Denial

Resistance

Exploration

Commitment

Stage

Launch
*start as you mean
to go on*

Communication
win hearts and minds

Education
skilling the end users

After go-live
build on success

Business benefits delivered

Activities

**Focus on senior management and
the user project team**
- establish a partnership with
  your sponsor
- build the user team
- create a project branding

**Focus on key influences and early
converts**
- define a communication plan
- AABBCC
- gather feedback
- surface resistance
- build communication skills

Focus on mass audience
- design safe learning situations,
  e.g. pilots, model office projects
- develop task-based training
  with real data
- build support mechanisms
- train key users

Focus on the best and the worst
- catch problems early
- stop and review, measure success
- encourage 'model' behaviour and
  build on the best practice

Fig 1.4 Four-phase model

mean abdication of responsibility – you should provide ongoing, active support and monitor people to ensure that their learning is positive and effective. For example, you might review a training guide or observe a practice training session and then provide constructive feedback. You must focus on the business benefits of the change you are introducing, and as a team share the responsibility for achieving them.

Having prepared the sponsor and the user side of the project team, you then need to launch the project to a wider user audience. At this early stage in the system's project lifecycle you probably won't have many facts about timescale or functionality, and the temptation is to say nothing in case going public means you will be held to account later. In fact the greater danger is that by saying nothing the grapevine will run riot and the rumours that spread about what the system can or cannot do could cause far more damage to your future reputation. Typically at this stage what people want to know is: why the system is being introduced, who is responsible from the business point of view for making it work, when it will affect them and some broad brush pictures about what it could do for the business and how this could be measured. Wherever possible you should try to ensure that these messages are delivered down the management line – starting with your sponsor rather than from the IT department.

Don't be afraid of saying 'I don't know', but be clear about what is known, and give dates that you are prepared to stick to for when you will be able to give more information. A 'countdown to go-live' chart is a good way of preparing people for a fairly lengthy build-up before they get their hands on the system. You might want to consider giving the project and the system a name and a visual branding, such as a logo, at this stage. This gives people something more tangible to identify the project by in the months before any new systems actually hit their desks.

Winning people's hearts and minds is the next step in implementing successful change. The key is to involve customer staff in the change. With help and coaching from the project team, users can find facts, analyse data, investigate needs, brainstorm solutions, produce reports and prepare training communications materials. A powerful way to start this process is to involve users in preparing a risk profile for the project. Inevitably, the pre-emptive actions for many of the risks will fall to the users themselves and immediately they are engaged in making the project work.

Winning hearts and minds also means communicating widely with everyone who will be affected by the new system. First, there needs to be a consistent way of describing the need for change. This often means finding ways of describing the problems with the present situation – what's pushing us towards a new system – and the vision, the opportunities offered by the new system – what's pulling us towards the new. You also need to plan the right vehicle for the communication. For example, use hot vehicles for sensitive or significant information, and cold vehicles for uncontroversial or detailed messages. Typical hot vehicles are face-to-face events like conferences and seminars, presentations, roadshows, team briefings, and regular management meetings. Cold vehicles are impersonal things like paper or electronic media such as videos, notices, posters, e-mails or the internal mail. Most of all remember communication is a two-way process – you need to make time to listen as well as to inform.

There is a useful model to remember when trying to win hearts and minds. It's not quite as simple as ABC, but it is as straightforward as AABBCC!

AA Identify audiences and the actions you want from them. Audiences and actions.

BB Identify the barriers which audiences might have that may prevent them from delivering these actions and tell them about the benefits that will come from the actions. Barriers and benefits.

CC Choose the communication channels to each audience and the controls and measures that you'll use to check that the messages have been received and understood. Communications and controls.

1.6   SKILLING THE END USERS

You need to continue winning hearts and minds right from when you first launch the project through to go-live and beyond, but as the systems get nearer to live use, the emphasis of user activities has to move from giving information to building new skills and knowledge; from communication to training. The two sets of activities must be closely linked, and it is often a good idea to use the same team to develop and deliver both.

The key to effective system training is to base it around the business tasks that users will perform, not just around the menus and functions of the system. Make the training examples as realistic as possible, use a copy of the live data if you can. By doing this people see the context in which the system will be used and you minimise implementation problems later. Don't be constrained by just thinking of conventional classroom training, consider delivering training in the work place, possibly using key users but make sure you select these people carefully and invest enough time in building their training skills. One successful approach is to create a model office in which you can rerun past 'real work' scenarios using the new systems and procedures. Well designed, these events can give the two-fold benefits of having powerful impact on the people involved (who have now been part of the future, for a few hours at least, and can then act as powerful advocates of the change with their peers) and also giving valuable feedback on the dependencies between the various technical parts of the project. Finally, make sure that training materials and user guides look professional. The quality of these printed materials will play a large part in forming users' initial expectations of the quality of the system itself.

1.7   AFTER GO-LIVE

As far as the system is concerned you may think your job is almost over as soon as it goes live but for the users the job is just beginning. For users to really make the most of the potential benefits of the system and for the project to achieve its business objectives, users still need your support after go-live. The job is much easier if the training has been designed to produce self-supporting groups, people who are confident in using the paper-based and on-screen documentation and know which of their colleagues to turn to for local advice. But in setting up a support system, there are a few broad lessons to bear in mind. Make sure that each level of support filters problems and resolves those that are their responsibility and doesn't just pass them on. Monitor help desk calls and when you find repeated problems produce short, targeted 'best practice' user guides to educate users to solve them themselves. Make sure that new recruits are properly trained in the current best practices and not just left to find their own ways of doing things. If staff turnover is high, computer-based training is an effective way of coping with new joiner training.

Finally, make sure you stop, review the benefits that users are delivering against the original objectives, and acknowledge the contribution that people have made. Because large projects never have a clear end point, it is all too easy to forget the need to celebrate successes, to identify what still remains to be done and to learn the lessons for next time.

1.8 SUMMARY

There is not an all-purpose, simple way to implement and manage change. Key ingredients in a change programme are to plan it properly as a sub-project in its own right, to ensure that communication and training work together to reinforce the messages of the change – the benefits of the new system. Involving the users throughout so that they manage their change rather than become victims of it is essential. Some final pieces of advice would include:

- Treat everyone with equal respect, making an effort to understand their motivations, viewpoints and perspectives.
- Being right doesn't count. You need to take people with you to get their buy-in.
- Always maintain your focus on the business benefits of the change.
- Take advice from, and use the help of, experts. You don't have to do it all yourself!

1.9 QUESTIONS

1 Figure 1.5 shows how bad an implementation can become. Action needs to be taken to prevent this kind of situation. What would you recommend should be done?

2 You are the project manager for a new management accounting system that will provide monthly profit and loss accounts to a chain of 30 computer dealerships, each of which is franchised to its local owner/manager. They've all done their own accounting before. What change issues would you expect to encounter? Does the fact that they are PC dealerships make any difference? Why might they have joined together in the chain?

3 Consider the organisation that employs you or where you study. What is its culture? Why does it have that particular culture? What organisational

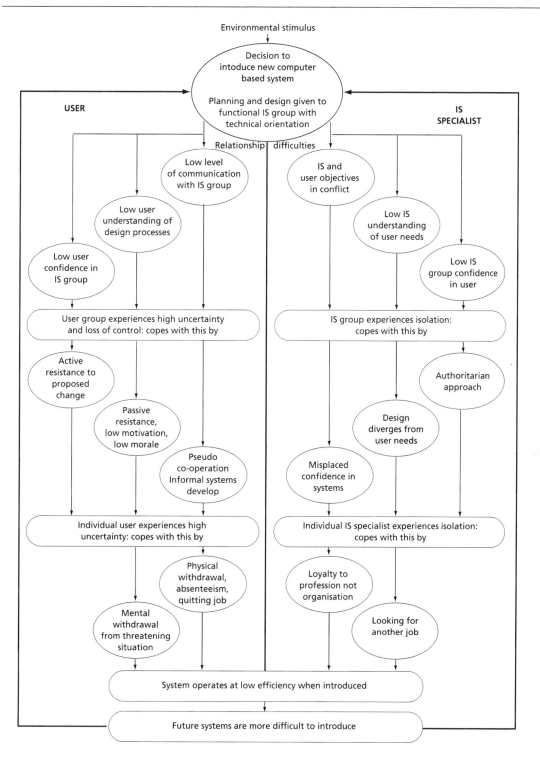

Fig 1.5   The risk of the traditional approach

culture would give you most satisfaction as an employee? Where might you find such an employer? Given your preferred organisational culture, what would it mean for you as an employee in terms of your responsibilities and obligations?

4 You have to design a 'hearts and minds' programme connected with the implementation of a new system for the recording and management of stock in a book-publishing company and for the supply of books to booksellers. What would be the main stages of such a programme?

CHAPTER 2

Business strategy and information systems

2.1 INTRODUCTION

This chapter is all about context: the business context within which systems projects are created; how the strategy of an organisation determines its shape and how that shape determines the business processes and their systems. In the first edition of this book we described this context as beginning with a 'systems planning activity' that determined which projects would be started according to the needs of the enterprise. The systems planning function enables business plans to be translated into developed computer systems to meet business goals. Typical business goals might be related to profit, or growth, or market share but could also focus on customer services, safety or staff development. Business goals lead to the identification of key result areas (KRAs) which specify in turn the need for new systems. IS management is therefore concerned with the development of new systems to

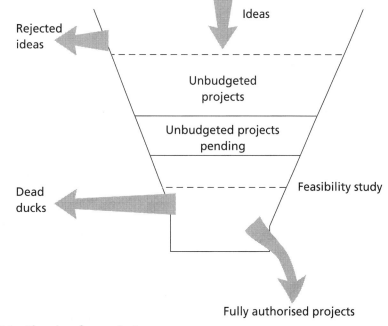

Fig 2.1 Planning for projects

contribute to the achievement of the business's key result areas. Figure 2.1 shows how this systems planning process can take place and how it can produce a range of possible systems projects.

We now want to look at what happens before the systems planning activity and address some of the issues around an organisation's strategy. With increasing expectations that computer people – especially analysts and project managers – will have an understanding of the wider environment within which organisations operate, it seems even more necessary to explore the wider context of how information systems fit into business strategy.

2.2   WHAT IS STRATEGY ALL ABOUT?

Firstly then, what is strategy? It is not some 20th century idea coming out of big business or the business schools – even though big business and the business schools have taken it to their hearts! We come across the concept of strategy in the development of military strategies in the time of the ancient Greeks over 500 years BC. First of all the word described the role of the general of an army – what the general did – then it became a civilian activity, but still in a national context, where it was concerned with a system of government, and finally it moved from the military and diplomatic or government worlds into business. Secondly, strategy is not an exact science. Indeed some writers have said that 'there is no single, universally accepted definition of strategy'. If this is true – and judging by the number of books and articles about strategy it certainly seems to be true – what can we usefully say here to give us a foundation for thinking about business strategy? We can begin with some general definitions of aspects of strategy and identify the components of an effective strategy.

James Quinn and also Michael Porter make the following observation about strategy:

> 'Strategy is the pattern or plan that integrates an organisation's major goals, policies and actions into a cohesive whole. In other words, it pulls together and gives meaning to everything an organisation does. A well formulated strategy helps to organise resources into a unique and viable force based on the competences and shortcomings of the organisation, on anticipated changes in the environment and activities by competitors.'

In other words, strategy is the result of a careful analysis and it is purposeful; it is a plan for achieving something. The problem with strategy though is that it can't be a plan for everything. How could it be possible to know all of the environmental changes that might take place in the lifetime of the strategy? How can the strategic planners know what competitors will do? Also, Henry Mintzberg – a leading American thinker and writer about strategy – says that strategies can emerge: they are not all formulated by strategic planners in quiet offices on the top floor but are formed by events that fall into patterns that are then recognised and further developed. Consistency of behaviour then becomes a strategy even though that's not how it started out. It's almost a post-event rationalisation of what looks like intuitive actions. This is why 'strategies' change and why strategic plans and the IS developments that support them get thrown out of the window and why systems projects are shut down for what seem like arbitrary or irrational reasons. 'We're killing this project, the strategy's changed.'

It is possible, however, to recognise a good strategy when we see it. We might find it difficult to define 'strategy' but we know a good one when we come across it. A good strategy is:

- *Clear*. The overriding goals for all units of the enterprise are clear enough to give continuity and cohesion to all of the tactical choices made during the lifetime of the strategy. Managers can answer the question: 'Does what I do now move us towards the strategy?' and answer it correctly.

- *Keeps the initiative*. A good strategy preserves freedom of action, supports empowerment and enhances commitment. It sets the pace and determines the course of action. Consequently people feel 'in charge' and motivated to achieve.

- *Concentrated*. A good strategy concentrates resources at the place and the time where they will generate maximum advantage. A good strategy defines what will made the enterprise superior to its opponents and organises the resources to achieve that advantage.

- *Flexible*. This isn't about changing the strategy but about being well balanced to take advantage of changes that occur. Is the opposition kept on the run by our consistent innovation?

- *Well led*. Successful strategies require commitment, not just acceptance. Good leadership is needed to turn a strategy into competitive advantage.

- *Full of surprises*. Our strategy is seeking to gain an advantage for us. We are in competition with other organisations, other ideas, other projects. We gain advantage out of proportion to the effort expended by doing the unexpected.

Just as we can recognise the criteria for a good strategy, it's possible – according to Mintzberg – to see strategy as:

- *A Plan*. People talk about having 'a strategy' for this sales visit, or for this meeting or for this game. Really it's just a plan or a consciously intended course of action to deal with a situation.

- *A Pattern*. This is different from a 'consciously intended course of action'. Strategy as a pattern means that intended or not we consistently behave in a certain way and that leads us to formalise this pattern of behaviour into a strategy.

- *A Position*. Our strategy describes how we position ourselves in our market. It therefore enables us to exclude areas of possible activity – 'Our position is here and we do this kind of thing, so we can't consider doing that'; 'We intend to be active in the public sector but not in local government';

'Our position is that we do business analysis, project management and high level design; even though we could do a lot of programming on this project, we don't, so we subcontract it out'.

- *A Perspective.* This is really attempting to describe strategy as a set of values. Strategy in this respect is to the organisation what personality is to the individual. It's the organisation's character or culture and it means that individuals are united by common thinking or behaviour. Strategy as a perspective can easily be applied to a project team which can create a shared vision of how the project team will behave and work together. So, in spite of the rather grand overtones that strategy formulation may have, you can use it directly on a project yourself.

2.3 DEVELOPING A STRATEGY

Knowing about strategy is useful only if we need to understand the strategy of the organisation for which we're developing new systems. To understand their strategy, it is helpful if we are clear, at least in outline, about how strategies are developed. If we look at the stages we go through when making a decision, we first of all:

- Investigate the situation to collect as much data as we can about the facts of the case, and people's views and feelings about them.
- Then we develop some alternative possible courses of action based on what we know about the situation under review.
- Next we evaluate these decisions in terms of their likely outcomes and consequences.
- Then we choose the decision to be implemented on the basis of the outcomes or consequences. We take account here as well of the likely risks associated with our choice.
- Finally, we implement our decision or solution and follow it up.

We can use this simple process to help us to develop a model of strategic management. The model, shown in Fig 2.2, is from Gordon Greenley's book *Strategic Management*.

- Analysing the environment is concerned with investigating the internal and external environments and developing a comprehensive understanding of our business, its strengths and weaknesses, our competitors and the market within which we all operate.
- Planning the direction determines the future that we want for our business. We might create a vision for the kind of business we want to be, our overall philosophy for doing business and the range of activities that are to be considered. This planning might be done at the corporate level, the division level and even at lower levels.

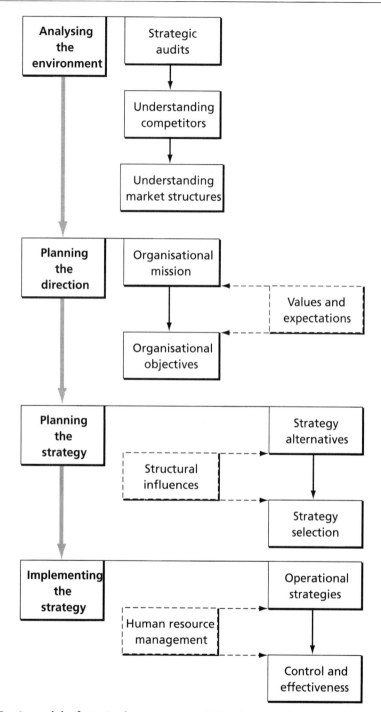

Fig 2.2   A model of strategic management (Gordon Greenley, *Strategic Management*, Prentice Hall)

- Planning strategy is all about designing the means for going in our planned direction. It addresses the issue of how we will achieve our goal. We might have several alternative approaches and we might pursue more than one of them at the same time. Organisational structures influence decisions taken here and equally organisational structures may be changed to speed up moves towards the planned direction.

- Implementing the strategy is putting it all into action and monitoring and controlling the implementation.

There are many analytical tools to help in this strategic management process, but most are concerned with offering ways of analysing the current situation of which the SWOT (strengths, weaknesses, opportunities and threats) analysis and the Boston Consulting Group (BCG) matrix are probably the best known.

A SWOT analysis identifies the strengths, weaknesses, opportunities and threats that face an organisation. Strengths and weaknesses are an assessment of internal factors, whilst opportunities and threats are ways of defining the external environment. A SWOT matrix would show strengths and weaknesses as in Fig 2.3.

In segment A for example we identify those activities in which we are strong and where good opportunities exist. We are playing from our strengths into a receptive market so our strategy for these activities is to overcome external threats that may arise, because the market is attractive to others, by eliminating any weak aspects of our overall performance. In segment B we identify that internally we have weaknesses even though there are external opportunities. So without some strategic internal action to eliminate these weaknesses, the opportunities will be taken by our competitors. Segment C is the worst place for a product or service; we are weak and there are external

Fig 2.3   A SWOT matrix

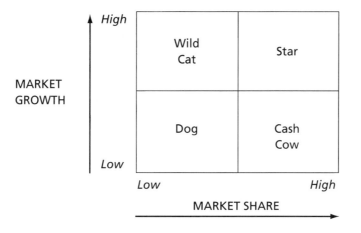

Fig 2.4 The BCG matrix

threats from competitors or the environment. We might decide to take action to reduce both the weakness and the threat – a difficult strategy to follow – or we might choose to discontinue our product or service, or leave this market. Finally in segment D we are strong but face external threats. A strategy here could be to use our strength to deflect the threat. It is generally not advisable to engage in unnecessary competitive battles. Overall the strategic actions taken by an enterprise are the result of this kind of SWOT analysis and could lead to new system developments.

The Boston Consulting Group (BCG) analysis technique models the relationship between a product or service's current and future potential and how management wants to deal with it. It is therefore a marketing analysis with market growth along one axis and market share along the other and it shows the products that are cash generators and cash consumers. Each of these will need to be managed differently and supported by different kinds of systems. Figure 2.4 shows how the BCG matrix works.

Wild Cats are the potential good businesses of the future. They are usually new products or services with a low market share but with a high potential for growth. *Stars* are the products that are profitable now and are expected to do well in the future. They are market leader products in growth markets needing investment to keep them there. It is hoped that as many Wild Cats as possible will become Stars. It is likely that organisations will invest in new systems for Stars. *Cash Cows* are the current high income earners. They provide the majority of current profit and are a source of investment funding for Wild Cats and Stars. They are not expected to provide significant future revenues, and investment in information systems will be around increasing the profit – by greater cost control perhaps – or by increasing their market share so that the Cash Cow can move back to becoming a Star. Finally, the *Dogs* are those products and services that make little or no contribution to today's profits and are not expected to make much contribution in the future. These are typically products that have lost market share to competitors or are in declining markets.

There is, then, a process for the development and implementation of business strategy, and a range of tools and methods to help in this process from which come the different types of systems projects that project managers are required to develop. We can't, however, leave this overview of business strategy analysis without considering the influence of Michael Porter's work and the impact that this has on information systems development.

2.4 COMPETITION AND STRATEGY

Porter's view is that, 'The essence of strategy formulation is dealing with competition'. He sees the competitive world as a violent environment within which the business position of an organisation is determined by five forces acting on it. Porter's five forces model is shown in Fig 2.5. The first force is the *rivalry* between existing competitors. This rivalry can be intense if there are many organisations of a similar size and there is often fierce price competition. We saw just this situation in the UK in 1995 with *The Times*, the *Daily Telegraph*, and the *Independent* all fighting each other for market share and making aggressive price changes in the process.

● *New entrants* also pose a threat. If the marketplace looks good and competition is weak, new entrants will want to enter the market. The seriousness of the threat they pose depends on the barriers that prevent them from joining, their determination to get over them and the potential retaliation from the existing competitors in the marketplace.

● *Substitute products or services* also threaten the existing competition. The advent of the word processor and then the powerful word processing

Fig 2.5 Porter's five forces model

packages on the latest-technology personal computers wiped out the type-writer industry. Technological change is often the driving force behind the arrival of substitute products.

- *Suppliers* can exert pressure on participants in an industry by reducing the supply of the product and by increasing prices. Suppliers are powerful if there are few of them and if they are bigger and stronger than the enterprises in the industry to which they sell.

- *Buyers* can also influence competition if they purchase in large volumes. We see this particularly with large supermarket chains and major retailers like Marks & Spencer who are all able to put competitive pressure on the suppliers competing for their business.

This five forces model of industry competitiveness offers a way of asking general questions about the role that information systems could play in generating competitive advantage. Wendy Robson has modified Porter's five forces model to show the opportunities for IS. This is shown in Fig 2.6. The Porter analysis would identify the major threats and then an analysis could be made of how information systems can be used to minimise these threats. For the Royal Bank of Scotland, the use of IS to support the Direct Line insurance business enabled the bank to generate new products and services. For the UK's supermarket giants, the Tesco Clubcard and equivalent products at Sainsbury's and Safeway use information systems to increase the cost to the customer of switching to a rival.

Fig 2.6   Robson's analysis of the five forces and IS opportunities

Taking the Porter analysis further, Robson identified three generic business strategies to respond to the five competitive forces:

- To go for a low-cost strategy and seek to be the overall cost leader and use IS to reduce overall costs.

- To distinguish or differentiate products and services from the competition's offerings and aim to use IS to enhance this differentiation and add additional features to the product or service.

- To concentrate on a particular market segment and to use IS to identify and support activity in these market segments or niches.

Robson also lists the IS applications that might support low cost and differentiation strategies. In pursuit of a low-cost strategy in manufacturing we might see process control system applications, stock planning and stock control. In sales and marketing, there could be applications to prioritise calls and track advertising and sales promotion activities, and in finance, applications for planning and budgeting and controlling costs. For businesses following a differentiation strategy, the manufacturing area might support Total Quality Management systems; in sales there could be order entry systems, order query systems and total customer care systems. In finance there could be office automation and business integration systems. Strategic direction therefore directly influences application development.

Finally in this section, what of generic IS strategies for organisations? Gregory Parsons offers six different strategies for the development of information systems in organisations. These are:

1 *Centrally planned* – where the planning cycles for business and IS are closely linked and where IS strategy is embedded in the planning of the business strategy. The IS function is a service provider and closely linked to the users it serves. We might regard this as an ideal model where it would be a pleasure to manage the development of IS projects.

2 *Leading edge* – where there is a belief that innovative technology can create organisational gains and that risky investment can generate big paybacks. The IS function is therefore the promoter of new ideas and technologies, always watching technological developments – but never realising the benefits perhaps?

3 *A free market* – where users make the decisions since they are the ones who have to live with the results and deliver the profits. The role here for the IS department is to behave as a competitive business unit – perhaps even a profit centre – achieving its financial targets through charging its users and relying on its knowledge of the business to give it an edge over external competitors. This has proved to be a very popular strategy in the 1980s and early 1990s as companies reorganised themselves into flatter structures with greater autonomy. However, it can also be seen as a move by top management to distance itself from the IS function by simply following the rule of 'if they balance their books and there's outside competition, everything is bound to be all right; we'll get a good deal'. There is unlikely to be a long-term corporate plan or use for IT, and the IS department may well find itself outsourced.

4 *Monopoly* – the opposite to free trade. It is founded on the belief that information is a corporate asset that should be available across the whole company and that this will happen only if there is a single supply source that everyone is obliged to use. The danger for the IS department is that it becomes slow moving and unresponsive to customers, concentrating on the delivery of large integrated systems that take a long time to deliver, by which time users' needs may have changed.

5 *Scarce resource* – where the scope of the IS function is deliberately limited by budget constraints and users' projects compete for service from the scarce resources using strict cost/benefit criteria. It has a negative impact on the development of information as a resource.

6 *Necessary evil* – where organisations see the development of information systems as a necessary evil and believe that information is not important to their business. The IT department's role is to provide a minimum level of resources and skill: not an attractive place to work.

Reviewing competitive strategies, and the IS applications that may result from them and the overall profile of the IS department itself, will give you an overview of the climate for development of information systems in the organisation, and of the context in which your project should be managed and in which it will be evaluated.

2.5 STRATEGY AND CULTURE

So far in this chapter, although we have recognised that the development of business strategy and the consequent information systems is an imprecise science, it has nonetheless been depicted as a scientific rather than an emotional activity. In this final section we want to redress this balance by addressing some strategic human issues that influence the way organisations are structured and managed and consequently influence how projects could best be managed in these environments. Later in the book, in Chapter 18, we consider the leadership role of the project manager; here we are concentrating on the context for leadership.

We begin by considering how strategy interacts with the way an organisation is structured, the systems it has and the style in which it operates. In other words, how strategy and systems link with organisational culture. The best way to do this is through an examination of the 7-S model developed by McKinsey, the management consulting firm. The 7-S model proposes that there are other factors than just strategy that make an organisation an effective one. It may be that strategy is not the most important. Organisational change to achieve better performance – and that's why we have new systems developed – depends on the relationship and on the interactions between:

● Strategy
● Structure

- Systems
- Style
- Skills
- Staff
- Shared values

In this McKinsey model, strategy is the action that an organisation takes based on its assessment of the environment which it defines as its customers and its competitors. Its strategy defines how it aims to improve its position against its competition. Clear ideas about strategy can enable organisation structures to be created that enable the strategy: a strategy of diversity may call for a decentralised structure for example. The model warns however that setting the structures that fit the strategy is not the only thing that has to be done. To understand how an organisation really works, you have to look at the systems. These are the things that keep the organisation going, day by day. Organisations can be changed by changing the systems without disruptive restructuring. A strategy to become more customer orientated can be implemented much more easily by discussing customers and markets at management meetings – and taking follow-up action – than by trying to reorganise the structure and create new marketing departments. How does 'style' fit into all of this? We should recognise the importance of management style and the power that it has in shaping the strategy and culture of an organisation. How managers spend their time shows what they think is important; is it poring over figures or out with customers? In the 'staff' dimension we can talk about recruitment, appraisal, pay scales, etc. and we can talk about morale, motivation, attitude, commitment, etc. Often top management is reluctant to get involved with these issues, yet top performing companies pay extraordinary attention to managing the development and progress of tomorrow's managers. All of the strategy, structure and systems in the world won't deliver the results without people and without the sixth S – 'skills', which here means the dominating attributes or capabilities of the organisation. The final S is shared values. These are the guiding concepts, the values and aspirations that make us want to work here, that give meaning to what we do.

You will have seen that four of the variables of an effective organisation are soft, informal variables – systems, style, skills and shared values. Each of them plays a powerful part in determining organisational success and, taking the project as an organisation, each lies in the gift of the project manager. Taken together they establish the culture of the organisation and are the elements that make project staff want to work for you again. Let's finish this chapter then with some summarised ideas about organisational culture.

An organisation's culture is an important feature of its life. You may well have experienced cultural differences yourself between one organisation and others. Do you think that Marks & Spencer's culture is different from Dixon's? Is BT's culture different to that of Mercury (Cable & Wireless) or Orange

(Hutchison Telecom)? In working with different organisations, knowing just the technical aspects of the new job will not be enough. Charles Handy has suggested that cultures are deep phenomena in organisations:

> 'In organisations, there are deep-set beliefs about the way work should be organised, the way authority should be exercised, people rewarded, people controlled. What are the degrees of formalism required? How much planning and how far ahead? What combination of obedience and initiative is looked for in subordinates? Do work hours matter, or dress, or personal eccentricities? Do committees control an individual? Are there rules and procedures or only results? These are all part of the culture of an organisation.'

What is this thing called organisational culture? It reflects the underlying assumptions about the way work is done, what is acceptable and what is not; what behaviours and actions are encouraged and discouraged. It is often thought to be the part of the organisational iceberg that lies beneath the surface and to consist of the unwritten rules of life. More and more organisations are however now writing down these unwritten rules and we recommend that your project does the same. Your project's mission will be well known to everyone – to achieve some deliverables within a time and within a budget. But do your team know the spirit with which you want them to work, do they see your vision, do they share it, for how you want your project to feel? It's not only captains of industry who need to give a vision, leaders at all levels need to do it. There'll be more about this in the leadership chapter later.

2.6   SUMMARY

In this chapter we have been addressing the topic of business strategy and how it is linked to IS strategy.

First, the nature of business strategy and the characteristics of a good strategy. We saw that strategies can be created from the top down, but can also emerge.

There are tools to help in the analysis of business, which is the starting point for the development of a strategy. The SWOT analysis, the Boston Consulting Group Matrix and Porter's competitive forces tools were described.

This led into a review of strategies for the development of IS functions and the impact of organisational culture on strategy.

2.7   QUESTIONS

1   Why is it important for project managers to understand the strategy of the organisation that uses their services?

2   If you knew about an organisation's strategy, could you suggest IS applications that would support it? For example, how could a large supermarket

chain use information systems for cost reduction, or for a strategy based on differentiation?

3 If you had to develop a strategy for a small software house employing 50 or so professional computer people, how would you go about it? What criteria would you use to test whether or not the strategy was sound?

CHAPTER 3

The organisational framework

3.1 INTRODUCTION

This chapter considers the organisational structure for project work. It is not concerned primarily with the organisation inside the project itself – though we do have something to say about the principal roles that might be encountered – but more with the framework which is needed around the project if it is to be a success. It is vital that this framework is established at the outset and well understood by all concerned since otherwise it will be impossible to get important decisions made and adhered to. Too many projects have set out with no clear idea of who the customer is and who is empowered to take these important decisions and a project which starts in this way is bound to encounter severe difficulties along the way even if it does not end in total disaster.

Consider this scenario. The IT director of a retail business engaged a systems consultancy to study the company's current systems and develop proposals for a new, integrated system that would enable the firm to manage its resources better and respond to changing market conditions. The IT director reported to a main board member who was not interested in IT matters. For the purposes of the project, another senior director was to act as the main user. Who was the customer in this scenario? The IT director? The main board member? The retail director? All of them? This lack of clarity bedevilled the whole project and meant that the consultants were unable to secure agreement on either the business or technical requirements of the new system.

Or this scenario, from the public sector this time. A public utility wished to introduce a corporate personnel system. The driving force behind this was the Management Services Director, who held the budget. But each of the various personnel managers in the organisation had a different view on what the system should do. It proved impossible to get consensus on a requirements specification, so eventually a package was bought which at least delivered something in a measurable timescale. The organisation then spent the next five years, and a great deal of money, trying to adapt the package to meet its real requirements. Who was the customer here? The Management Services Director? The personnel managers?

These two examples show why establishing a sound organisational framework is so important. In this chapter, we shall consider organisation from a general perspective and then look at the structure offered by the PRINCE project management method.

3.2 PROJECT ROLES AND RESPONSIBILITIES

First we shall examine the principal roles encountered in a project. In real projects, the people concerned may not be known by these titles but it is important to establish who they are nevertheless.

Sponsor

The sponsor is the person who is accountable to the business for the investment represented by the project and for the achievement of the project's *business objectives*. The sponsor therefore will:

- Define the business aims of the project.
- Justify the project to the board, or whatever the overall management body is called in the particular organisation.
- Define the project's objectives and its priorities in terms of the 'triple constraint' of time, cost and quality/performance.
- Specify the minimum requirements that the project must meet if it is to achieve its business objectives.
- Obtain approval for any capital expenditure involved.
- Initiate the project and appoint the project manager.
- Monitor the progress of the project from a business standpoint.
- Monitor also the business environment to ensure that the project still meets the business needs.
- Keep the board or higher management informed of progress.
- If necessary, terminate the project.
- Account for the success of the investment.
- Provide high-level support as a 'champion' for the project.

The sponsor is thus the 'owner' of the project as a piece of business and the sponsor will, ultimately, be responsible for its success or failure in delivering business benefit to the organisation. The sponsor does not necessarily need to be a user of the proposed system and, in some ways, it is preferable if the sponsor is not, as he/she will then be better able to make disinterested value judgements on whether a particular feature or facility is really essential or not. The sponsor must, however, have the necessary authority to make major decisions on the project and this implies that the sponsor should be a senior manager or director in the organisation.

User

The user is the person who will make use of the facilities of the system in his or her everyday work and is therefore the person most directly affected by the project. The user will:

- Define the detailed requirements for the system to the developers.
- Review the developers' specification to ensure that it supports the business functions.

- Work with the developers in introducing the system into the organisation.
- Conduct, or at any rate witness, the acceptance tests to ensure that the system meets its specified requirements.

The user therefore requires a detailed understanding not just of what processes are to be included in the system but also of how they work. This often means that there is not one but several users with whom the project team must communicate in order to define the system. Inevitably, different users will have different requirements of the system and they will also adopt varying attitudes towards it, from warmly supportive to overtly hostile. The developers will try to reconcile these differences themselves but, at the end of the day, it may be necessary to refer contentious issues to the sponsor for resolution.

Project manager   The project manager is appointed by the sponsor and is responsible for the management of the project on a day-to-day basis and for the achievement of the *project objectives*. The project manager's role is to:

- Achieve the project's objectives within the time, cost and quality/performance constraints imposed by the sponsor.
- Make or force timely decisions to assure the project's success.
- Plan, monitor and control the project through to completion.
- Select, build and motivate the project team.
- Keep the sponsor and senior management informed of progress and alert them to problems – especially if these could have an impact on the project's achieving its business objectives.
- Recommend termination of the project to the sponsor if necessary.
- Serve as the principal point of contact between the sponsor, management and contributors.
- Select and manage subcontractors.

The project manager's role and responsibilities are considered in more detail in Chapter 22.

These are the principal project roles but, within the project, other roles may be encountered. Not all of these will be found on every project, and several roles may well be combined, but the main responsibilities are:

Risk manager   On a large project, risk management may be a significant part of the project manager's work and it may be necessary to appoint someone to assist with this. The project manager retains overall responsibility for project risk but the risk manager will control the process of identifying, classifying and quantifying the risks and for chasing people to carry out their risk reduction actions. Risk management is discussed more fully in Chapter 13.

Quality manager   Again, on a large project, it could be worthwhile to appoint someone as quality manager. Under the guidance of the project manager, this person will write the quality plan, develop the quality control procedures, check that these procedures are being followed and provide advice and guidance to team members on quality related issues. Quality is the subject of Chapter 12.

Chief analyst   This is a senior and experienced business or systems analyst who will, under the direction of the project manager, lead the analysis work. The chief analyst will advise the project manager and project team on analysis methods and techniques and, with the quality manager, ensure that appropriate standards are being followed. It is useful to have as chief analyst someone with extensive experience of the type of *business* being studied who can authoritatively discuss business issues at the highest levels in the user organisation.

Chief designer   Like the chief analyst, the chief designer works under the direction of the project manager to control the work of the design team, and probably that of the programmers as well. The chief designer will have extensive experience of the *technology* being used and can provide advice and guidance to the project team as well as develop any project-specific standards that are required.

Database administrator   The database administrator will be the principal custodian of the database and of its supporting data dictionary. The database administrator will develop and enforce standards for the use of the database product, the naming and placement of data items and so on. Usually, the database administrator will work closely with the chief designer in the development of the design and with the programming teams in using the database.

Configuration librarian   Configuration management is discussed in Chapter 12. Someone needs to assume responsibility for operating the configuration control procedures and, on a large project, this is often a full-time role.

Team leader   The project manager is responsible for the overall direction of the project, but detailed management of the staff is often delegated to a number of team leaders. Typically in charge of a small group of, for example, programmers, team leaders plan and direct work on a day-to-day basis and either review or organise reviews of the team members' work.

Project office   A project office provides administrative support to the project manager. This includes things like the collection and recording of timesheets, the organisation of meetings and the dissemination of information. It is quite common to find a project office that supports a number of discrete projects.

3.3   ORGANISING THE ROLES

The various roles we have described may be organised in different ways, depending on a number of factors including the type of project, whether the work is being done in-house or under contract and the culture of the organisation. In the simplest case, the sponsor appoints the project manager and these two, plus the user, make the important decisions for the project. Usually, though, the situation is more complex and less clear-cut and other bodies that may be encountered are the steering committee and the user group.

The steering committee

This body is set up to control the development of a particular project – or perhaps a group of related projects – and has representation from the various interested parties. Typically, it might have a senior user representative, or representatives if there are multiple users, plus people from other departments or functions affected by the project – finance, purchasing, personnel and so on. A steering committee is a fine idea provided that either it, or one of its members, possesses the authority to make decisions on the project. Unfortunately, this is not always the case and sometimes one encounters steering committees that lack one vital member – the project's sponsor. Where this is the case, the steering committee risks becoming a 'talking shop' which has to refer all real decisions to the sponsor or some other authoritative person or body in the organisation.

The user group

Where there are several users for a planned system, it is sometimes useful to create a forum where they can come together and discuss and reconcile their disparate requirements. Unless the sponsor is a member of the user group – perhaps chairing the meetings – this body's role will be advisory only and the final decisions will have to be made elsewhere in the organisation. What usually happens is that low-level decisions – for example on the layout of a proposed report – can be made at the user group with the more fundamental policy issues, probably involving the project budget, being referred upwards. Quite often, the user group will continue to meet after the project has delivered and will then become the conduit through which changes and enhancements are passed to the maintenance and support team.

The risk management committee

On large projects, the management of risk can assume great importance. Rather than burden the steering committee or user group meetings with another large agenda item, it may be found useful to form a committee expressly to review and control the project's risks. Typically, the function of this group would be to review the current status of risks, assign owners to the risks and check that the identified avoidance or mitigation actions are being carried out. It should be noted that the risk management committee does not remove overall responsibility for managing risk from the project manager but acts in support of the project manager.

There are other bodies that may be encountered on projects or set up on an *ad hoc* basis – for example, a technical committee or a quality assurance group. The important point, however, is that the project manager must ensure that the final responsibility and authority for the project is clear and unambiguous. There must be an identifiable sponsor who will decide what the project must do and the constraints within which it will operate. Without this, there are bound to be problems of direction and authority and it will be very difficult, if not impossible, to secure sign-off for the project at the end.

3.4 PRINCE ORGANISATION STRUCTURE

PRINCE stands for **P**rojects **IN C**ontrolled **E**nvironments. PRINCE is a structured approach to project management developed for and championed by the UK Government. PRINCE was originally intended for the management of IS projects but most of its principles are equally applicable in other areas and newer versions will explicitly broaden its use into other disciplines. PRINCE offers a number of features that are of benefit in the management of IS projects:

- A defined management structure.
- A system of plans.
- A set of control procedures.
- A focus on product – that is deliverable-based planning.

We shall examine each of these features of PRINCE in this book and we shall start by examining the PRINCE management structure, which is illustrated in Fig 3.1.

At the top of the PRINCE hierarchy is the *IS Steering Committee*. This body sets the overall IS policy for the organisation. It is assumed that this policy is designed to support the organisation's business objectives, so the IS Steering Committee will probably be composed of, or at least include, members of the organisation's main board. Below this is the *IT Executive Committee* which takes the IS policy and translates it into specific projects, ensuring that these projects each support the business objectives set for them.

We now come to the top level of management for individual projects, which PRINCE calls the *Project Board*. The Project Board represents three constituencies with an interest in the project:

- The *Executive* chairs the Project Board. He or she is appointed by the IT Executive Committee and represents the business interests of the organisation. The Executive provides overall guidance throughout the project and is 'first among equals' on the Project Board.
- The *Senior User* represents the interests of the business areas that are affected by the new system and has the authority to speak for all users of the system.

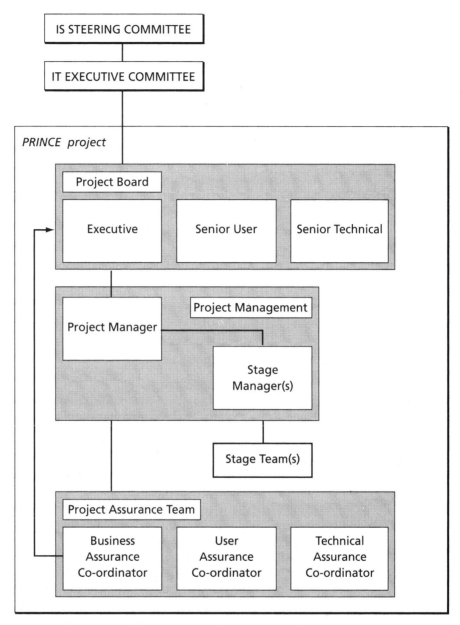

Fig 3.1   PRINCE organisation structure

- The *Senior Technical* person represents those who control the technical aspects of the project, in other words the developers. Probably, someone like the organisation's IT director or systems development manager would assume the Senior Technical role.

In practice, the Project Board may be a somewhat larger body than this. There is usually only one Executive and one Senior Technical member but there may be several Senior Users if this is appropriate.

The actual day-to-day management of the project is the responsibility of the *Project Manager* and one or more *Stage Managers*. The Project Manager's role is what one would expect but the Stage Manager idea is fairly novel to PRINCE and perhaps requires some explanation. It is assumed that a PRINCE project will go through several stages, with each stage being signed off and the plans reviewed before moving to the next stage. Since a different blend of skills may be required at each stage, it is possible that a different Stage Manager will be required for each. In practice, there are several ways in which the Project Manager/Stage Manager roles could be operated:

- There may be one Project Manager throughout the project, with a different Stage Manager for each stage.
- The Project Manager may also assume the Stage Manager role.
- A succession of Stage Managers may be appointed, with each also assuming the Project Manager role for that stage.
- In a customer and supplier context, the customer may supply the Project Manager, with the supplier providing the Stage Manager or Managers.

The Project Manager is given authority to manage the project within constraints of time, cost and quality set by the Project Board. The Project Board will also assign some tolerances around these constraints within which the Project Manager may make adjustments to the project if necessary. Tolerances are discussed in more detail in Chapter 5. Reporting to the Stage Manager is the *Stage Team* that actually carries out the work.

In PRINCE, too, there is the concept of a *Project Assurance Team* (PAT). This works for the Project Manager but also has a responsibility to the Project Board. The Project Assurance Team represents the same three interest groups as the Project Board but works at a more detailed level. Whereas the Project Board sets the general direction of the project, the Project Assurance Team reviews the detailed plans and products emerging from the project from three perspectives. The members of the Project Assurance Team are:

- *Business Assurance Co-ordinator*. The BAC assists the Project Manager in preparing the plans and collects the project monitoring information on the Project manager's behalf. The BAC assists the Project and Stage Managers in the preparation of reports and evaluates the business aspects of any proposed changes to the project.
- *The User Assurance Co-ordinator*. The UAC represents the interests of the system's users. The UAC is responsible for ensuring that the user's require-

ments are properly addressed, for establishing the acceptance criteria for the project, for assessing changes and for assisting in the quality review of products from the users' perspectives.

● *The Technical Assurance Co-ordinator*. The TAC assists in defining the technical strategy for the project, advises on quality criteria and other technical methods and standards and ensures that these standards are being adhered to.

Where an organisation is undertaking a number of projects simultaneously, the various Business Assurance Co-ordinators and Technical Assurance Co-ordinators can be grouped into a *Project Support Office*. This makes for more effective use of resources and allows for the co-ordination of common methods and standards across projects. The User Assurance Co-ordinator for each project must, of course, come from the user area(s) affected by the project.

The PRINCE structure provides a very sound basis for the management of an IS project. It ensures that projects have as their primary focus the achievement of business objectives and it ensures that IS projects grow out of the business strategy. It also ensures that the interest groups affected by the IS project are properly represented and that there is a proper decision-making body that can control and direct the progress of the project.

3.5 SUMMARY

It is vital to the success of an IS project that there is a clear understanding of who the customer is, who will make the major decisions about the scope and direction of the project and who will ultimately accept the project.

It is necessary to identify the sponsor of the project within the organisation. Various bodies may be formed to guide and advise the project, including the steering group, the user group and the risk management committee.

The PRINCE project management method offers a convenient and effective structure for the management of IS projects.

3.6 QUESTIONS

1   How many different types of customer may there be for a systems development project? Who are they? What kind of relationship and reporting arrangements should the project manager have with the sponsor?

2   In a PRINCE project structure there are formal committees, a project board and specific roles. What is your opinion about the value of this kind of arrangement? How do you see it working in large and small projects? Could it be useful for projects outside IT?

CHAPTER 4

System development lifecycles

4.1 INTRODUCTION

In this chapter we shall consider the project lifecycle and the various approaches to system development which may be used on IS projects. These approaches are sometimes more formally termed *lifecycle models*. Various models exist, many of which are developments or refinements of earlier ones. It is important to define the terms 'system development lifecycle' and 'project lifecycle'. Generally speaking, the system development lifecycle covers the whole life of a system. This will cover not only feasibility study, analysis, specification, design and development but also the operation, maintenance and enhancement aspects which take place after the system has been accepted by the end users. A project can be defined as 'a management environment set up to ensure the delivery of a specified business product to meet a defined business case'. In terms of systems development, this can generally be taken to mean the delivery of the specified information system within given constraints of time, cost, resource and quality but a project may not cover all stages of the system lifecycle. As a project is defined as something which has an end, it is unlikely – although not impossible – that ongoing maintenance would be included in the scope of a project. Similarly, the objective of the project may only cover the delivery of a specified product, for example a feasibility study report or requirements definition. In other words, the project lifecycle covers the delivery of whatever has been defined as constituting the end product of the project.

There is another important difference as well. The system development lifecycle often covers only the technical deliverables whereas the project is concerned with all aspects leading to the delivery of the project's objectives. This therefore includes not only the delivery of technical products, but also the associated management and quality products necessary to a successful project.

The government-sponsored project management method known as PRINCE explicitly divides the project lifecycle products into three groups:

- The *technical* products – these products are concerned with the actual deliverables for the information system – the software, user manuals and so on.

- The *quality* products – these are used to define the required quality criteria and controls to be applied to the project and to the deliverables from the project.

- The *management* products – these are used to manage the project itself – the organisation, plans, reports and the like.

There is more detail on PRINCE in Chapter 6 on project planning.

Many of the system development lifecycle models, particularly the earlier models, were concerned solely with the work required to produce the actual system. It is now accepted that, following the failure of many computer projects to deliver information systems that met business needs, aspects of system development other than the delivery of technical products need to be addressed. These aspects, which include quality, planning, control, risk analysis and so on, are therefore being increasingly incorporated in development approaches.

The selection of an appropriate system development lifecycle model is important for the project. It is clearly better to go into the project with a clear idea of the general form that the development is going to take. The decision about the 'model' to follow may not be determined by the project manager of course; the project may be handed over with the development approach already set out, possibly in the project's terms of reference or in the initiation document. The organisation for which the project is being carried out may have sets of standards in place which dictate how system development is to take place. Another possibility is that the project may form part of an overall strategy in which a number of systems are being developed and this strategy may have defined the approach to be followed.

Alternatively, and this is rather less likely nowadays, the project manager may have the power to decide on the most appropriate development model to be used for the project. In this selection, there are many factors to be taken into consideration to determine the best approach. In any case, whether the project manager gets to choose or not, the project has to be planned with the system development approach in mind.

There are only two basic system development lifecycle models: the waterfall model and the spiral model. All other well-used models tend to be variants or refinements of these two. This chapter looks at these models and how they can be used in a project context. It describes them together with their strengths and weaknesses to help you understand them fully. The chapter also considers a number of development approaches which make use of these two basic models.

4.2 THE WATERFALL MODEL

In the early 1970s, it became apparent following a number of high profile failures that computer projects required a greater degree of formality than had previously been the case. The waterfall model was originally published in 1970 by W Royce in order to introduce this level of formality and the original is shown in Fig 4.1. In the waterfall model, system development is broken down into a number of sequential sections or stages represented by boxes, with each stage being completed before work starts on the following stage. The outputs from one stage are used as inputs to the next. This is illustrated by the 'flow' from one stage to the next. For example, using Fig 4.1,

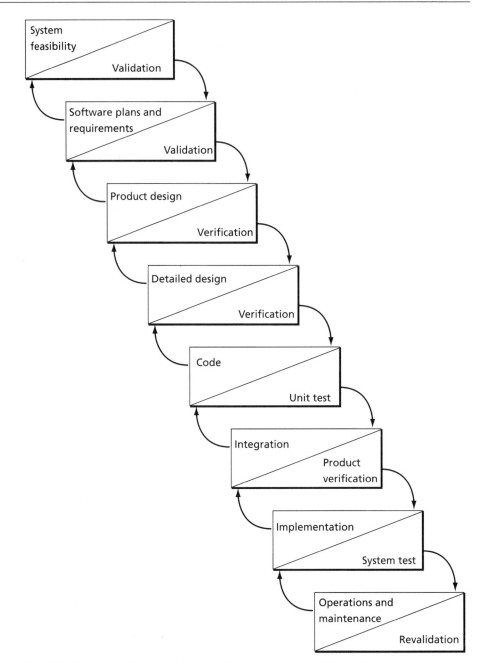

Fig 4.1 The waterfall model of system development lifecycle
(*Computer*, May 1988, © 1988 IEEE)

the Product Design products are completed and accepted before being used as inputs to the work of the next stage, Detailed Design, and so on.

Each stage is divided into two parts: the first part covers the actual work being carried out in the stage; the second part covers the 'verification and validation' of that work. *Verification* is taken to mean establishing the correspondence between a product and its specification – in other words, are we building the product in the right way? *Validation*, on the other hand, is concerned with whether the product is fit for its operational mission – in other words, are we building the right product? Typically, there is a degree of iteration of work and products within a stage but very little between stages. Rework, where necessary, is carried out in succeeding stages and the original stage in which the product was produced is not revisited. For example, if a new requirement is identified during Detailed Design stage, the project will not return to the Software Plans and Specification stage but will incorporate the reworking within the current stage. This may mean that some of the previously delivered products need to be amended however.

Nowadays, the waterfall model is generally taken to mean any sequential model divided into consecutive stages and having the attributes of the original model. The identification and naming of the stages are not fixed and can be modified to suit particular project characteristics.

The model has a number of good points. Apart from the sequencing of activities, it addresses elements of quality management through verification and validation, and configuration management by baselining products at the end of the stage. It does not have explicit means for exercising management control on a project, however, and planning, control and risk management are not covered. Nevertheless, the stage-by-stage nature of the waterfall model and the completion of products for the end of each stage lends itself well to project management planning and control techniques and assists in the process of change control. Many projects still use versions of the waterfall model, generally with some of the shortcomings of the original one addressed, and the model is used as the basis for many structured methods such as SSADM. Waterfall models work best when the level of reworking of products is kept to a minimum and the products remain unchanged after completion of their 'stage'. In situations where the requirements are well understood and the business area in general is not likely to undergo significant business change, the waterfall model works well. In situations where the business requirements are not well understood and where the system is likely to undergo radical change, a different approach to that suggested by the waterfall model may be more appropriate.

4.3 THE 'b' MODEL

One of the weaknesses of the waterfall model is that the maintenance phase is not adequately covered. 'Operations and Maintenance' is treated as a separate stage as if it had a separate start and finish like the other stages. There

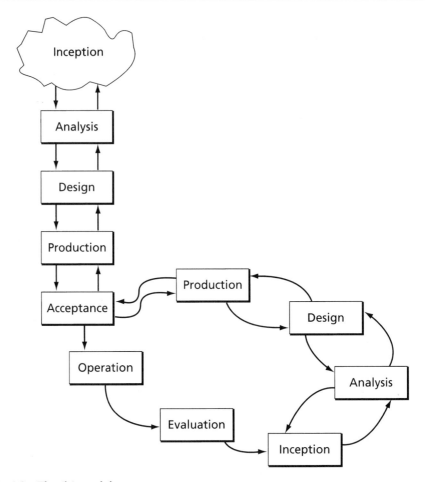

Fig 4.2   The 'b' model

is no acknowledgement that maintenance is different in nature from the other stages in that it is ongoing and open-ended. It should be borne in mind that most of the effort which is expended on a system over its whole life is during maintenance and that it can typically be greater than 70 per cent of total life-cycle costs. The 'b' model, illustrated in Fig 4.2, was devised by N Birrell and M Ould to address this shortcoming in the waterfall model. It takes its name from its distinctive 'b' shape, with the maintenance and enhancement of the information system shown as a series of cycles each of which follows the same general sequence as the original development. In other words, each change or correction to the system will go through feasibility, analysis, design, production, acceptance and finally operation. These changes may not be implemented separately, of course; they may be combined into 'packages' for implementation.

4.4   THE 'V' MODEL

In this model, which is another variation of the waterfall model, the successive stages are shown in a 'V' formation. An example of the 'V' model is shown in Fig 4.3. On the diagram, the left, downward leg of the V shows the progress from analysis to design to programming and the increasing breakdown of the system components. The right, upward leg shows the progressive assembly and testing, culminating in the delivered product. The important feature of this model is that it shows correspondence between the different stages in the project. For instance, the individual programs or modules are tested against the individual module designs, the integrated set

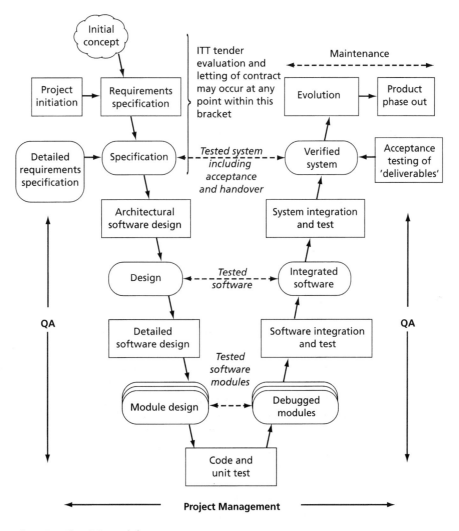

Fig 4.3   The 'V' model
(Reproduced with permission of the National Computing Centre Limited from the *STARTS Guide 1987*, which was supported by the Department of Trade and Industry)

of software is system-tested against the system design and the final system is user acceptance-tested against the requirements specification. This model demonstrates elements of quality assurance in its treatment of this correspondence.

The 'V' model also introduces something else of interest to the project manager. In the situation where the development work is being provided by external contractors, it enables the procurement and delivery stages to be clearly defined and the deliverables of each stage to be validated. This model is used in the next chapter where a particular project is examined in some detail.

4.5 THE INCREMENTAL MODEL

This is another variant of the waterfall model and it is illustrated in Fig 4.4. This model is used where the total functionality of the system is to be delivered in phases over a period of time and it is sometimes termed 'phased delivery'. This makes the delivery and testing more manageable as it introduces the new system to the organisation over a period of time, allowing familiarisation with the changes. It can be difficult to break the delivery of systems down into phases which are internally consistent and it does introduce overheads in that the latest phase has to be integrated with the earlier ones and the whole system retested. Incremental delivery is an implementation issue and the total scope and definition of requirements must be completed before the increments are defined. The incremental model is not appropriate where the scope of the project is poorly defined or undecided, or where there is lack of clarity of some of the requirements.

4.6 THE SPIRAL MODEL

The spiral model differs from the waterfall model in that it introduces an evolutionary or iterative approach to systems development. The waterfall model concentrates on a stage-by-stage process with the end products from one stage being finalised before the next stage is begun. This works reasonably well where the requirements of the system are well understood by the users and the environment is stable. There are often occasions where the requirements are not well formed or understood by the users, where it is difficult to specify the requirements, or where it is difficult to determine how a proposed solution will perform in practice. In this situation, an evolutionary approach may be appropriate. This involves carrying out the same activities over a number of cycles in order to clarify the requirements, issues and solutions and it effectively amounts to repeating the development life-cycle several times.

The original spiral model was developed by Barry Boehm and it is shown in Fig 4.5. The project starts at the centre of the spiral and progresses

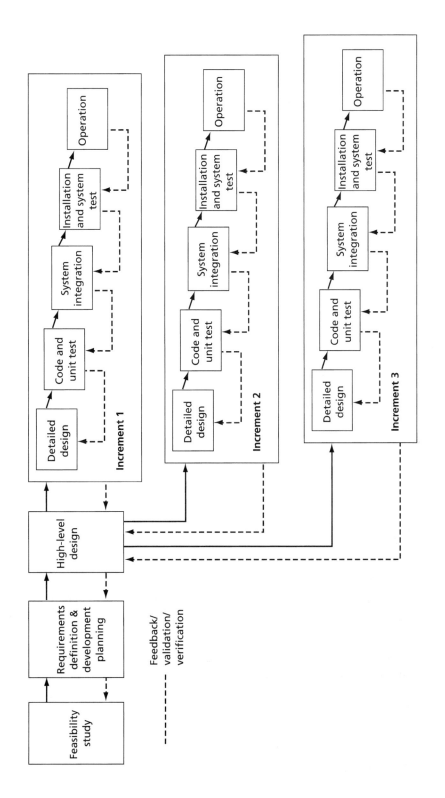

Fig 4.4 The incremental approach

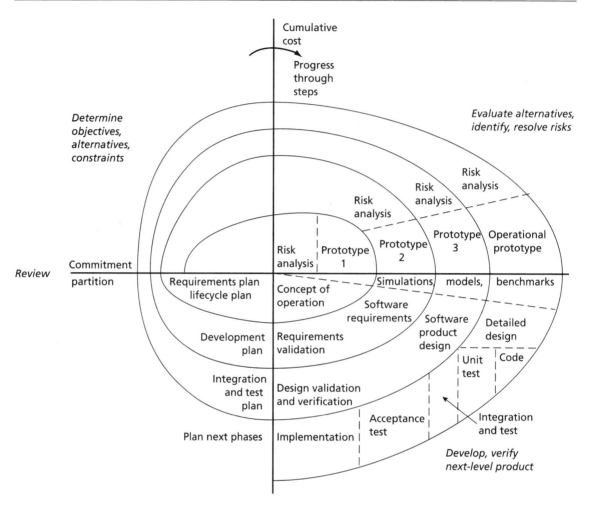

Fig 4.5 Boehm's spiral model
(*Computer*, May 1988, © 1988 IEEE)

outwards. At the centre, the requirements will be poorly understood and will be successively refined with each rotation around the spiral. The total cost of the project will increase as the length of the spiral increases. The model is divided into four quadrants.

- The top left quadrant is where the objectives are determined and the alternatives and constraints identified.
- The top right quadrant is where the alternatives are evaluated and the various risks are identified and resolved.
- The bottom right quadrant is where the development takes place. This effectively covers the same area as the more conventional waterfall model.
- The bottom left quadrant is where the next phase or iteration is planned.

The Boehm spiral introduces the important concepts of objective setting, risk management and planning into the overall cycle. These are all very desirable from a project management point of view as they apply explicitly to factors which may affect the timely delivery of the system within its defined constraints.

4.7 THE TRADITIONAL APPROACH

In this model, 'traditional' tends to mean unstructured and somewhat non-specific and most traditional approaches are based on variations of the waterfall model. Although the overall picture will probably be familiar, the actual methods of developing the systems are almost as numerous as the projects themselves. A diagram of a representative traditional approach is shown in Fig 4.6. This shows three of the stages:

- *Analyse requirements.* In this stage the analyst considers the current system and investigates any problems associated with it. The users are also interviewed to obtain their views of the problems and to get their ideas for improvements. Other sources of information about the system and the new requirements would also be investigated at this time. The output from this stage would probably be no more than a set of notes put together by the analyst.

- *Specify requirements.* In this stage the analyst considers the information that has been accumulated and produces a requirements document. This is likely to be a mix of business requirements, functional and non-functional requirements and an overview of the proposed hardware and software. Elements of the physical specification in terms of screens and printed output reports might also be included.

- *Produce high-level design.* The designer would consider the requirements document and, on that basis, produce a high-level design for the system setting out the database design, the input and output specifications, the menu structure and the overall program design and breakdown.

This approach is characterised by the lack of user involvement, the use of text-based, as opposed to diagrammatic, documentation and an emphasis on *how* things are going to be achieved rather than *what* is going to be achieved. Although there is a stage-by-stage approach, it is difficult to see how the stages link together or to follow an audit trail of individual requirements. Typically, in project management terms, there is no business case or defined acceptance criteria for the system, which make it rather difficult to gauge success or failure. The lack of user involvement is demonstrated in many ways. The users would be involved at the initial analysis stage but the only point where they would be formally required to review anything would be when the Requirements Specification has been completed. Following this,

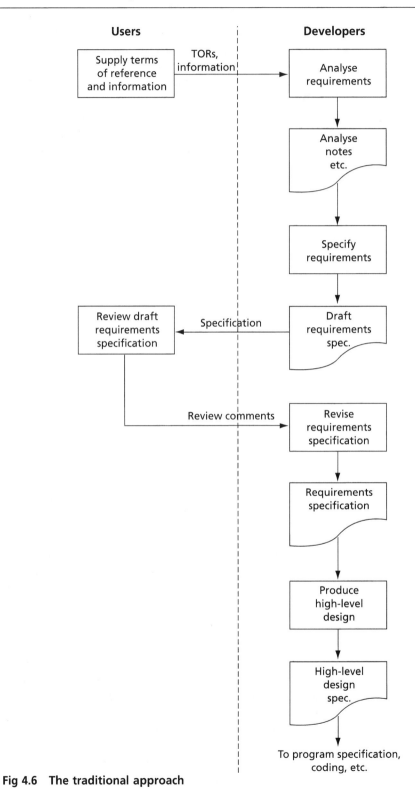

Fig 4.6   The traditional approach

their next contact with the computer system would probably be when the system is delivered!

On the other hand, this method of working suited many analysts and users. It allowed the analyst to use 'intuitive' methods of working and made limited demands on the user's time. The documentation was relatively easy to understand, being mostly in English, and there were no special techniques to be learnt in order to understand it. Unfortunately, text tends to be ambiguous and interpreted differently by different people and misunderstandings were common. This lack of user involvement and 'ownership' for the system often resulted in a poor quality system and an abdication of responsibility by the users and blame for the developers.

4.8 STRUCTURED METHODS

Structured methods have largely taken over from the traditional approach in the development of IS projects. Most of these methods offer a set of techniques and tools to carry out the systems development work within a defined framework. Structured methods are largely characterised by:

- *User involvement*. The users are involved with the review of the products throughout the project and with formal agreement or acceptance of them.

- *Separation of logical and physical*. There is a clear separation in the design of the system between *what* is to be achieved and *how* it is to be implemented. This has the advantage of allowing business benefits to be focused on, rather than being diverted by physical implementation issues.

- *Emphasis on data*. Most structured methods concentrate on the data rather than the processing required by the system. This is because the data tends to be more stable and less likely to change over time.

- *Diagrammatic documentation*. Diagrams rather than text-based documentation are used as much as possible to avoid the problems inherent in large textual documents.

- *Defined structure*. Most structured methods have an overall structure associated with them which ensures a more consistent and complete approach to the work. This allows the progress in the work to be fully charted and there are no sudden unconnected and unexplained jumps between stages or activities.

In general, structured methods are considered to offer improvements over traditional methods but there are drawbacks and criticisms. The users and analysts/developers need to be trained to understand the documentation; this is important as there is no value whatsoever in producing documentation to be reviewed and signed off if it is not fully understood. The users also need to accept that the amount of time required from them will be much increased. This is a project management issue, of course, and full user commitment must be obtained if the final system is to be a success. However, the major criticism levelled against structured methods is that they lead to increased levels of documentation and therefore of bureaucracy. Unfortunately, there is an element of truth in this as, in inexperienced or ill-informed hands, the use of structured methods can lead to the adoption of a 'cookbook' approach. This is where the various steps and activities of the method are followed blindly without considering the reasons why they should be carried out. The needs of the particular project should always be examined before embarking unthinkingly on the use of a method in order to ensure that best use is made of the method. It is usually disastrous to assume that the method, rather than the analyst, will do the work.

4.9 SSADM

The Structured Systems Analysis and Design Method (SSADM) is an example of a structured method. It is a non-proprietary product and was originally developed for use by the UK Government in 1980. It is now widely used in all areas of business and commerce in the UK. SSADM covers analysis and design but does not cover the whole system development lifecycle, providing only a general approach to feasibility and ending with physical design. It generally conforms to the structured method description in the last section and additionally has links to the project management method PRINCE, although it may be used with other project management methods. The method has been developed over several years and includes a comprehensive set of techniques. The major techniques include business activity modelling, logical data modelling, dataflow modelling, entity behaviour modelling – incorporating entity life histories, function definition and conceptual process modelling. These techniques provide alternative views of a system that cross-check each other to ensure that an accurate and complete picture of the system is formed. We do not go into any detail on these techniques in this book but several good books exist which explain the method fully.

SSADM has a 'default structural model' which suggests an order to the system analysis and design work to be carried out. The default structural model consists of five modules:

● Feasibility.
● Requirements Analysis.
● Requirements Specification.
● Logical System Specification.
● Physical Design.

Each module is decomposed into one or two stages, each stage into a series of steps and then the tasks of each step are defined. The default structural model is based on the waterfall model. There is also a product breakdown structure which shows the composition of the products to be delivered. For an explanation of product breakdown structures, refer to Chapter 6 on Project Planning.

In response to accusations of an over-prescriptive and bureaucratic approach, SSADM4+ (released in February 1995) has highlighted the need to tailor the method for individual projects. It has introduced the concept of a template of activities known as the 'System Development Template'. The System Development Template defines a number of areas of activity where work must be carried out during the development of a system. This template shows the interaction between techniques during the analysis and design of a system. Along with the default structural model, this template provides a mechanism for developing an approach for the analysis and design of a particular system. This has to be done with care, however, and ideally should be carried out by people experienced in the use of the method. SSADM also proposes the use of prototyping at various places and may involve a limited use of the spiral model in order to elicit and clarify requirements.

4.10 RAPID APPLICATION DEVELOPMENT (RAD)

Rapid Application Development (RAD) is an approach which is gaining in popularity. With business changes taking place at an ever-increasing rate, traditional organisational structures being redrawn, technology continuing to change quickly and user expectations of IS increasing, there is pressure to do it 'quickly'. There are many 'RAD' approaches and some are more formalised than others. The one thing which all RAD approaches appear to have in common is the 'rapid' part and RAD has become popular because of the commercial pressures to provide a competitive advantage by putting in a system quickly, often accepting that the implemented system may not be perfect. In the same vein, a business opportunity may arise which has a fixed and limited life and which, if missed, will render the development a waste of time. An advantage of developing systems rapidly is that external changes are reduced and are made easier to control as there is less elapsed time for change to become necessary than with a conventional and longer development cycle. The spiral system development lifecycle model is generally used for at least part of the project.

Generally, the RAD approach involves a number of techniques which enable the requirements, and subsequently the system, to be developed via a series of iterative activities generally involving the use of prototypes. The use of prototyping does not necessarily imply RAD, however, as prototyping techniques may be used in other types of development approach. Within a RAD project, prototyping may be used in many ways including:

● Assisting users to define and confirm requirements by demonstrating possibilities.

● Investigating the effectiveness of novel methods of working.

● Testing performance implications.

● Assisting in considering work practice.

Once developed, prototypes allow the system to be examined and reviewed by the users and modifications and refinements can be made quickly and easily. The prototypes then become the final delivered system. One of the major differences between RAD and the more conventional structured methods is that iteration and rework are seen as being an integral part of the RAD approach and not something to be avoided if possible, which is the view of most structured methods.

There are several schools of thought on RAD. One says that RAD should only be used where there is a completely stable environment in that:

- The application is not complex and the scope is well defined.
- The organisational environment is fixed and mature.
- The technical environment is neither technically advanced nor novel.
- The application fits in well with the existing infrastructure.

Another RAD school of thought is more radical and advocates a truly evolutionary approach to development. In this situation, the requirements may not be clearly defined and even the scope of the project may be 'fuzzy'.

Most RAD approaches do have a number of things in common:

- The success of the approach depends on users and technical staff being empowered to make decisions without having to obtain explicit approval from their senior management.
- All deliverables are reviewed for their business fitness rather than their adherence to a 'requirements' document. The reason for this is that requirements are often not completely accurate and this may ultimately lead to a poor system.
- Testing is seen as being an integral part of the iterative cycle.
- All changes are viewed as being reversible. This means that going down a dead end is not seen as being a mistake but rather as an integral part of the process.
- Incremental delivery is acceptable and so a partial system may be implemented initially and refined by subsequent increments.
- The concept of a 'timebox' is used to develop a system with a predefined scope within a short time limit. The limit for each timebox is set before work starts and delivery is limited to what can best be achieved within each timebox.
- Joint Application Development (JAD) brings together the system developers and all key stakeholders from the user organisation. Typically, workshop-type methods are used to develop requirements and agree priorities.

An emerging standard for RAD is Dynamic System Development Method (DSDM), which sets out nine key principles in a framework for this type of development. These principles, which are briefly set out below, are broadly in line with those in the previous discussion of RAD.

- Users must be actively involved.
- Teams must be empowered to make decisions.
- Products are delivered frequently rather than perfected.
- Each product should be fit for its business purpose.
- Iterative and incremental development is an integral part of the approach.
- All changes are reversible.
- The high level scope of the system should be agreed at a level which does not make it difficult to change it later in development.
- Testing is an integral part of the lifecycle.
- All stakeholders must co-operate and collaborate.

The final thing to be said about RAD is that it can create difficulties for the project manager. RAD methods imply speed and, to a certain extent, a lack of structure to the development. The lack of clearly defined requirements, possibly even of the overall scope of the project, and the iterative nature of the specification and development process, make it very important that control is properly exercised if the project is to deliver the 'rapid' benefits of the approach.

4.11   INFORMATION ENGINEERING

Information Engineering (IE) is representative of a number of approaches which offer something additional to the models and approaches already described. IE was developed in the 1970s and, although there are a number of variants, the Information Engineering Method (IEM) from James Martin Associates is probably the main proprietary version currently available.

IE offers complete support to the whole cycle of systems development in a number of ways. It incorporates the use of information systems at the highest levels of business planning. It adopts a strategic approach by the production of business-wide corporate data models and an integrated approach to the development of individual systems. It makes use of integrated CASE tools and of application generators.

In order to be fully effective, IE has to be used on an enterprise-wide basis and this makes it expensive to set up. It also requires the full commitment of senior management and a high level of centralised control. In many ways, IE is running against current thinking as decentralisation and end user empowerment are currently in vogue. Similarly, long-term strategic objectives are now often considered too inflexible and business requirements change too fast to make the IE approach effective. Finally, IE probably works best when introduced to an environment where intensive use is not currently made of IS. The problems in introducing a concept like IE to an IS-literate organisation are considerably greater when the range of current and disparate computer systems have to be considered than when introducing it to relatively virgin territory as all the currently accepted methods have to be replaced by the all-enveloping IE. However, where IE is appropriate and the IE environment has been implemented properly, the project and the project manager will benefit considerably from the comprehensive level of support provided and the detailed definition of the approach.

4.12 SUMMARY

It is important to appreciate the difference between the project lifecycle and the system development lifecycle. Although this book is primarily about project management, the project manager needs to have an appreciation of the different models used in developing systems as it may be necessary to select an appropriate system development lifecycle in order to meet the constraints of time, cost, quality, resources and risk which have been placed on the project. In any event, the project manager will need to have a knowledge of the problems, pitfalls and good points of managing a project using each of the lifecycles.

There are basically two system development models, the waterfall and the spiral, and most other models are based on them. The waterfall model adopts a stage-by-stage approach with each stage being carried out once only and a stage starting only on completion of the one before. The spiral model is iterative in nature with several cycles being carried out in succession with the system under development being refined at each cycle.

The 'b' model, the 'V' model and the incremental model are variants of the waterfall model. There are a number of development approaches which make use of these models and each has advantages from the point of view of development. Most structured approaches make use of a waterfall model. The important application of the spiral model at present is rapid application development which adopts an iterative or evolutionary approach to system development.

4.13 QUESTIONS

1 You have been asked to take charge of a system development where the customer requires about 50 per cent of the functionality very urgently to meet a business opportunity but the remaining functions can be delivered over the next few years. Which of the various development lifecycles do you think would be most suitable for this project and why?

2 What would you say are the principal advantages and disadvantages of the sequential approach to system development offered by the waterfall and 'V' lifecycle models?

3 Some critics have said that the use of structured methods, such as SSADM, increases both delivery time and bureaucracy. Do you think these criticisms are justified and what are the claimed advantages in the use of structured methods?

4 Increasing interest is being taken in the use of *rapid application development*. Why is this, and are there any dangers associated with the RAD approach?

5 Consider how you would organise your project team for a RAD-type project. What leadership practices would it require from the project leader and what would the team members have to do? How, and at which points, would you involve the users?

CHAPTER 5

The profile of a project

5.1 INTRODUCTION

In the previous chapter we looked at a number of system development life-cycles and considered some of the general project management issues that affected them. In this chapter we will look at a particular project in some detail and at the work involved at each stage of the project. We will then examine a generic 'process model' which can be tailored to suit the project in question. Rather than looking at an 'in-house' project where the information system is to be developed for the organisation by internal staff, we are going to consider the situation where an external supplier will carry out the technical development work alongside the company's users. In the remainder of the chapter therefore we'll refer to 'customer' to mean the organisation commissioning the work and 'supplier' to mean the external company brought in to carry out the development work.

The IS project to be considered will be the delivery of a specified information system within given constraints of time, cost, resource and quality. We shall assume that a feasibility study has been carried out and that the scope of the project and the overall requirements have been specified as part of the procurement process to select the supplier. The project will come to a conclusion with the acceptance of the system by the customer and there will be no element of on-going maintenance or enhancement as part of the project. The work will be carried out by the supplier on the customer's premises and will be developed, tested and finally installed on hardware owned by the customer. Any additional hardware procurement will be handled by the customer and will not form part of the remit of the supplier.

We shall also look at the issues involved in systems delivery with this type of arrangement as the views of the customer and supplier can be rather different and it is useful to be aware of both sides, irrespective of which 'side' the project manager represents. Obviously the overall objective is the same from both sides: the delivery of an information system acceptable to the customer in terms of quality and delivered by the supplier within the allotted budget and timescale. Projects of this type are usually carried out in one of two ways: 'fixed price' or 'time and materials'. In a fixed price contract, the cost of the work is agreed at the outset and is based on delivery of the stated requirements. A time and materials contract is less rigid and means that the supplier is paid on the basis of the effort which is put into development. There are pros and cons to each arrangement which are different for customer and supplier. Fixed price means that the requirements need to be specified to a high level of detail in order that both customer and supplier have a clear understanding of what is to be delivered. The risk with this kind of project is carried by the supplier as they receive the same amount in payment irrespective of how much resource has been put into delivering the system. If the supplier underestimates the amount of work involved, they will reduce, or even eliminate, their profit. Conversely, if they can deliver the project efficiently, there is scope for maximising the profit. This type of arrangement also means that change control is very important; the customer is likely to find that the cost of the project is increased with every change which is required to the original requirements specified at the outset. From the customer point of view, this can be frustrating and lead to a deterioration of working relations with the supplier, perhaps unfairly. Time and materials arrangements, on the other hand, mean that the customer is required to pay for all effort expended by the supplier and leave the customer exposed to inefficient and poor quality work by the supplier. The advantage of this arrangement for the customer is that it is more flexible, allows the requirements of the project to be varied more easily and minimises reworking and renegotiation of the contract.

5.2   THE PROCESS MODEL

Although all projects are different and have unique features, there are elements which are common to most projects. The concept of a 'process model', which shows a generic framework, can be useful. A process model needs a set of features which:

- Are adaptable to a wide range of applications.
- Provide a complete and adequate definition of any project to which they are applied.
- Are easy to assimilate, with the key tasks and points of interest highlighted.
- Are suitable to act as an *aide-mémoire* and checklist to ensure that everything is covered.
- Do not impose any unnecessary constraints on the use of tools, techniques or methods during a project.

A typical process model is shown in Fig 5.1. This model shows the project divided into a number of stages which are followed in sequence from start to finish of the project. There are a number of stages which are carried out in parallel with the main stages and these are also shown. The major deliverables from each stage are indicated by the 'shadowed' boxes.

A process model can be helpful to a project manager in planning the project but obviously cannot be followed blindly and must be tailored to meet the

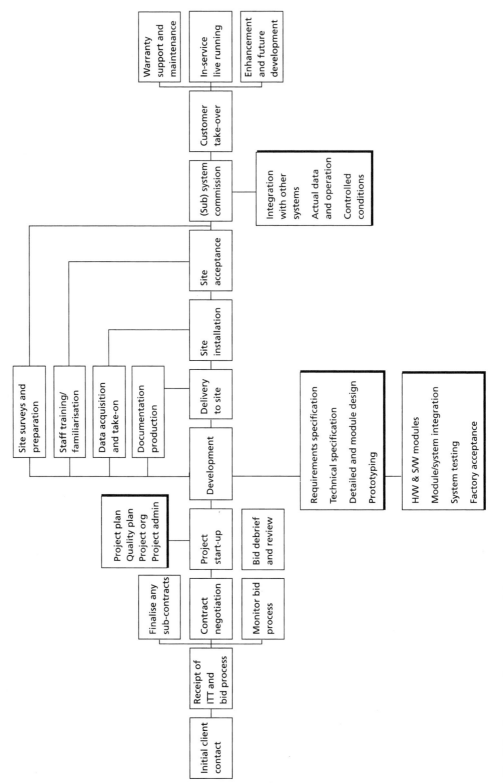

Fig 5.1 A general process model

requirements of the particular project. Not all of the elements of the process model will be appropriate but the model can be used as a checklist to ensure that nothing important is missed from the project. Within the process model, the system development lifecycle must be considered and an appropriate model chosen. This was discussed in some detail in the previous chapter. The process model is also used to help define what is required of the project manager at each stage in the project and to define the inputs and outputs of each stage.

The particular process model shown perhaps implies a 'waterfall'-type system development lifecycle model due to the sequential nature of the activities. However, the process model does allow a number of different system development lifecycles within the Development process box. This typically covers the analysis, design, programming and testing aspects of IS development but does not prescribe how, or in what order, these activities should take place. For example, a full 'waterfall' model approach would have analysis, design, programming and testing carried out in sequence with each activity starting only when the preceding one had been completed. With a phased delivery approach, the analysis and high-level design would be completed followed by sets of detailed design, programming, and system testing for each delivery phase. Similarly if a spiral model approach were adopted, the analysis, design, programming and testing would be repeated for each turn of the spiral. The generic process model would cater for all of these different approaches without substantial modification.

The generic process model shown will be used in our consideration of the 'example' project. For the purposes of 'our' project, we are going to assume that the initial stages of the process model have been completed and the first stage which we shall consider will be Project Start-up. This means that the scope and overall requirements of the project have been broadly agreed between the customer and supplier, and the contract between the two parties has been signed. We shall now look in some detail at a number of the stages of our project and how they relate to the process model. These stages are:

- *Start-up or Initiation Stage* – this includes the Project Start-up Stage on the process model
- *Development Stage* – this includes the Development Stage on the process model
- *Completion Stage* – this includes the Site Delivery, Site Installation, Site Acceptance, System Commission and Customer Take-over Stages on the process model
- *Operational Stage* – this includes the In-Service Live Running and Enhancement Stages on the process model.

5.3 PROJECT START-UP

This stage covers the work which is carried out at the beginning of the project when the basic framework is put in place. This stage is sometimes called the Initiation Stage. This is an important stage of the project as it is where the foundations are laid. Much of the future work of the project is based upon these foundations and the importance of the Start-up Stage should not be under-estimated. There is also pressure at this point to start the 'real' work; this should be resisted as effort spent in getting the basic infrastructure of the project correct is generally time well spent.

It is instructive to look a little more deeply into the overall organisation of the project. In a sense there are likely to be two project managers in this project. The customer project manager, or project director, as this person is sometimes termed, is responsible for the overall project which involves co-ordination of the customer/user resources and all issues relating to the customer's liaison with the supplier. This person's responsibility is to arrange for the appropriate user involvement, specifically during the production of the requirements specification and for customer acceptance of the system. The users may be required to be involved at other times too. Prototyping, training and production of user manuals are some of the other activities which require user input.

Depending on the terms of the agreement between customer and supplier, there may also be an on-going review of products by the customer's staff other than the users directly involved in the project. This may be considered necessary by the customer as part of the general assurance of the project, to ensure that it is 'on-course' and continuing to meet the business objectives and to ensure that certain standards, technical policies and strategic aims are being adhered to. In a PRINCE project, this work would be carried out by the Business Assurance Co-ordinator and the Technical Assurance Co-ordinator. In terms of the overall organisation of the project, the project director should be in overall charge of the project as it is owned by the customer and not by the supplier. It is important also that the customer side is involved in the project planning as many projects fail, not through technical resourcing problems, but through lack of available user resources at appropriate points in the project.

The supplier project manager is responsible for the delivery of the technical products which make up the information system. As was described in Chapter 2 this role is often called the stage manager and the stage manager is viewed as being responsible for the delivery of a specific stage of the project. There may be a number of stages within the project for which the supplier is responsible. The supplier may use the same manager for each stage or may change the manager to meet the differing technical requirements of the particular stage. For the remainder of this chapter we shall refer to the customer project manager as the project director and the supplier project manager as the project manager. It should be noted that both have responsibilities which relate to project management. It is important that these demarcation lines are clearly agreed and documented at the start of the project as misunderstandings and problems over responsibilities can arise later in the project if the roles are not clearly defined.

It is useful to look at the different elements of Project Start-up under the headings of What, Why, Who, How and When headings. This information is often combined into one document and PRINCE calls it the Project Initiation Document or PID.

- *What* is to be carried out?
- *Why* is it being carried out?
- *Who* is going to do it?
- *How* is it to be carried out?
- *When* is it to be carried out?

What. This documents the objectives, scope, constraints and interfaces which apply to the project. Most of this information will be available from other sources such as feasibility study report, project brief, project terms of reference and contract documents. It is important to re-examine this information, however, and confirm that it is still accurate and that it is consistent.

Why. Every project should have a Business Case which sets out the main problems or opportunities which are to be addressed. The main part of the business case contains details of the costs of developing and maintaining the system as against the benefits which are expected. This cost/benefit analysis provides a justification for the project and can be used at any point in the future to confirm that the benefits which are to be realised are still cost-justified. This is important as circumstances can alter and changes to the business requirements or in development costs, due to under-estimates or time overruns, can result in the project no longer being a cost-effective proposition. Many projects in the past have continued with open-ended development when a re-examination of the business case, had one existed, would have made it obvious that the project should be terminated.

Who. This covers the project organisation. For our 'example' project with the Customer/Supplier situation, it is particularly important that the roles and responsibilities are clearly set out in order to avoid contractual issues clouding matters.

How and **When.** These elements are covered in the plans for the project which are developed at this stage. The planning process is covered in detail in Chapters 6, 7 and 8. It is usual at the Start-up Stage of a project to produce a high-level plan for the whole project and to produce a detailed plan for the next stage. This process is continued at each stage with the overall project plan being successively refined and a detailed plan for the following stage produced. In reality, there is more than one type of plan and all of the following plans should be covered in some form or other:

- A general plan description which, as well as a narrative description, also details the project prerequisites, the external dependencies and the planning assumptions.

- A technical plan which sets out the products to be delivered, the activities required to produce them, the times/dates and durations of each activity and the dependencies between activities.

- A resource plan which identifies the type of resource – analyst, programmer, user and so on, and the amount of effort required from these resource types to carry out each activity. 'Non-people' resources should also be covered. This includes the provision of PCs, desks, CASE tools or any other items required for the smooth running of the project.

- A project quality plan which sets out the quality strategy to be followed and cross-references any quality management system, quality manuals, and development approaches which the organisation has decided are to be used. The quality plan should also set out the quality criteria which are to be applied to each of the products.

- Risk analysis which sets out the risks to the project, the probability of each identified risk and its impact, and any countermeasures which are to be taken. Risk is covered in more detail in Chapter 13.

- The configuration management plan which sets out how control is to be exercised on the products of the project and how changes to these products are to be managed. Configuration management is covered in more detail later in Chapter 12.

Resources need to be addressed as early as possible in the project, especially when particular resources are identified as being required. From the customer side, the project director has to ensure that the appropriate end users are available at the right times. This may involve negotiating with their line managers who may not be keen to have their staff diverted to project work, possibly to the detriment of their everyday duties. The project director also has to assemble the 'experts' in the various assurance functions if their expertise is to be used in monitoring the project. Some organisations have dedicated groups for just this purpose. The project manager from the supplier organisation is responsible for locating resources from within the organisation and ensuring their availability. There may be conflict between different managers within the organisation for the same resources, particularly if these resources are scarce. The use of additional contract staff may have to be considered to make up shortfalls.

Ensuring that resources other than people are available is equally important and often overlooked. Because of the limited life of a project and the varying number of people involved at different times, accommodation can be a troublesome issue and ensuring a place to work for all the project staff can be difficult. Similarly, the infrastructure to support their work is important if valuable time is not to be wasted. Analysts probably need access to CASE tools and to PCs to produce the project documentation. The development environment also needs to be ready for the programming staff with appropriate support tools for module building and testing. The list of resourcing issues is long and requires a lot of careful thought if nothing is to be overlooked.

5.4 THE DEVELOPMENT STAGE

The Development Stage of the project is where most of the supplier's work is carried out. Although overall control of the project should be exercised by the customer's project director, many of the activities are under the day-to-day control of the supplier project manager. If we assume that the system development lifecycle approach in our project is based on a waterfall model, then the analysis, design, programming and system-testing activities come into this stage. It should be noted that these activities are more likely, particularly on a medium or large project, to be divided into separate stages themselves in line with the boxes in the waterfall model. It is instructive to consider the 'V' model again as this is a frequently used model in the type of customer/supplier situation in our example. The 'V' model is shown again, in a slightly modified form, in Fig 5.2. This version shows more explicitly the products that link the production activities of the left-hand part of the 'V' with the validation and verification activities on the right. These validation and verification activities are largely carried out by the supplier although, as stated previously, the customer may wish to apply checks and assurance procedures on these products.

The Development Stage has several distinct parts and these have varying amounts of user/customer involvement. The different parts of the development stage are set out below. All projects will vary to some degree depending on the precise nature of the project, but the following is fairly typical of a customer/supplier type of project. The parts considered here are:

- Requirements Definition
- Design
- Implementation
- Integration and Test
- System Test.

Requirements definition

In this part of the project, the customer's requirements are specified in detail. Much of this information will have been supplied in some form in earlier documents, perhaps the initial contract documents, and confirmed in the Start-up Stage output document. The purpose of this work is to ensure that all the requirements are captured and documented, that the requirements themselves

Pre-contract stage   **Completion stage**

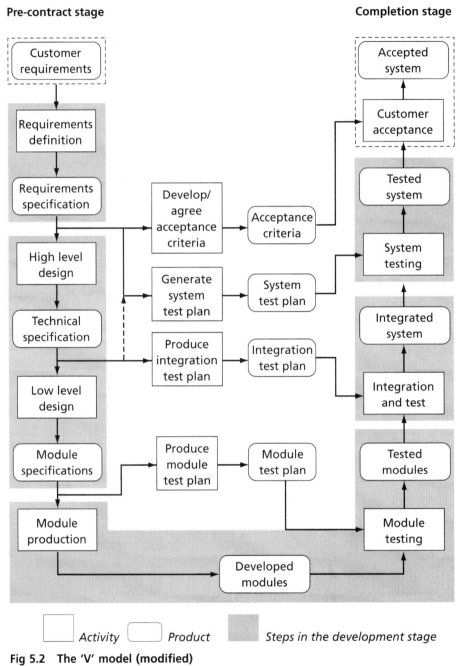

Fig 5.2   The 'V' model (modified)
(© Sema Group UK Ltd 1992)

are complete and consistent with each other, and that they are recorded in a precise and unambiguous manner. These requirements must, of course, be in a form such that it is possible to tell at a later date whether they have been met by the information system which is delivered. The representatives of the customer, the users, will be much involved in this part of the project and it is imperative that these users are able to commit the required time to carrying out the work properly. This issue should have been addressed in the planning activity of the Start-up Stage. From the customer point of view, the requirements should be framed to support the overall business needs for which the system is being developed as well as meeting the needs of the end-users of the system. The supplier will be looking at the requirements from a slightly different point of view. If the project is being delivered on a fixed price basis, the supplier will need to check whether the requirements are in accord with what was originally agreed in the contract documents and that the customer has not increased the overall scope of the project. A good requirements specification is the foundation of all the rest of the development stage work and the work of the project manager should from now on be relatively straightforward, at least in the sense that the 'target' has been clearly defined. This requirements specification document will be a major deliverable for the customer as it will form the basis on which the delivered system will be accepted, or otherwise, by the customer. The specification should include acceptance criteria which set out in a clear and unambiguous manner what the information system is expected to do. These acceptance criteria should link with the requirements themselves and be stated in quantitative terms wherever possible to avoid later disputes on the acceptability of the system.

Design

The design is the first part of the project which addresses *how* the requirements of the project are to be met. As we saw earlier in Chapter 4, most projects now adopt a structured approach to systems analysis and design, and one of the key points of structured methods is the separation of logical and physical designs. It is important that all design work stems from the requirements specification and that there is a clear link, an 'audit trail', from requirements to the design components. The techniques used to produce the design and the form which the documentation of that design takes will be determined by the method or approach being used. The design will be broken down into smaller, more manageable components which will form the basis of the program or module specifications. It must be possible to identify easily how these low-level components fit together to form the overall design – the audit trail again. In terms of the 'V' model, the design will be used to form the basis of the integration tests and system tests later in the project.

Implementation

The implementation part of the Development Stage is where the programming and unit testing take place. This will depend to a great extent on the programming environment to be used on the project and is probably the part where the customer has the lowest level of involvement in the delivery of the products. This is not to say that the project director will not be continuing to monitor progress and to take corrective action when necessary, as the overall progress of the project is the project director's responsibility, even if the day-to-day control of the technical work is being carried out by the project manager. At the end of the implementation part, there should be a complete set of modules which have been tested and signed off as conforming to the specification to which they have been built.

Integration and testing

This part is concerned with integrating the individual components and checking that they work properly together. For instance, it is essential that the data passed from one module to the next is in the form which the second module expects. Integration testing must be designed to ensure that all components communicate in the expected way.

System testing

System testing is carried out by the supplier to check that the whole system behaves according to the specification in the design documents and meets the requirements specification. The supplier should also check that the acceptance criteria set and agreed in the Requirements Definition part have been met, as there is little point in delivering the system to the customer for deficiencies to be pointed out when the system is subjected to acceptance testing by the customer.

There remain a number of issues that are relevant to all parts of the stage. Change control is an important issue if the project is not to be allowed to overrun its timescales or cost constraints. The project should have a procedure for dealing with change in all its forms. It should be remembered that changes can arise at any stage of a project, from near the beginning to almost at the end. Although the general procedure to be followed should be much the same, whatever the stage at which the change occurs, the impact of such a change is likely to be considerably greater, the later that it takes place in the project. As an extreme example, a change which is raised late in the project could necessitate a re-analysis of the requirements for consistency, a major redesign and attendant modifications to a number of programs, and the rerunning of system testing.

The need to make changes to project products can arise in a number of ways. There may be a genuine change in the requirements raised by the users because some element of the business has changed or simply because they have realised that something necessary has been omitted from the requirements. When this happens it is necessary to carry out a thorough impact analysis to ascertain what effect the implementation of this change will have on the project. This will need to take into account the effort, time and cost of reworking any components which have been completed, of specifying and building any new ones and of modifying any which have still to be constructed. It is important to identify every component affected by the proposed change and to estimate the likely cost of modification. The total cost of implementing the change must be calculated along with the probable delay to the project. The authority for accepting changes is generally the steering committee or project board or whoever has been given executive authority for the project. It is usual, however, for the project director to be allowed a tolerance of time and cost for each stage of the project and to be able to authorise the implementation of changes of this nature as long as the tolerance is not exceeded. Tolerance is generally agreed at the Start-up Stage of the project and may be defined as an amount of money or a number of days of effort. In a fixed price contract any change of any significance is likely to increase the cost of the contract if it leads to more work being carried out by the supplier.

Changes may be required to products for other reasons. Errors may be discovered during integration testing or system testing, which will result in reworking components, retesting them and possibly revising estimates for other uncompleted components. Errors of this type become progressively more expensive to put right the later they are discovered and therefore it is sensible to attempt to eradicate them as early as possible. The general procedure to be followed is similar to that for changes to requirements. The contractual position regarding who has responsibility for paying for this type of correction will depend on what was agreed between the customer and the supplier at the outset of the project.

Configuration management is another important element of any project and is closely related to change control. The configuration management plan should contain details of how this is to be handled. Configuration management is concerned with managing the numerous components – plans, program code, technical documentation and management documents, which will be in varying stages of development or change throughout the project. Configuration management is concerned with four basic disciplines:

- *Configuration identification* – the process of uniquely defining each component, or configuration item.
- *Configuration control* – the mechanism for controlling change to configuration items and for recording their status, e.g. undergoing development, baselined.
- *Configuration status accounting* – the means of extracting information about configuration items such as the number of outstanding changes.
- *Configuration audit* – for verifying the completeness, accuracy and security of the configuration items.

Throughout the whole of this stage the project director and project manager will have paid particular attention to tracking the progress of the work, monitoring this progress against the plans, taking action to resolve problems as they arise and modifying the plans accordingly. If it appears, at any time, that the stage is going to exceed its agreed tolerances in terms of cost or time, a report should be prepared for the project board or steering committee in order that they can consider the continued viability of the project. At the end of the stage a report will be produced for the project board or steering committee setting out the cost, time and resource figures for the stage.

5.5 COMPLETION STAGE

The Completion Stage begins when the information system has been completed by the supplier and has been subjected to the full rigours of a system test and every error and problem eradicated. The associated technical documentation, user manuals, operating instructions and any other documentation should also have been finished. This stage is where the customer receives the finished product and carries out a number of examinations and tests in order to confirm that the system meets the specification which was agreed between customer and supplier. This culminates, hopefully, in the acceptance of the completed system by the customer.

There are a number of steps in the completion stage:

- Delivery to the customer of all the elements of the system including software and documentation.
- Training and documentation for the end users, system administrators and operators.
- Carrying out of acceptance tests by the customer on the delivered products.
- Acceptance by the customer.
- System commissioning.
- Final take-over by the customer.

Not all of these steps will necessarily take place. For example, the customer may wish to carry out the training and produce the user manuals without assistance from the supplier. Similarly, commissioning the system in preparation for live running may be implemented directly by the customer using internal resources. It all depends on the agreement between the customer and the supplier or on the terms of the original contract.

Delivery to the customer

This should take the form of a formal handover with all the deliverables being held under configuration management. Software should be available in an appropriate electronic form together with paper records of source code or whatever was agreed in the project plans. All documentation should be handed over as agreed, with appropriate numbers of copies, and generally should be in electronic as well as paper form.

Training and documentation

This may have been taking place over a period of time as it is generally unwise to leave all training until the last minute. If the supplier is to be responsible for training and for the production of user and operator documentation, the numbers of staff involved and the definition of the training will have been agreed beforehand.

Acceptance testing

This involves the customer applying a series of tests to the delivered system and associated documentation to check that it meets the specification. These tests will take a number of forms and can be divided into four categories:

- *Functionality testing.* To check that the functionality specified in the Requirements Specification document has been met. The customer will consider the requirements and the acceptance criteria and carry out a full test to confirm this. The 'V' model shown in Fig 5.2 illustrates the correspondence between the requirements specified for the system and the customer acceptance testing.
- *Performance testing.* This will check that the system meets its performance criteria in terms of response times at terminals, numbers of transactions handled per hour, numbers of users logged on, or whatever. Recovery testing should also be included. If the system is running under test conditions which are different to live running conditions, the results of these tests must be treated with care, by both supplier and customer.
- *Interface testing.* This will confirm that the delivered system works with other systems with which it has interfaces and that the communications between the systems are functioning correctly.
- *Environmental testing.* This relates to power consumption, heat dissipation, noise and other environmental factors.

The activity of user acceptance testing is the responsibility of the customer and should be planned and managed in the same way as any other part of the project and not allowed to become open-ended. There should be a formal procedure in place for reporting faults and errors – or more correctly, issues, as they may turn out not to be faults at all – and proper records should be kept on progress to resolve them. When there are faults to be corrected, the supplier manager should plan the redelivery of the system in a sensible fashion. For instance, it would not be wise to redeliver the system in response to each individual fault, unless perhaps the number of faults was very low indeed.

Acceptance by the customer

When all of the above tests have been successfully passed, or the number of faults is low enough to be acceptable – this will have been defined in the acceptance criteria – the system will be officially accepted by the customer.

System commissioning

Following acceptance of the system by the customer, the system will be set up in its final environment for live running, connected to other systems and loaded with real data. Many of the tests previously carried out during acceptance testing will be repeated as, in some instances, these tests can only properly be carried out in a production environment. For instance, capacity and stress testing are better carried out in conditions which are as close to live running as possible. In some cases it is possible that the acceptance testing and commissioning activities will be combined in order to save time. This is probably what would happen in the example project as all development and testing is being carried out on the customer's premises and using the customer's equipment, and there would be limited gains by repeating much of the testing.

Final customer take-over

This is the point where the customer formally accepts the system and the project comes to an end. It is possible that the system will be accepted with some minor faults on the basis that they will be corrected within a specified period of time. The project director should prepare an end of project report for the project board or steering committee which is responsible for officially accepting the system. This should set out in summary form information relating to the whole project and whether the time, cost and quality objectives have been met.

The project director also prepares a second report on the project, from the project management point of view, in order that the organisation benefits from this experience. The focus of the report should not be on blame allocation for anything which went wrong but on lessons for the future. This is sometimes called a *project evaluation report*.

5.6 OPERATIONAL STAGE

The Operational Stage takes over when live running begins. This does not form part of the project, as such, unless some type of guarantee or support arrangement has been negotiated between the customer and supplier. Business requirements change, however, and it is likely that the system will require maintenance and enhancement. Faults will arise during live running which were not discovered during testing of the system. Perhaps the system will be used in a way not envisaged by the designers and this may lead to faults becoming apparent. Changes to requirements or additional requirements will become necessary with the passage of time. The management process of applying these changes in a controlled way is essentially the same as when the project was being developed and the documentation produced during the project phase should be maintained and kept up to date.

Some time after live running has started, usually after about six months, a post-implementation review should be carried out. This effectively reconsiders the business case produced at the beginning of the project and assesses whether the business objectives of the system have been met. This concentrates, not so much on whether the requirements have been met, as on whether the organisation has achieved the business benefits from the system which it expected.

5.7 SUMMARY

In this chapter we have looked at a particular project from beginning to end. We have considered the use of a generic process model and identified the likely stages of a project. These stages are:

1 **The Start-up or Initiation Stage** which is more concerned with 'pure' project management than with direct delivery of information system products. The start of a project has been looked at under the following headings:

   • *What* – the objectives, scope, constraints and interfaces.

   • *Why* – the need for every project to have a business case.

   • *Who* – the project organisation to define the roles and responsibilities on the project.

   • *How* and *When* – the plans which need to be developed to ensure that the project has a firm base.

2 **The Development Stage** which is concerned with the traditional analysis, design, programming and testing aspects of system development.

3 **The Completion Stage** which is where the finished product is delivered by the supplier, and tested and accepted by the customer.

4 **The Operational Stage** where the information system goes into live running.

For each of these stages, project management issues which are likely to be encountered have been discussed and considered from the viewpoint of the customer and the supplier and we have noted areas of possible dispute.

5.8 QUESTIONS

1 Describe the products that typically result from the following project stages: *Project start-up; Analysis of requirements; Design integration and testing.*

2 Explain the incremental approach to testing represented by the sequence: *unit (module) test; integration test; system test; acceptance test.*

3 From what product should the *acceptance criteria* for a project be derived and why?

4 Why is it important that the project team and the users develop and agree a process model for a project?

CHAPTER 6

Project planning – understanding the work

6.1 INTRODUCTION

In this chapter, and the two that follow, we shall examine some of the steps involved in planning an IS project – or most other types of project for that matter. We shall present a systematic model for the development of sound and practicable project plans and we shall contrast two approaches to breaking the project down into controllable chunks – the work breakdown structure and the product breakdown structure.

A First World War German general once remarked that 'no plan survives first contact with the enemy'. Translated into the more peaceful sphere of project management – at least we hope it is more peaceful! – this might become 'no plan survives the start of actual project work'. If this is the case, the question might be asked, why do we bother to plan at all? Why don't we just roll up our sleeves and get on with it, a project management approach that has been called 'JDI' – 'just do it'? Although this might seem like a silly idea, the fact is that many – too many – IS projects have been attempted using JDI and most of them have ended in disaster. Project managers come under a lot of pressure to JDI, not least from their customers who want to see some 'real work' in progress.

So why do we need to plan? There are some very compelling reasons:

- Developing an information system is a very complex undertaking, generally involving the synthesis of various elements – hardware, software, data capture, user training and so on. Something of this complexity is only likely to succeed if it is planned carefully in advance.

- The people involved in a project need to know exactly what their role is, what they are expected to produce and when it is wanted. The project plan communicates this information to all concerned.

- Customers want to be confident that the developers know what they are about. The plan is a tangible demonstration that thought has gone into the work and that the developers have a clear idea of where they are going.

- Unless there is a plan, how can the project manager know whether the project is on schedule, ahead or behind and whether corrective action is needed?

This last reason, of course, explains why a plan is needed even though it won't survive first contact with the enemy. If there isn't a plan, the project manager has no information on which to base management actions – it is rather like driving a car with one's eyes closed, not knowing whether one should be steering to left or right, or even putting on the brakes.

Altogether we have devoted three chapters to project planning. In this chapter, we shall examine how to break down the project into manageable chunks that we can plan and estimate. We also discuss the dependences between activities and introduce the concepts of the network diagram and the bar chart. In Chapter 7, we review some different methods available for estimating the work to be done, and in Chapter 8 we see how the estimates and the dependences are combined to create workable schedules for the project.

One final point. The planning *process* itself has a value irrespective of the actual plan that results. This is that it gives the project manager the opportunity to sit down and *think* about what the project is about and how it is to be achieved. What are the deliverables and when are they wanted? What skills do we need and where do we get them? What are the problems we are likely to encounter and how shall we tackle them? What are the risks involved and how shall we manage them? Risk management is such an important subject that it gets a chapter to itself later in the book. Planning for quality, too, is addressed as a specific topic. In the rest of this chapter, we consider how to develop the basic project plan, specifying the work to be done, the sequence in which it will be performed and who will undertake it.

6.2 UNDERSTANDING THE REQUIREMENT

The starting point for a good project plan is a proper understanding of the requirement – what is it *exactly* that the project is supposed to achieve? Obviously, if an IS project is to be successful, then all concerned must know *in detail* what they are trying to do. Unfortunately, in too many instances, this is very far from being the case.

In an ideal world, the project would start with a requirements specification of some sort. Exactly what this covers, and the level of detail involved, will depend on where we are in the project lifecycle. For example:

- If we are about to start an IS strategy study, then the requirement may be very broad indeed – for example, the study might be to include all activities that contribute towards the business's market strategy.

- A feasibility study would have a narrower focus – for example, to examine the practicality of automating stock checking in a warehouse.

- A full IS project – covering the analysis, design, specification, development and implementation of an information system – requires a much more precise definition of the requirements from which to start.

It is evident, then, that the further along the IS lifecyle we are, the more precision we require in order to get going. The very generalised briefing given for a strategy study is quite inadequate for an actual development project. It is the project manager's responsibility to ensure that the requirement is specified in enough detail for the project to get off to a clear start.

But what if the specification is not detailed enough? What if you are a systems company, or an in-house IT department, that has been asked to quote for a development project against a very high-level specification? The logical response to such a situation would, of course, be to decline to bid and to ask the customer to refine their ideas more precisely and come back later – but we live in the real world and developers are often forced through commercial pressures to tender against quite inadequate specifications. The practical answer is that the project manager must conduct a very thorough risk analysis of the project and identify where all the 'holes' are in the specification. These must then be discussed with the customer and any assumptions must be documented and accepted by both customer and project manager. This is a non-trivial activity and probably involves some hard bargaining, but it is essential if the interests of all parties – the customers in getting what they want and the developers in limiting their exposure – are to be protected.

This analysis of the work is the first and perhaps most important stage in the planning process. At the end of it, the project manager should have a pretty clear idea of what the project is supposed to achieve, its business objectives and the assumptions inherent in the proposed approach.

6.3 BREAKING THE WORK DOWN

Having looked at the objectives of the project, it is time to consider what needs to be done to meet those objectives – what are we trying to produce and how shall we go about it? There are two basic approaches to this – the work breakdown structure and the project breakdown structure – though, as we shall see, these converge in developing a detailed list of the activities needed to execute the project.

6.3.1 Work breakdown structure

This is the more traditional approach and has been widely used in many industries for a long time. The basic idea is to take the overall 'work' – the project – and to break it down progressively into smaller and smaller chunks until we end up with individual tasks, or work packages, that we can estimate sensibly and assign to team members. To understand how this works, let's consider a small IS project, say, a feasibility study in a builder's merchant to see if there is scope for introducing a computerised stock control system. If we consider the project as a whole, we might decide that the work breaks down into two main components, as shown here in Figure 6.1.

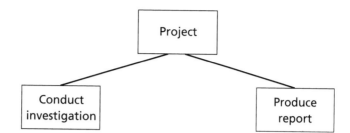

Fig 6.1   Work breakdown structure: top level

If we look in more detail at the first of these components – conduct investigation – we could break it down further, as shown in Fig 6.2.

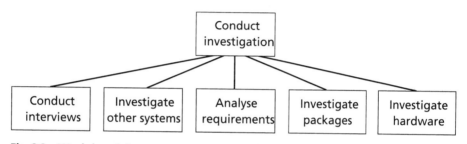

Fig 6.2   Work breakdown structure: second level

We now have five work packages but these are still too large to estimate properly or to plan from. So, we need to subdivide some more, as shown for example in Fig 6.3.

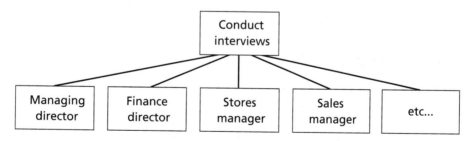

Fig 6.3   Work breakdown structure: third level

And we might decide to subdivide each interview once more, as shown in Fig 6.4.

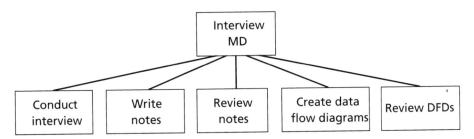

Fig 6.4 Work breakdown structure: bottom level

Actually, in this case, we probably wouldn't subdivide the work this far. We would probably decide that a single interview – conducting it, writing it up and reviewing the results – is a small enough work package, say a day's work. But this does illustrate the principle involved.

The idea, then, is that we continue to break down each activity until we arrive at tasks that:

- Are fairly atomic, that is do not readily lend themselves to further subdivision – or to assignment to more than one person.

- Are small enough to estimate with reasonable accuracy – from, say, about half a day to two days' duration.

Some IT departments and system companies have developed standard work breakdown structures (WBSs) based on their experiences over a number of projects. If these are available, they provide a very useful starting point for the creation of a project-specific WBS and they make it more likely that the project manager will not forget something. The danger of using a standard WBS – or a standard anything else for that matter – is that each project has some distinctive features and it is important not to try to fit the project to a standardised approach; if anything, the standardised approach must be customised for each project.

6.3.2 Product breakdown structure

In recent years, another approach to project planning has emerged, based upon the idea of considering the products that will result from the project. This approach underpins the PRINCE project management method. There are several advantages claimed for the product-based approach, including:

- It ensures that the project's focus is on *what* is to be achieved rather than *how*; in other words on the ends rather than the means. This is valuable in that projects are not undertaken for their own sake, but to achieve some wider purpose, and keeping their eyes on the products helps remind the project team of this fact.

- When approaching a new area of work, it is sometimes difficult to envisage exactly what you need to *do* – in other words, the work. However, it is somewhat easier to consider what you have to develop – in other words, the products – and starting from the product end is more productive.

● Project managers who have used the product-based approach report that it is less easy to forget something in the plans than it is when using a work breakdown approach.

● Once you have identified all of the products, then you can associate other things with them: what quality standards will be applied; who will review them; what the configuration management regimes will be; and so on.

As with a work breakdown structure, product-based planning works by progressively decomposing the project products into smaller products until we reach a sensible, unitary product level. To illustrate this, we shall use the standard PRINCE approach.

In PRINCE, the top-level of products is known as 'project products'. These subdivide into three main categories as shown in Fig 6.5.

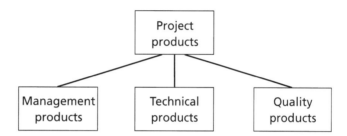

Fig 6.5   PRINCE product breakdown structure: top level

1   **Management products** are those products associated with the planning and control of the project. They include, for example, the project initiation document, the project plan, the quality plan, the acceptance criteria, the regular checkpoint reports and so on.

2   **Quality products** are associated with the definition and control of quality and include the product descriptions, quality review reports and project issue reports.

3   **Technical products** are those things that the project has been set up to create. In the case of our example project, the top-level technical products might be those shown in Fig 6.6.

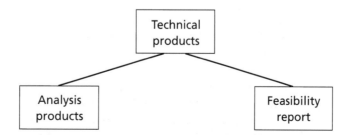

Fig 6.6   PRINCE product breakdown structure: second level

We could subdivide the analysis products further, as shown in Fig 6.7.

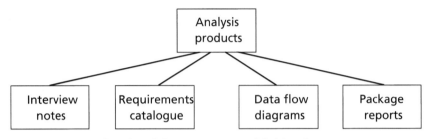

Fig 6.7   PRINCE product breakdown structure: third level

Finally, the products may be subdivided one more time as shown in Fig 6.8.

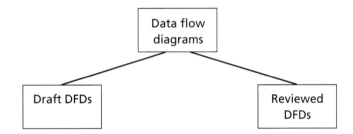

Fig 6.8   PRINCE product breakdown structure: bottom level

At the bottom level, we find an individual product for which we can write a **product description**. This contains a very precise specification of the product including:

- *Composition* – for example, what makes up a data flow diagram?
- *Derivation* – where the product comes from, how it is created.
- *Quality criteria* – how we shall check that it is correct.

Once we have completed our product breakdown structure, or PBS, we have a complete list of the products that the project will develop. Some of these will be final, deliverable products, like the feasibility study report. Others will be transitional products, created on the way to our final product but not deliverable. A good example of this might be the minutes of weekly team checkpoint meetings.

With our list of products, we can now consider the work we will need to do to create the products. PRINCE uses a technique known as a **product flow diagram** for this. The idea is simple enough – we look at the products in relation to each other and consider how one product is transformed into another. For example, say we have conducted our interviews for the stock control feasibility study. We have our interview notes and we need to transform them into entries in our requirements catalogue and into data flow diagrams. We can represent this as a product flow, shown in Fig 6.9.

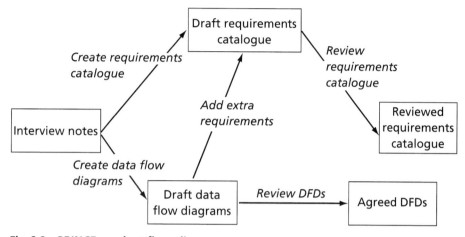

Fig 6.9   PRINCE product flow diagram

In this diagram, we can see that our interview notes are transformed into requirements catalogue entries by the activity *Create requirements catalogue*. Similarly, the draft data flow diagrams are transformed by the activity *Review DFDs* into a set of agreed DFDs.

The product flow diagram provides two important inputs to the planning process:

● A set of activities, for which we will need to estimate effort.

● An understanding of the dependences between activities.

We shall discuss dependences more fully in the next section.

Just before moving on, however, there are two more points to make in relation to PRINCE and products. The PRINCE manuals, and many of the textbooks on PRINCE, provide outline product breakdown structures for projects. These are quite detailed in respect of the management and quality products, less so for the technical products – necessarily, since all projects are different. However, when PRINCE is used in association with SSADM, then SSADM provides a more detailed product breakdown structure for its technical products, as well as detailed product descriptions. Thus, a project manager using both PRINCE and SSADM will have available a very good general product breakdown structure from which to develop a project-specific structure.

6.4   UNDERSTANDING DEPENDENCES

Dependences are fundamental to planning a project and, later, in understanding the effects of any problems encountered. Yet many IS project managers do not conduct a proper analysis of project dependences, arguing that for most IS projects they are obvious: one has to analyse a requirement before specifying a solution and write a program before testing it. Although this is true enough in this case, these arguments apply only to simple projects, with a few people involved in them. Where, as is often the case nowadays, there are several teams at work, each of them developing a specific part of a system, the need to understand the often-complex dependences becomes paramount.

Essentially, understanding dependences is simple. If activity B can only begin when activity A is complete, then we have a dependency. So, in our example project, we can only begin to develop data flow diagrams once we have conducted our interviews. However, dependences are often more complex than this. Do we, for example, need to have completed all of our interviews before we start any of our DFDs? Probably not. Quite possibly, we could produce a high-level DFD having interviewed the managing director and then develop it further as other interviews are completed. With multiple teams operating, they become more complex still as we need to know exactly which components from one team are required before that, or another, team can start on something else.

We can analyse dependences using a **network diagram**. A network diagram for our example project is shown in Fig 6.10.

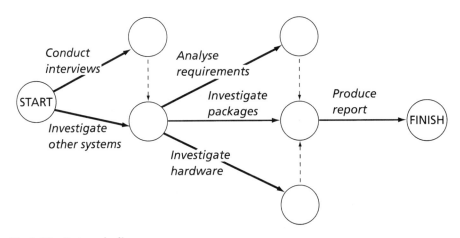

Fig 6.10   Network diagram

This diagram has been drawn using a format known as *activity-on-arrow*, which means that the lines represent project tasks and the circles the connections between tasks. From the diagram, we can read the following:

- Once the project starts, we have two activities – *Conduct interviews* and *Investigate other systems* – that can proceed in parallel.

- But the results of both activities have to be brought together before we can start the next three activities: *Analyse requirements*, *Investigate packages* and *Investigate hardware*. We show this bringing together by using a 'dummy' activity, one with zero duration, indicated by the dotted line.

- The three activities are then brought together – again using two dummy activities – before we can start the last task of our project, *Produce report*.

This very simple structure has already told us one important thing about our project: we can use more than one person on it if we wish, working independently until such time as their work must be brought together.

Once we have estimated the effort involved in each activity, however, we can use the network to establish another important feature of the project. Let us suppose that we have estimated the effort for each activity as follows:

- Conduct interviews   8 days
- Investigate other systems   4 days
- Analyse requirements   3 days
- Investigate packages   8 days
- Investigate hardware   5 days
- Produce report   5 days

Using this information, we can enhance our diagram as shown in Fig 6.11.

This now shows those activities that are on the **critical path** of the project – in other words, those that, if they are delayed, will delay the whole project. For example, *Conduct interviews* will take eight days whereas *Investigate other systems* will only take four days; so a delay of up to four days in *Investigate other systems* will not delay the start of the three successor activities. On the diagram, the critical path has been indicated by the use of thicker lines. We know, too, that if we wanted to shorten the project we would need to shorten

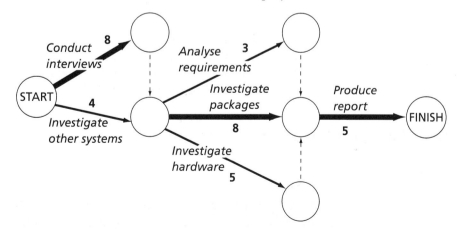

Fig 6.11   Network diagram with durations and critical path added

the critical path tasks – perhaps by adding an extra analyst to *Conduct interviews* and *Investigate packages*.

On a small project like this, we could probably have a good guess at the critical path activities without constructing the network diagram. But what about the project illustrated in Fig 6.12?

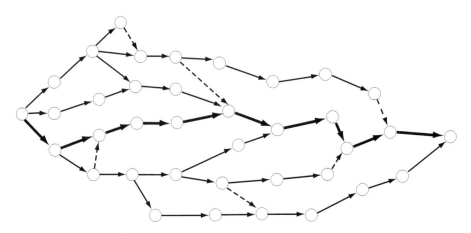

Fig 6.12   Network diagram for more complex project

It would be rather difficult, to say the least, to spot the critical path through this project without a network diagram and it would be practically impossible to work out what would be the effect of slippage on the non-critical activities.

The usefulness of the network diagram becomes clear once the project gets under way and snags are encountered – as they surely will be. If an activity gets behind schedule, the network lets the project manager assess the effect on other activities and on the final outcome of the project. If the late activity is not on the critical path, and there is enough 'slack' to accommodate some delay, then perhaps the project manager just needs to keep a careful eye on it to ensure it doesn't slip further. But if it is a critical-path activity, then the project manager can consider adding more resources, or assigning more experienced staff, or otherwise taking action to bring the activity back on schedule. We shall have more to say on this in the chapters on Monitoring progress and Exercising control (Chapters 9 and 10).

6.5   BAR CHARTS

Another widely-used planning tool is the bar chart, often called a Gantt chart after H L Gantt, an industrial engineer who pioneered its use during the First World War. Bar charts provide a highly visual way of illustrating the sequence of activities in a project but, because they do not show dependences very readily, they are less useful for actually managing progress on a project.

Figure 6.13 is a bar chart of our feasibility study project. We have drawn it on the assumption that one analyst will be performing all the work and that therefore the activities are arranged in a simple linear sequence.

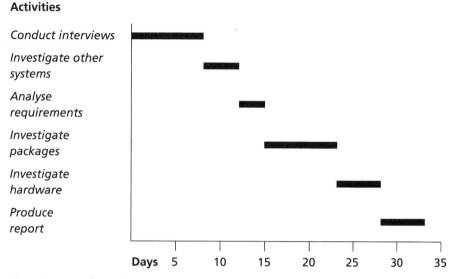

Fig 6.13   Bar chart showing sequential activities

In fact, of course, we know from our network diagram that some activities can proceed in parallel and this is shown in Fig 6.14.

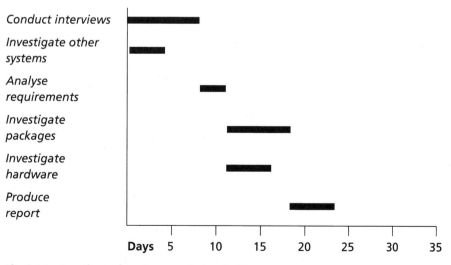

Fig 6.14   Bar chart showing parallel activities

This illustrates well why bar charts are so poor for indicating dependences. Although the bar chart seems to indicate that *Analyse requirements* cannot start until *Conduct interviews* is complete, this may not in fact be the case; the chart might just be reflecting the fact that the person who is to carry out *Analyse requirements* is not available for a few days.

Some project planning software tools try to show dependences on bar charts but the result usually ends up looking messy, as in Fig 6.15.

Activities

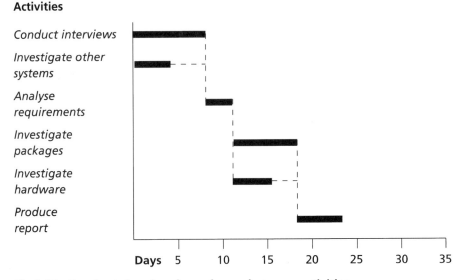

Fig 6.15   Bar chart showing dependences between activities

Generally, it is much better to keep a network diagram to indicate dependences and to use bar charts for what they are most suited – as a means of indicating to those involved in the project the overall sequence of activities. We shall return to bar charts in Chapter 8 when we consider how they are used to create the schedules for the project.

6.6   PLANNING FOR QUALITY

So far, we have mainly discussed *what* is to be done on the project – what activities are required and the order in which we shall carry them out. But this is only part of the planning process – we also need to decide *how* we shall carry out the work, in other words what methods and techniques we shall use and what quality standards we shall apply to our work.

Chapter 12 discusses the issue of quality in some detail. For now, we need to note that planning for quality is an important element of the planning process. The *quality plan* may be a document in its own right or it may be part of the project plan – different organisations have different approaches to this. But whether there are two documents or one, the essential thing is that quality must be considered when planning the project's activities, since quality reviews, inspections and rework arising from inspections are tasks that must be planned for like any others. Moreover, the nature of the project needs to be considered: a critical piece of command software for a nuclear power plant is likely to need more rigorous quality control applied to it than a little spreadsheet-based system to support a local cricket club.

6.7 TOLERANCES

The PRINCE project management method uses the idea of tolerances, and we shall explore these now. Projects are set up in order to achieve certain objectives and these are usually expressed in terms of the 'triple constraint' of time, cost and quality. So, for example:

- The new system must be in place in two months.
- The budget for the project is £1 million.
- The system must enable us to process 500 000 transactions per week, with an average transaction time of two minutes.

However, the three criteria quoted are all absolutes and we need to know whether there is any latitude associated with them. Would the system still be worth having if it took three months to develop? Or four? Would the cost justification for the project be compromised if the final cost was £1.1 million? Or £1.2 million? Would a transaction time of 2.5 minutes be acceptable? There may, in fact, be some flexibility in these criteria and they may be interlinked. For example, it may be acceptable for the budget to rise to £1.2 million provided that the system was delivered in two months. It is important that (*a*) it is known what tolerances there are in a project and (*b*) it is clear who is allowed to use the tolerances. A PRINCE project is 'owned' by the Project Board which delegates authority to run the project to the project manager – along with some tolerances within which the work must be done. This gives the project manager some flexibility to make adjustments to the project as necessary, whilst keeping overall control within the business. If it looks like the tolerances might be exceeded, the project manager must return to the Project Board and present a case for exceeding them – to which the Board may or may not assent.

6.8 USING PLANNING TOOLS

It will probably have occurred to you by now that creating the various diagrams and charts for a project is likely to be a time-consuming business. In addition, as we have said, plans are not produced at the start of a project and then engraved in stone; they will require constant adjustment and revision as the project progresses. All of this points towards the use of computerised planning tools to take the drudgery out of the planning work and to make re-planning less of a chore.

There are many project planning tools on the market today. Most of these have been created for use on personal computers but some of the most powerful tools require a mainframe computer. In a work such as this, it would be impossible to present a proper survey of the available tools – and in fact, it would become out of date as soon as it was published. Instead, we shall consider some of the pros and cons of planning tools in general.

Let us start with the advantages, of which there are several.

Ease of re-planning

Plans are generally created iteratively. We produce a project breakdown, create estimates and produce a schedule. This doesn't work, so we re-schedule. We go back and review our estimates and produce another schedule. And so on. If we are drawing our plans by hand each time, we will soon run out of patience and settle, perhaps, for a less than optimal solution. With a planning tool, however, there should be no such reluctance and we can make minor or major adjustments to our plan at will. The result should be that we plan more thoroughly and produce a much better end product.

Quality of presentation

A plan is a means of communication from the project manager to the project team, to the users, to senior management and to customers. Planning tools generally have flexible presentation and reporting facilities capable of producing high-quality output in a variety of formats. Although presentation isn't everything, the fact is that a well-presented plan is both easy for its audience to assimilate and has greater credibility than a handdrawn plan.

What if? analyses

Perhaps the most valuable feature of a planning tool, though, is the ability to perform 'what if?' analyses of various scenarios. What if the activity *Investigate other systems* takes more than four days? What if we don't get information on packages in time to complete *Investigate packages*? What if the customer asks us to conduct an extra four interviews? Without changing our working plan, we can model the effects of each of these changes and decide how we would handle them. It is very difficult to do this without planning tools and, without them, project managers' responses to change are likely to be based on instinct and feeling rather than proper analysis.

Tracking progress

Most planning tools have facilities to track progress on a project. The data may have to be input manually by the project manager or support staff or, if they are lucky, it may be possible to link the tool to a time recording system and capture the input that way. In either case, though, the project manager will be able to compare the actual progress with the plan, to identify where problems seem to be arising and to investigate them and decide how to respond to them.

However, planning tools also have some disadvantages, of which we would mention the following two.

Hard to use   Although very powerful, some project planning tools can be rather difficult to use. Indeed there is the usual trade-off between ease of use and functionality. Generally, those designed to use a Windows or Macintosh type interface are easier to use, but some packages have had a Windows interface grafted on to an older product, with less than satisfactory results. Some products, too, are rather finicky about the sequence in which the plan is set up – if you start out the wrong way, it can involve a lot of hard word to reshape the plan later. The answers to this, of course, are to read the manuals thoroughly, get properly trained and, best of all, find a local 'expert' who can help you out when you get stuck.

Means become ends   There are some project managers who become quite besotted with their planning tools. They sit at the screen day after day, tuning and tweaking their plans and trying to achieve perfection. In the meantime, the project is proceeding merrily – or probably quite disastrously – without them. This is not an exaggeration and, with all the facilities available on some packages, it is quite easy to see how IS project managers – who probably started out as technicians – get hooked on their use. However, the planning tool is a means to developing a workable plan more quickly and not an end in itself and the project manager needs to keep this in mind!

6.9   SUMMARY

- Planning is essential to the successful execution of an IS project.
- Planning involves thinking hard about the project, what it is to achieve and how the team will go about it.
- The starting point for a good plan is a proper understanding of the requirement and the project manager must ensure that this is done before planning begins.
- The work to be done is analysed using either a work breakdown structure or a product breakdown structure. In either case, the product is a set of activities that will need to be performed to complete the project.
- With the activities identified, the next step is to understand the dependences between them.
- A network diagram shows these dependences and can be used to identify the critical path through the project.
- Bar charts provide a very visual means of showing the sequence of activities in a project, but are less useful for assessing the progress of work overall.
- The project manager needs to understand the tolerances – of time, cost and quality – within which the project must operate.
- Project planning software can take much of the drudgery out of the planning process, produces high-quality output and facilitates 'what if?' analysis of various scenarios.

6.10 QUESTIONS

1 Give three reasons why it is essential to plan an IS project in detail before starting work on it.

2 Ideally, the requirement for an IS project would be specified in some detail before planning begins. If the requirement is not detailed enough, what steps can the project manager take to improve the likelihood of the project's success?

3 Essentially, there are two basic ways of breaking down a project into plannable chunks: the use of a *work breakdown structure* or a *product breakdown structure*. Contrast the advantages and disadvantages of these approaches.

4 What do you understand by the term *dependency*? How can project dependences be represented for planning purposes?

5 Network diagrams and bar charts have different parts to play in planning a project. Where is each of these tools used and what does it show?

CHAPTER 7

Project planning – estimating

7.1 ESTIMATING FOR INFORMATION SYSTEMS PROJECTS

We need to admit at the outset that the reputation of estimating for information system projects is not exactly glorious. Too many projects have gone badly over time and exceeded their budgets and the blame has often been put on the original estimates. Before we look at estimating methods, therefore, it might be as well to consider the special features of IS projects that make estimating for them so difficult.

The first, and perhaps most important, characteristic is that IS projects tend to be one-off affairs. The project is undertaken to achieve some specific business objective, very often nowadays to secure some competitive advantage, and this means that there will always be a degree of innovation involved. The project may be using familiar methods and standards, established programming languages and proven hardware but it will almost certainly be using these components in a combination that is in some way unique. The implications of this are obvious, in that it will be difficult to obtain reliable experience on which the estimates may be based. In addition, there will very likely be no metrics available to assist the estimators or, if there are, they will have to be examined very carefully to ensure that they are suitable for the new project.

The second feature of IS projects is that the initial estimates are often prepared long before there is a detailed specification of the requirement on which to base them. In commercial systems development, for example, companies are often asked to tender for a development based upon a 'user requirement specification' which is a long and ill-defined 'wish list'. Even where in-house IT departments are planning for projects, they are frequently asked to prepare budgets long before the detailed specification of the system has been pinned down.

A third aspect of IS estimating is that it is seldom performed by professional estimators. Generally, estimates are prepared either by the project manager, by salespeople or by any staff who are spare at the time. Although one could argue that estimating is a project management skill, the fact is that a project manager is not a disinterested party. Still less impartial are salespeople and the fact that someone happens to be available does not mean that they possess the skills and experience to create realistic estimates.

There are some additional factors that can influence the estimating process and these are considered later in this chapter. Before proceeding, however, it is worthwhile to compare the approach found in IS with that of a more established profession, to see if there are any lessons we can learn.

7.2 ESTIMATING IN ENGINEERING DISCIPLINES

In order to see how IS estimating might be done better, we could look at civil engineering, to see how the practitioners there go about things.

The first thing we observe is that, usually, civil engineering projects use well-established techniques and equipment. This permits the use of generally-agreed and reliable metrics. There is, for example, hundreds of years' experience available of bricklaying, with bricks of all types used in all conditions and positions. The result is that an estimator can go to a 'blue book' of metrics for various building operations and find out, to a very reasonable degree of accuracy, how long it will take to perform such-and-such a task in a particular set of circumstances. Now, it is clearly nonsense to claim that civil engineering projects do not involve innovation. Many do – for example the Sydney Opera House and the Channel Tunnel. It is noticeable though that where, as in these two projects, there is a large degree of innovation, the civil engineers prove no better at producing accurate estimates than do the information technologists. Nevertheless, a civil engineering project can usually be broken down into components for which reliable metrics can be found. However, an important aspect of civil engineering estimates is that they are prepared against very detailed specifications. The architects and structural engineers will provide a comprehensive design and the estimators will stick rigidly to that. If, subsequently, the design is changed, then that will trigger a variation to the contract. Finally, estimating is a distinct specialism in civil engineering. An estimator does nothing else and is judged, and rewarded, according to the accuracy of the estimates produced. The result is that there is greater professionalism in civil engineering estimating than is usually found in IS.

The lessons for estimating for information systems are therefore:

- We need to identify the known, rather than the innovative, components of our project and base our estimates around them.
- We should be very careful that firm estimates are only offered on the basis of firm specifications.
- We should be more active in compiling metrics on our projects, to help progressively to improve our estimating accuracy.
- An effort should be made to achieve a degree of specialisation in IS estimating.

All of these things are of course more easily said than done but project managers can help themselves by taking a tougher attitude towards estimating and insisting that it be done as well as possible before signing up to an incompletely defined commitment.

7.3 ESTIMATING METHODS COMPARED

In the following sections, we examine a number of the most commonly used methods for preparing estimates for IS projects. Clearly, in a chapter of this size we cannot provide an exhaustive treatment of each method but we do aim to give an outline of each approach and a comparison of the pros and cons of each. For more detailed treatments of the methods, you are recommended to get hold of some of the books mentioned at the end of the chapter. A word of warning, though. All estimating methods are prone to error and all depend to some degree on subjective views of the size and complexity of the task ahead. No single method is going to give a 'right' result and, in fact, a 'right' result is probably unachievable. Estimates are a means by which the project manager can get a handle on the scale and scope of the project and make important decisions on how it will be tackled. Inevitably, factors will arise that will invalidate many of the estimating assumptions and there will be a need to revisit the estimates for the later project tasks once work is under way. So don't expect the methods described here to produce the correct result for your project every time. Use them as a means to an end, as a pointer to the development of your own approach to project estimating.

7.3.1 Analogy method

This is one of the oldest, but one of the most reliable, of methods and depends on finding a project similar to the current one which has been undertaken in the organisation before. The similarity should ideally extend to:

- The type of business involved.
- The overall size of the applications.
- The general scope of the systems – for example, the proportion of on-line to batch functions, whether there is a major communications component and so on.
- The technical methods, standards and languages used.

Where there are differences in any of these areas, suitable adjustments must be made. For example, if the historical project was developed in COBOL, but the new one is to use a fourth-generation language and perhaps a code generator, then the programming effort – though not the analysis or design – should be less this time.

In addition, some judgement needs to be made if there are likely to be other significant differences between the historical project and the new one, for example:

- The customer's company culture.
- The customer's level of computer literacy.
- The degree of management support for the project.

The major advantage of the analogy method is that it enables a broad-brush estimate for a whole project to be developed fairly quickly, perhaps during the preparation of a bid or a proposal. The great danger, of course, is that there are actually fewer similarities between the two projects than initially appears to be the case. If the older one turns out to have been much more complicated, and/or broader in scope, then the result might be an over-estimate which could make the bid uncompetitive. If the newer project is the more complex, perhaps involving new and untried techniques, then an under-estimate might be produced, resulting in loss if the company wins the business.

7.3.2 Analysis effort method

This method is most suited to producing the initial estimates for a project, probably before detailed analysis has begun. The general idea is to estimate the effort required to perform the analysis work for an assumed number of project functions and then to derive the estimates for subsequent project stages via the use of ratios to the analysis effort. For the purposes of this method, a somewhat simplified systems development lifecycle is assumed:

- There is some **analysis** work, leading to a functional specification.
- **Design** work, resulting in a system design, is followed by the writing of program specifications.
- Programs are coded and unit-tested (**CUT**).
- The programs and modules are combined and subjected to an integration test and finally full system **testing** is performed.

As a starting point, some idea is needed of the overall range of functions which are to be provided. This overview could have been obtained from a feasibility study or from the Invitation to Tender, supplemented by further questioning of the prospective customer. Once the functions have been identified, the estimator assesses the effort needed for the *analysis* of each function. This should include *only* the analysis effort itself, not ancillary activities like familiarisation, training or project management; these are examined later in this chapter. In producing the estimates, the estimators will use their own skills and experience, discuss their ideas with others and, perhaps, use statistics from previous projects which have tackled similar functions before. With the analysis estimates available for the individual functions, these can be totalled to give figures for functional areas – groups of functions – for subsystems and for the overall system.

The next step is to make some assessment of three 'key factors' which will apply to the project in terms of its *size*, *familiarity* and *complexity*. Each of these will need to be classified in some way; for example:

Size

The size, or S, factor relates to the number of people who, it is expected, will be involved in the project at its peak. A suitable scale might be:

S = 1   One person project.
S = 2   Small project (up to 4 people).
S = 3   Medium project (up to 12 people).
S = 4   Large project (up to 30 people).
S = 5   Very large project (more than 30 people).
S = 6   Size cannot be determined at this point.

Familiarity

The familiarity, or F, factor concerns the familiarity that project staff are likely to have with the type of work and with the business and technical environments. This factor may be classified as:

F = 1   All factors known by the people likely to work on the project (usually because it is very similar to a previous project).
F = 2   Application or techniques well known to the developers but using unfamiliar hardware, operating system, language or other software package.
F = 3   Unusual application or specialist techniques known only to a few people within the development organisation and who are unlikely to work on the project but using familiar hardware, etc.
F = 4   Application or techniques new to the developers but more common in the IT industry generally, such as using familiar hardware, etc.
F = 5   Application or techniques new to the developers but standard in the IT industry, using unfamiliar hardware, etc.
F = 6   Large element of innovation with considerable uncertainty over outcome.
F = 7   Familiarity cannot be assessed at this time.

Complexity

The complexity, or C factor, takes into account the type of technical issues likely to be associated with the project. Definitions might be:

C = 1   Straightforward algorithms, simple data structures, few files, few interactions.
C = 2   One of the above factors not true.
C = 3   Two or more of the above factors not true.
C = 4   Severe constraints on storage, timing or performance.
C = 5   Complexity cannot be assessed at this time.

Using the S, F and C factors, tables are used to determine the ratios between analysis – for which an estimate is now available – and design, CUT and testing. These ratios can then be used to calculate an effort figure for these other stages and hence for the whole project. Each organisation will develop tables of ratios based on its own experience but to illustrate the approach, Table 7.1 shows an example from an actual table. The table relates to projects where the S (size) factor is 3, that is to a medium-sized project with up to 12 people involved.

Table 7.1 Part of a table of ratios for the analysis and programming effort methods

F	C	Analysis	Design	CUT	Testing
1	1	2	14	59	25
1	2	2	14	55	29
1	3	5	14	47	34
1	4	7	16	43	34
2	1	2	15	63	20
2	2	2	14	59	25
2	3	5	15	51	29
2	4	7	16	47	29
3	1	5	16	59	20
3	2	5	16	55	24

If we assumed that our F (familiarity) factor was 2 and our C (complexity) factor 3, then we can read off stage ratios for our project as follows:

Analysis	5%
Design	15%
CUT (code and unit test)	51%
Testing	29%

Since we have estimated the analysis effort, we can use these ratios to extrapolate the effort for the other project stages and for the project as a whole. The ratios must not be followed blindly however and the estimator must use judgement as to whether special factors apply. For example:

● If a very efficient code generator is being used, the coding effort may well be reduced somewhat compared with the analysis. But coding is only a part of CUT as defined here and unit- and link-testing effort is unlikely to be reduced in proportion. So care should be taken if considering a revision of the analysis/CUT ratio.

● If part of the functionality is to be provided via some packaged software, then the design and coding is likely to be reduced; but link testing and integration testing (included, respectively, in CUT and testing) may actually be increased.

● If there are no interfaces planned with other systems – rare nowadays, but possible – then no integration testing will be needed. In this case, the estimator may decide that some of the testing figure should be removed from the final estimate. However, if many interfaces are required, or if the system itself is very complex with lots of test 'threads' to explore, then it may be sensible to increase the test figure.

The estimator therefore needs to examine the particular features of the current project and make any adjustments required to the ratios. If this is done, the nature of the adjustment, and its justification, should be fully documented so that someone else can review, and comment upon, the estimates.

Testing itself can generally be further subdivided as follows:

Planning test	10%
Test preparation	25%
Running tests	65%

The estimates arrived at using the analysis effort method cover the main project activities. However, they do not encompass the range of supporting activities – such as project management, team leading, quality control and so on – which are needed on every project. These activities should be estimated for explicitly, and some guidance on this is given later in this chapter.

7.3.3 Programming method

This approach starts from a different point from the analysis effort method, namely that of examining the programming effort required and deriving values for the rest of the project tasks. The same project lifecycle definition is used as for the analysis effort method, with the project being broken down into analysis, design, CUT and testing. The programming method generally requires that some preliminary design work has been carried out, but it could be used early in the project if it is possible to obtain, perhaps from the user requirement specification, some idea of the number and types of programs that will ultimately be required. The programs will be related to the functions used in the analysis effort method in the sense that each function may consist of one or more programs.

The simplest way of assessing the programs is to decide if each is likely to be small, medium or large. The estimator then uses metrics from other projects or personal experience to establish an average effort figure for code and unit test (CUT) in each of these categories. For a COBOL (or similar 3GL) environment, suitable figures might be:

Small program	5 days
Medium program	10 days
Large program	15 days

A slightly more refined approach is to make another assessment, as well as of its size, of each program's likely complexity. If three categories, simple, average and complex, are used, a grid can be constructed. For COBOL, this might look like that shown in Table 7.2.

In general, on-line programs are simpler than batch programs because they do not need the same error-handling – problems can simply be referred back to the users. Programs with involved rules and processing logic will be more complex than straightforward enquiries or reports. More complex systems of classification can be evolved, with programs broken down by language type,

Table 7.2 COBOL grid

Size	Complexity		
	Simple	Average	Complex
Small	5	5	10
Medium	5	10	15
Large	10	15	20

for example 3GL or 4GL, as well as by complexity. It may be that the source documentation, an invitation to tender for example, does not contain enough detail to permit such a detailed analysis of the programs. In this case, the estimator may notionally decide that all programs will be assessed as medium/average for estimating purposes. As always, the basis on which the estimates have been prepared should be documented.

At this point, the programming method converges with the analysis effort method. An assessment is made of the size, familiarity and complexity of the system as discussed earlier and the project stage ratios are used to extrapolate effort figures for all stages from the CUT estimate. Where a 4GL is to be used on the project, special consideration must be given to how this will affect the project estimates. Generally, using a 4GL decreases coding effort (in CUT) but does not affect either design or testing. A revised procedure which suits this situation is:

- Estimate for programming as described above but using person/day figures for CUT that have been adjusted for the appropriate 4GL.

- Estimate the programming again, this time using the figures for the COBOL environment.

- Use the COBOL programming estimates when looking up the ratios for other project stages.

- Obtain the total project estimate by using the 4GL CUT effort added to the COBOL estimates for the other stages.

As with the analysis effort method, the estimates arrived at here cover the main project activities. However, they do not cover the range of supporting activities such as project management, team leading, quality control and so on which are needed on every project. These activities should be estimated explicitly and added to the estimates for mainstream tasks and some guidance on this is given later in this chapter.

7.3.4 Direct estimation based on project breakdown

This is the most detailed estimating technique and depends upon having some sort of breakdown of the work to be performed. The two principal methods for breaking down the work – using a work breakdown structure or a product breakdown structure – are discussed in Chapter 6. Once a detailed list of the project tasks is available, the estimator, or preferably several estimators so their results can be cross-checked, review the tasks and assess the effort to perform each. The effort required for each project stage and for the project as a whole is then arrived at through summation. Provided the estimators have sufficient knowledge and experience, this method probably produces the most reliable results but, for a variety of reasons, it is not always possible to use it:

- At the start of a project, there is probably insufficient information to enable the full set of products or tasks to be identified.
- The method takes a great deal of time and effort, neither of which – and especially the former – may be available in, say, a bid situation.
- Even if time is available, the costs of direct estimation may not be justified if an acceptable result can be obtained by other means – through analogy, for example.

Direct estimating is therefore generally used in developing plans for the immediate stage or sub-stage of a project, with other, more approximate, methods being used for the later stages until sufficiently detailed information comes to hand.

7.3.5 The Delphi technique

The Delphi technique is based on the idea of obtaining estimates from suitably qualified people and then synthesising them to produce the final estimate. Since people have differing levels of experience of estimating, and of the underlying hardware and software to be used, the approach has a number of stages:

- Each estimator is given a specification of the work – activity, task or whatever – and asked to provide their estimate for it; these are filled in anonymously.
- The estimates are then summarised anonymously and the summary is circulated to each estimator.
- Estimators reconsider their own estimates in the light of the summary and provide a revised estimate if they wish.

The above processes are repeated as many times as necessary to achieve a reasonable consensus.

The principle involved here is that, by keeping the estimates anonymous, personal disagreements are kept out of the process. In addition, the technique avoids a possible outcome of a round-table discussion which is that the person who shouts loudest, rather than the person with the best estimate, will win the day. Individual estimators can reconsider and revise their ideas in the light of other people's estimates without public 'loss of face'.

7.3.6 CoCoMo

The **Co**nstructive **Co**st **Mo**del was developed by Barry W Boehm and is described in great detail in his seminal book *Software Engineering Economics*. The model, which exists in three versions, presents formulæ for calculating the effort and elapsed time needed to develop software based on an assessment of the amount of program code to be developed expressed in thousands of delivered source instructions or KDSI. For the purposes of the model, delivered source instructions are program instructions developed on the project which are turned into machine code by compilers, assemblers, pre-processors or some combination of the three. The **Basic CoCoMo** formula for development effort is:

MM = 2.4(KDSI)$^{1.05}$

where MM = effort in person/months. So, if we estimate that our project will result in 10,000 delivered source instructions, we can calculate that the development effort will be:

$2.4 \times (10,000)^{1.05}$ = 27.92 or about 27 peson/months

In the CoCoMo formulæ, a person/month equates to 152 working hours or 19 working days, so effort figures can also be expressed in person/hours, person/days or person/years.

The elapsed time is calculated using the formula:

TDEV = 2.5(MM)$^{0.38}$

where TDEV = total development time. So, for our example, the elapsed time would be calculated as:

$2.5 \times (27.92)^{0.38}$ = 8.74 or about 9 months

These basic formulæ are concerned with the total development effort for a whole project and produce estimates which should lie within a factor of two of the actual outcome about 60 per cent of the time. As such, the formulæ are mainly useful in the early stages in planning a project or to provide a cross-check on estimates made using other methods.

Intermediate CoCoMo takes the process a stage further and takes into account many more of the variable factors which can influence project outcomes. These include such things as the attributes of the product (reliability, complexity, etc) of the target computer (execution time, main storage, etc), of the personnel (capability, general experience, language experience, etc) and of the project (use of modern tools, etc). This version of the method takes much more time to use but should produce results within 20 per cent of the actual outcome 68 per cent of the time.

Finally, **Detailed CoCoMo** considers the different factors which apply during the different stages of a system development and produces more detailed estimates on a phase-by-phase basis.

While the full CoCoMo approach is not always followed, one of the major formulæ – that relating effort to elapsed time – is quite widely used. To reiterate, this stated that the elapsed time for a project was defined as:

$$2.5 \times \text{(estimated effort in person/months)}^{0.38}$$

Boehm's formula was derived from close analysis of a large number of projects and can therefore be claimed to be based firmly on reality. What Boehm's work and that of other researchers show is that it is very unlikely that the schedule for a project can be compressed below about 75 per cent of the nominal elapsed time calculated as above. In turn, this suggests that adding staff to a project to try to shorten its timescale will probably not work – and may, in fact, have the opposite result from the one intended.

The main disadvantage of the CoCoMo equations is that they depend upon an assessment of the number of delivered source instructions – more or less, lines of code. The obvious snag with this is that it is not possible to estimate accurately the likely numbers of lines of code until quite late in a project. In addition, it is not entirely clear how the CoCoMo formulæ should be interpreted for projects using more advanced programming tools and fourth-generation programming languages. The elapsed time formula, however, is extremely valuable and seems to work pretty well whatever the environment.

Despite these reservations, however, all serious students of software development should study Boehm's book because of the insight it provides into the dynamics of the software development process.

7.3.7 Function point analysis

The technique of function point analysis was developed in the USA by A J Albrecht and J E Gaffney. The method has three stages:

- Analysing the system in terms of its information processing requirements at a logical level, independent of implementation considerations. Components of the system – inputs, outputs, logical files, interfaces and enquiries – are counted and each is assigned a number of **function points**. These are then totalled and the result is a score for Unadjusted Function Points (UFPs).

- A Processing Complexity Adjustment (PCA) is calculated to allow for technical considerations such as ease of use, distributed processing, maintainability and so on.

- The Unadjusted Function Points are factored by the Processing Complexity Adjustment to derive the final function point score for the project.

These ideas were further developed by Charles Symons in the UK to produce Mk II Function Point Analysis (FPA). This version considers three aspects of a system:

- Its information processing logic size, derived from the system's inputs, processing and outputs.

- Its technical complexity, whether batch or on-line, if it involves demanding criteria for performance or ease of use.

- Performance influencing factors, such as the general development environment, available staffing and so on.

The method provides formulæ which can be used to estimate both the effort and elapsed time for a project. It is recommended that organisations calibrate the formulæ to match their own experience based on collected metrics, but there are some default metrics, derived from cross-industry research, which can be used until organisation-specific metrics are available.

FPA is suitable for use on transaction-oriented business application systems, on-line or batch, which manipulate data stored in files and databases. It is not applicable to other types of application, for example operating systems or command and control systems. FPA depends upon an understanding of the information processing, derived from the entities and data attributes involved in the processing, and on knowledge of the proposed system's balance of on-line and batch transactions. It is clear therefore that, for the method to work properly, a completed Requirements Specification is needed. However, FPA can be used earlier in the development process if certain assumptions can be made about system functionality; as always in estimating, the basis of such assumptions should be documented for future reference. FPA is particularly suitable when the project is to be developed using the Structured Systems Analysis and Design Method (SSADM) as the project stages used within FPA are the same as those in SSADM's default Structural Model.

The basic procedure in FPA is described below but this is, necessarily, a great simplification of the complete process. For a detailed description of the method and the rules for function counting, you should read one of the books listed at the end of the chapter.

1 Determine the size of the system
This should be performed by calculation based on known facts about the number and types of transaction, etc. In the absence of that, properly-documented assumptions may be used. Input attribute-types, output attribute-types and entity types referenced during processing are counted or assessed and a number of function points assigned to each. These are known as *unadjusted function points*.

2 Adjust the unadjusted function points for technical complexity
A *technical complexity adjustment* is calculated based upon an assessment of 19 factors, including:

- Data communication.
- Distributed functionality.
- Performance.
- Operating restrictions (for example, use of a shared processor).

- Transaction rates.
- Percentage of on-line data entry.
- Ease of processing required.
- Percentage of on-line updates.
- Complexity of processing.

and so on.

The unadjusted function points are then multiplied by the technical complexity adjustment to get the overall system size in function points.

3   Calculate normative effort and elapsed time
The system size in function points is converted into an effort figure by using tables showing productivity rates (3GL or 4GL) in terms of function points per work hour. Other tables, of function points delivered per elapsed week, are used to determine the elapsed time for the project.

4   Distribute effort and elapsed time by project stage
More tables are used to distribute the total calculated effort and elapsed time over the various stages of a project.

5   Consider estimates and adjust for risk factors
Various risk factors are considered which could influence the calculated effort and elapsed times. These include such things as whether the project is larger than the organisation has handled before; the degree of technical innovation involved; and also 'political' issues within the user organisation.

6   Consider the effects of time or manpower constraints
Finally, the calculated elapsed time is compared with the available time for the project. If the available time is less than the calculated elapsed time, then an assessment is made of the likelihood of being able to compress the project into the shortened timeframe.

The product of Function Point Analysis is a set of estimates covering:

- The effort needed to complete the project.
- The elapsed time needed to complete the project.
- The likelihood of being able to deliver the project in the time actually available.

As we have indicated, FPA is most suitable when there is a Requirements Specification available to the estimators. If FPA is used earlier in the project, then the recommended procedure is to revisit the estimates whenever more detail is available, to re-evaluate if the original assumptions are still valid.

7.4 ESTIMATING FOR SUPPORTING ACTIVITIES

Whilst it is probably true that some projects go over time or budget because activities were under-estimated, usually it is because activities were missed out altogether. It is relatively easy to identify the main tasks of the project, such as conducting interviews, writing code and performing system tests, but there are scores of other activities which seem insignificant by themselves but which can amount to a lot of time over the length of a project. For example, an activity may have been defined for 'review program specification X' – but what about dealing with the results of that review, like:

- Revise program specification X after review?
- Re-review program specification X?
- Rework program specification X after second review?

It is very important that all these supporting activities are catered for in the estimates. An important aid to this is a standard work breakdown structure or product breakdown structure as described in Chapter 6 but, as with everything concerned with estimating, this should not be followed blindly. The project manager needs to consider carefully if there are any specific tasks which apply to *this* project and which should be taken into account.

There are two basic ways of accounting for these supporting activities:

- By estimating for them explicitly, such as by adding a task called 'quality review' and allowing a number of days to carry it out.
- By adding a percentage on top of one of the basic activities – say 10 per cent on top of program specification for quality reviews.

As long as the allowances are feasible, it does not matter too much which approach is adopted. However, it is important that the method used is documented properly so that, for example, a programmer with 15 days available for a program does not believe that quality review is additional when it is included as a percentage in the task estimate.

The supporting activities which should be taken into account are discussed below. Some of these activities can be calculated as a proportion of other, specifically estimated, tasks; for example, one might add 5–10 per cent on top of a design task to allow for quality reviews. Other activities, such as project management, are more related to the elapsed duration of the project.

7.4.1 Proportional activities

Team leading/ supervision

There is a long-established, and generally quite reliable, 'rule of thumb' that a team leader should be capable of running a team of up to five people. This means, in effect, that team leading should represent 20 per cent of the programming effort during coding, unit testing and system testing. However, this ratio only works for 3GLs such as COBOL. With the increased programmer productivity of 4GLs, a lower ratio of team leading to programming should be used – say 1:4 or 25 per cent. Team leading during other phases of a project is less easy to estimate. During analysis and design, a lot will depend on the experience of the individual analysts and designers. A figure of 10–20 per cent of the effort for functional specification, system design and program specification is a useful starting point.

Documentation This refers not to design documentation, the production of which is the specific purpose of the analysis and design activities, but to documentation such as the User Manual and Operations Manual, which result from the programming work. A good approximation to use here is 7 per cent of CUT.

Quality control The project manager has to decide what form the quality control should take – for example, will it be supervisor reviews, peer reviews, structured walk-throughs, Fagan inspections or something else? Then, some allowance needs to be made on top of the analysis or CUT figure for the work involved.

Quality assurance Projects are also likely to get involved in some sort of external QA review – either from the developer's own QA specialists or as part of a regular ISO9001 surveillance and re-accreditation process. The project manager should discuss this question with the quality department when the project starts and schedule QA reviews as explicit activities in the project plan.

Staff technical training This does not refer to generalised training, which may affect the elapsed time on the project but should not impact on the project's budget. What this involves is training specifically designed to enable team members to under-take their project work – perhaps training in a new language or version of the language. There can be no reliable yardstick for this and project managers will have to assess the requirements of the project in each case and allow for attendance at training courses as necessary. It should be remembered that not only is there a staff cost associated with this, but probably there has to be some budget for paying for the training provided.

Familiarisation Team members may need familiarisation in any or all of:

- The customer's business.
- The customer's rules and regulations, especially if working on restricted or safety-critical sites.
- The standards and methods to be used on the project.
- The technical environment – operating system, programming language, CASE tools and so on.

The effort to be devoted to familiarisation differs considerably from project to project. The project manager must make some assessment of how much familiarisation, and what sort, is required given the skills, experience and background of the staff assigned. There may also need to be some allowance for the development of, for example, team-briefing materials.

Customer reviews Once again, the requirement here varies from project to project. At the very least, customers will be asked to review major documents such as the Functional Specification and some allowance must also be made for:

- Possible presentations of the documents to customer representatives.
- Discussions with customers to amplify or explain points of detail.
- Revisions to the documentation arising from the reviews.

In some cases, it may be necessary to provide training to customer representatives to enable them to play their full part in the development work – in reading SSADM documentation, for example.

Some customers will take a very detailed interest in the development and, particularly in safety-critical or mission-critical situations, may want to examine even technical documentation such as program specifications. It is important that the project manager discusses these requirements with the customer at the start of the project and makes sufficient allowance for the review work.

Data conversion and system migration The difficulty of converting data from an old system and managing the migration of data to the new one is very often either forgotten or underestimated. This can be a very time-consuming activity and may involve the use of additional personnel, such as data preparation staff if direct data conversion is not possible.

Reviewing third-party work If subcontractors are being used to perform some of the work, some allowance must be made for applying quality control to their work: 10 per cent of the estimated effort of the third-party is a good general guideline.

Post-implementation review Some effort should be allowed for performing a post-implementation review at the end of the project. This enables the lessons of the project, good and bad, and also the ever-valuable metrics to be captured for the benefit of later projects.

7.4.2 Elapsed-time activities

The problem with elapsed time activities is, of course, that the duration of the project only becomes apparent once some detailed project planning has taken place. In this sense, therefore, estimating and scheduling can be seen to be iterative processes. However, Boehm's formula for working out the likely duration of a project can be used to give an initial idea of the likely project duration and this, in turn, can be used in calculating the elapsed-time activities.

In the sections that follow, we use a figure of 18 days per month for a full-time person. This is based on the following calculation:

Total working days per year (52 × 5): 260

Less holiday (say): 25

Less other non-working time (training, sickness, etc): 15

Leaves: 220

Divided by 12 to give days per month: 18.33

Where there is, on average, more or less annual leave and/or sickness and training, then some other figure may be more appropriate.

Project management

A major decision needs to be made whether:

- A full-time project manager is to be used on the project.
- If a part-time project manager is to be used, does he or she perform some other activity, perhaps as a business analyst, on this project or fill in the remaining time with work on another project?

In general, it is preferable to have a full-time project manager where the overall volume of work supports this. The main problem with part-time project management is that other commitments, on the current project or another project, always seem to clash with some vital management task and the project suffers accordingly.

For a full-time project manager, the allowance should be 18 days per month during the length of the project. The duration, as we have seen, can be derived from Boehm's formula, thus:

$$\text{Elapsed time (months)} = 2.5 \times (\text{estimated effort in person/months})^{0.38}$$

Part-time involvement can be calculated in a similar way so that, for a half-time project manager, 9 days per elapsed month would be allowed.

Systems management/ technical support

This role may be needed from design onwards. If it is, full-time involvement can be calculated at 18 days per month, with lesser involvement reduced accordingly.

Configuration management

An allowance must be made for setting up the configuration management procedures at the start of the project and operating them thereafter. On a large project, there may be a full-time configuration management role, in which case 18 days per month should be allowed. A less than full-time involvement should be factored proportionately.

Implementation management

If a full-time implementation manager is needed, then they will need several weeks for preparation plus the usual 18 days per month during implementation itself.

Data administration

Another non-trivial activity, particularly on a large project where a full-time role may be identified.

Project office   Having a project office, or at any rate some sort of project support, is very valuable and cost-effective. It frees the project manager from some routine work, like recording timesheets, and enables him or her to get on with actually managing the project. In addition, it is useful for analysts and designers to have support staff who can copy and distribute documents, arrange meetings and so on. If a full-time person is used, then the estimate should be for 18 days' effort per month over the duration of the project. If the project shares the use of project office support, then a suitable *pro rata* allowance needs to be made.

Subcontractor management   If subcontractors are involved, effort must be devoted to managing them. Quality control of subcontractors has already been mentioned but, depending on the size of the subcontract, there may also be a need for:

- Regular meetings to review progress.
- More meetings to agree and later review the contractual arrangements.
- Checking and authorisation of invoices.
- Interviewing subcontractors' staff.

and so on.

7.4.3   Other factors influencing estimates

So far, in discussing estimating, we have tended to assume that all analysts are interchangeable, that programmers have equal levels of skill and ability and that all projects have similarities. However, it is obvious that none of these things is true in the real world and estimates must be adjusted to take account of the variations which can occur between people and from project to project. Some of the estimating methods we have reviewed – detailed CoCoMo and Function Point Analysis – contain adjustment factors which enable the circumstances of particular projects to be taken into account. However, in using other methods, the project manager will have to consider them and decide how their raw estimates should be adjusted. In this section, we consider some of the factors to be considered but, of course, the list is not exhaustive and project managers will develop their own checklist as they gain in experience of estimating and planning.

Use of inexperienced staff   The productivity difference between experienced and inexperienced staff can be very marked. The first two or three programs written by an inexperienced programmer can take twice as long as the standard metrics will suggest. An experienced programmer, using a new language for the first time, is also slower at first, although the difference is less marked. New analysts or designers, too, are more hesitant and hence slower than experienced people, particularly if they are working in a business or technical area with which they are unfamiliar. Familiarisation has already been discussed, but the prudent project manager will also allow some additional time to complete the analysis and design work with inexperienced staff. It should be remembered, too, that if the analysis or programming work takes longer, the amount of supervision has to increase proportionately.

Use of contract staff
Increasingly, companies are making use of contract programmers. In theory, a contract programmer should possess good technical skills and so productivity should not suffer. However, outsiders are always an unknown quantity – unless they have worked for the company before – and there may, in any case, be some initial slowness as they get used to the local methods and standards.

User involvement and availability
The project manager needs to form a view, before work starts, on how available and committed the users will be to the project. If users are enthusiastic and interested in a development, then getting access to them for fact-finding and reviews is fairly easy; if they are suspicious, antagonistic or just uninterested, access is more difficult and things will inevitably take longer.

Although a lack of user access initially affects elapsed time, it does also impinge on the effort estimates since, unless they can juggle their work around, staff may end up sitting around doing nothing useful but booking to the project nevertheless.

User support during acceptance
Again, users can adopt varying approaches to this. Some happily conduct the acceptance tests themselves, others simply want to watch tests, perhaps the system tests, conducted by the developers. The responsibilities for testing should have been spelled out in the contract but some allowance should be made in the estimates for supporting the users during acceptance testing.

Installation and commissioning
Depending on the number of locations at which the system is to be implemented, this could be quite a sizeable activity and should be allowed for in the estimates.

Warranty
The type and duration of warranty will have been discussed and agreed during the contract negotiations. However, some allowance needs to be made for possible warranty work and this is most easily assessed as a proportion of the total development effort. Some guideline figures are:

3-month warranty	5%
6-month warranty	7½%
12-month warranty	10%

7.5 HUMAN FACTORS AFFECTING ESTIMATING

One of the main reasons why estimates often turn out to be hopelessly wrong is that they aren't real estimates at all – they are numbers contrived to meet a political situation, such as making the bid low enough to be competitive. Now, it is clearly important for IS companies to win business, and to do this they have to offer competitive pricing. But the price at which some work is offered is a very different thing from the cost. The price is determined by what the market will bear, the profit margin that the company wants to obtain, the strategic reasons for wanting the business and a host of other factors. The cost on the other hand is, or should be, some scientifically-quantifiable measure of the resources required to perform the work and not influenced by market factors.

The typical problem that arises, however, is that the estimators on the bid team look at the requirement and come up with what they believe to be a realistic estimate. The salespeople then say, 'Oh come off it, it can't cost that much', and there follows a period of haggling until the final 'estimate' is arrived at. It is of course quite legitimate for salespeople to question estimates especially if, as does happen, the estimators are conservative and trying to build in some contingency against disaster. But, at the end of the day, the estimators must stick to their guns if they believe their figures are correct. This can be pretty unpleasant for the estimators, and it is one of the reasons why project managers require considerable self-confidence in order to withstand the resultant pressure, but it must be done if the project, once won, is not to be compromised.

If cost – and hence, once profit is added, price too – really is an issue, then perhaps the bid team should consider a more innovative way of doing the work. They might try Rapid Application Development, or phasing the project, or delivering a cut-down core system, or using cheaper resources, or a quicker programming language. What they should *not* do, however, is fool themselves that they can reduce the estimates arbitrarily across the board and still have a chance of delivering the project within time and budget.

It is quite legitimate for project managers to be asked to re-check and justify their estimates, to prove that they are not building in excess 'padding' to give themselves an easy life. They may, too, be asked to agree to a 'challenging' target that requires tight project control and considerable drive to push the project forward. But this is not the same as signing up to do the impossible and sometimes project managers just have to fight their corner and keep on insisting, patiently but firmly, on the quality of their estimates and the inadvisability of committing themselves to an unachievable target.

This is not easy and the pressures on the project manager can become very intense and unnerving. There is no simple remedy for this, and obviously a fairly strong ego will be a help. But so does:

- Ensuring that the estimates have been thoroughly researched and based on realistic metrics.
- Making sure that more than one person has contributed to the estimates and that a high degree of consensus has been obtained.
- Using several different estimating methods and formulæ and cross-checking the results.

● Insisting on a proper risk assessment on the probability of achieving the planned targets.

If, then, it is decided for commercial reasons to go with a price and/or timescale that is not supported by the estimates, the project manager can insist that the responsibility for the resultant disaster is shared by those making the commercial decision.

7.6 PRACTICAL EXPERIENCES WITH ESTIMATING

In this section, we present some practical tips on improving the quality of the estimating process.

Building up metrics
Systems developers are not usually very good at this, but a reliable body of metrics is the best way to take the uncertainty out of estimating. The objections raised here are that collecting metrics takes time and effort and that metrics from one project cannot necessarily be applied to another.

While there is no doubt that metrics collection does take time and effort, statistics on effort expended are probably collected anyway as part of the project monitoring process and/or to support billing the customer. So the basic figures are there – all that is needed is to collect also some definition of where the effort went. Thus, we may know that J Soap spent twelve days coding program XY123B; if we can define that program in some way – for example, as batch or on-line, simple, medium or complex, written in Ingres – then we have the start of a collection of metrics. Ideally, of course, metrics would be collected across an organisation. Even if there is no organisation-wide metrics initiative, however, individual project managers can still collect metrics for themselves – to use on their own projects later or, perhaps, to use when they get dragged in to work in a bid team. The second objection is that metrics from one project cannot necessarily be applied to another, so what is the use of collecting them at all? Although this is true to some extent, metrics can be applied more widely than is necessarily apparent at first sight. For example, although Ingres and ORACLE are very different environments, experience shows that the approach to using them both is very similar, that staff can cross-train very quickly and that productivity rates are very similar. So, if no ORACLE metrics are available, you might try using some metrics from an Ingres project instead. Or, again, if you have estimated for a COBOL development, you might like to cross-check against the Ingres estimate; if the Ingres estimate doesn't come out rather smaller, then there is something wrong somewhere.

Using standard project structures
Although each IS project has its distinctive features, there are also areas of commonality between projects which can be used to the project manager's advantage. One of these features is that projects seem to follow a fairly common lifecycle from analysis, through design to coding and testing – we

are ignoring the so-called Rapid Application Development for the moment. Because of this, and making allowance for certain variables, ratios from one project may well be applicable to another. So, if you are using, say, SSADM, it is reasonable to assume that the ratios of one stage to another should be similar to those in previous SSADM projects. This is, of course, one of the great advantages of using a method like SSADM since the work content is clearly defined and experience from previous projects is readily applicable. It also assists in the collection of useful metrics of course.

Getting more than one view

Estimating is one area in which two heads, or better still several heads, really are better than one. Different people will approach an estimating problem in different ways and each is likely to spot something the others have missed. So it is worth getting several people to contribute to the estimating process and comparing their answers. The Delphi technique that we have already described provides a very structured way of doing this. An extension of this is to use more than one method to produce the estimate. You may, for example, use function point analysis as your primary method and then perform a cross-check using the analysis effort. Where the different methods produce different results – as they are almost bound to do – the worst thing you can do is to 'split the difference'; there may be good reasons why, in the particular circumstances, one of the methods is more likely to be right than the other. Therefore, the only solution is to sit down and consider the two estimates carefully, the data available as input to each and their underlying logic, and reason out where the probable answer is. Having done this, it is important to document the reasons for arriving at the final estimate.

Qualifying estimates

However good the estimates are, they are going to be based on some assumptions – that you will need to conduct 20 interviews during the analysis work, that customers will turn round review products in 10 days, that you have adequate access to a development machine and so on. The estimates must, therefore, be qualified by stating these assumptions. Though it is sadly true that a customer will remember your estimate long after they've forgotten the assumptions around it, stating any qualifications or assumptions clearly and unambiguously helps in two ways. First, it reminds you of the basis on which you prepared your estimates – how you were going to tackle the work, for instance. And, second, if the assumptions have been carried forward properly into the contract, it gives the project manager some bargaining chips if, say, the customer falls down on their part of the development.

Documenting the estimates

It is extremely important that the estimators document their work as they go along and that this documentation is kept somewhere safe and accessible. The reasons are threefold:

● There may be a need to compare the results of different estimating processes and, if so, a record of the assumptions and thought processes, as well as the actual calculations, of the estimators, will form part of the arbitration process.

- During the project, if slippage occurs, the project manager can examine the basis on which the estimates were prepared to see if similar slippage is likely in tasks yet to come.

- After the project is over, the estimates can be compared with the actual time spent and the results used to calibrate and fine-tune the estimating process for future projects.

Unfortunately, documenting estimates is tedious and time-consuming and, in the pressure to get the estimates out, is often left to tomorrow – which never comes. Although it does require some extra work, the effort is repaid with interest later in the project and on future projects.

Estimating and risk analysis   Chapter 13 discusses the important issue of risk management in IS projects. The initial risk analysis on a project should include an examination of the estimating methods used and an assessment of their reliability and likely accuracy. So, the estimates should be revisited after the initial risk assessment, to take the results of that assessment into account and to make any necessary adjustments.

7.7   SUMMARY

Estimating for IS projects has a very bad reputation, generally attributable to the number of cost and time overruns on such projects. Although there are some specific problems that arise on IS projects, most of the estimating difficulties can be put down to the lack of a proper approach to the process, as practised in more mature engineering disciplines. No single estimating method will produce the 'right' result for a particular project. The project manager must use several different methods and compare the results critically before settling on 'the' estimates to underpin the project plans. In the longer term, the careful collection of metrics should lead to an improvement in the accuracy of IS estimating.

Finally, remember that, however difficult IS estimating is, project managers can help themselves to a great extent by using the approaches described here and by not allowing themselves to be bullied into producing or accepting estimates that are commercially or politically acceptable. In the end, the project will come out as it will and the only result of starting with over-optimistic estimates will be to increase the chances of it appearing to be a project management – rather than a commercial – failure.

Further reading

The first three books recommended here were written some time ago but they still remain, in their various ways, extremely valuable to the project manager:

Software Engineering Economics, by Barry W Boehm
This is more or less a standard work on the subject of software estimating. It does not cover the most modern techniques such as Function Point Analysis but it does contain a lot of original research material showing why and how software projects work out as they do.

Controlling Software Projects, by Tom De Marco
Another seminal work, this analyses the roots of estimating failures and suggests various remedies. Sadly, despite being published originally in 1982, few of the central recommendations seem to have been widely adopted more than a decade on. It is also very readable – amusing even.

The Mythical Man-Month – Essays on Software Engineering, by Frederick P Brooks, Jr
This is mainly about estimating but also contains a number of insights into the management of software projects generally. Brooks was project manager for the development of IBM's System/360 computer and OS/360 operating systems, so knows what he is talking about. The book is also small and relatively inexpensive.

The next two books are more recent and provide detailed information on the use of Function Point Analysis:

Estimating with Mk II Function Point Analysis, by Ian Drummond
This is the definitive guide to its subject and has the advantage of being brief and to the point (67 pages).

Sizing and Estimating Software in Practice, by Stephen Treble and Neil Douglas
A very comprehensive guide by authors with a lot of practical experience of applying FPA on projects.

7.8   QUESTIONS

1 Explain three reasons why estimating for IS projects has a poor reputation and a bad track record. What can be done about these problems?

2 The analogy method of estimating is often used to produce 'broad brush' estimates at the start of a project. Why is this method particularly suited to this application?

3 The analysis effort and programming methods both rest on the principle of extrapolating the total development effort from detailed estimates of one phase of the project. Describe the approach taken in each of these methods and show in what circumstances each might best be employed.

4 The *Delphi technique* aims to achieve a consensus estimate from the efforts of a number of estimators. How is this achieved and what is the advantage of the Delphi technique over, for example, a round-table discussion?

5 Describe how you would go about estimating for the following supporting project activities and why you would take your chosen approach to each:
  - project management;
  - team leading/supervision;
  - quality control;
  - familiarisation.

6 State three factors that could influence the estimates for an IS project and how you would attempt to adjust the estimates for these factors.

CHAPTER 8

Project planning – scheduling and resourcing

8.1 INTRODUCTION

In Chapter 6, we saw how a project is broken down into elements of work that are small enough to estimate with some accuracy and which can act as 'work packages' for individual team members. We also showed why it is important to understand the dependences between activities and the permissible sequences in which activities can be carried out. In Chapter 7, we reviewed various approaches to estimating for IS projects. In this chapter, we shall show how the dependency information and the estimates are brought together to produce a workable schedule for the project. We also present a format for documenting the completed plan and examine the plans used in the PRINCE project management method.

8.2 SCHEDULING

8.2.1 Effort and elapsed time

The project schedule, which usually takes the form of a bar chart, shows two things:

- The sequence in which the work will be carried out.
- The dates at which we plan activities to start and finish.

Bar charts can also be made to show who will be responsible for each activity.

Development of a workable schedule is invariably an iterative process. We make some initial assumptions, develop a first-cut schedule, compare the results with our desired outcome – particularly in terms of the project end-date – and reschedule as many times as are needed to achieve an acceptable plan.

Before turning to the scheduling process, however, we need to explain the difference between effort and elapsed time, since this difference is crucial to an understanding of the scheduling process. Let us suppose, for example, that we have estimated a task as requiring 20 days' effort. Assuming that we only have one person available to do the work, then – if our person has no absence during the period – this 20 days' work will take 20 elapsed days to perform. If we have two people available, and the work can be partitioned, then the 20 days' work can be accomplished in 10 elapsed days. With four people, it would take five elapsed days. In practice, for reasons we shall discuss later in this chapter, partitioning of activities is not usually as straightforward as this but it does illustrate the point. In producing our project schedule, it is vital that we keep the distinction between effort and elapsed time in mind. Usually, the project manager cannot do much about the effort required to perform an activity, since the amount of work is inherent in the task itself. But the project manager can and must seek to influence the elapsed time by committing the right amount of resources to each task.

8.2.2 Developing the schedule

To illustrate the approach, we shall use the simple feasibility study that we described in Chapter 6. The dependency network shown there, with estimated effort figures for each activity, is shown in Fig 8.1.

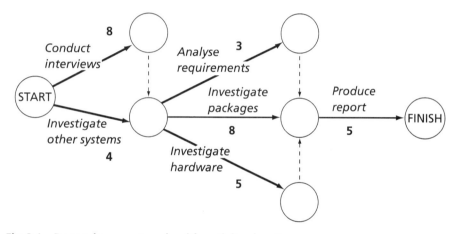

Fig 8.1 Dependency network with activity durations

To develop our initial schedule, we might decide to see how long the project would take with one analyst assigned to the work. Since, in this case, the activities have to be carried out in sequence, we would get the schedule that is shown in Fig 8.2. This shows that the elapsed time for the project would be the sum of all of the activities: 33 days. We know, however, that our customer wants the feasibility study more quickly than that, so we have to examine our network to see if any activities can be performed in parallel. We find that:

● *Conduct interviews* can be progressed in parallel with *Investigate other systems*.

● *Analyse requirements* can be done in parallel both with *Investigate packages* and *Investigate hardware*.

Activities

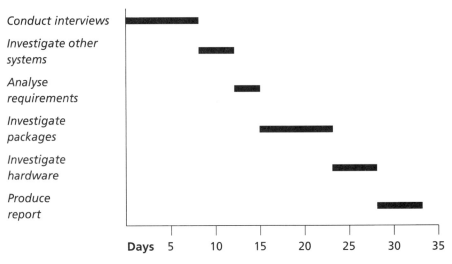

Fig 8.2   **Schedule for one-person team**

If we have a second analyst available, then we can take advantage of this parallelism as shown in Fig 8.3.

Activities

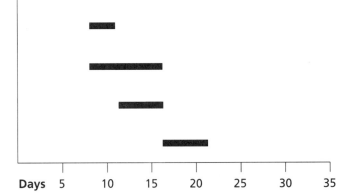

Fig 8.3   **Schedule for two-person team showing parallel activities**

In this plan, we have used one analyst on *Conduct interviews* and the other on *Investigate other systems*. Then, while one analyst is engaged on *Investigate packages*, the other first performs *Analyse requirements* and then *Investigate*

Activities

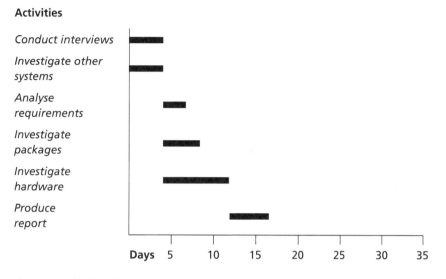

Fig 8.4   Schedule for three-person team

hardware. By doing this, we have shortened the elapsed time of the project to 21 days. If our customer were very demanding, however, and if we had a third analyst available, we could partition the work again and shorten the timescale still further. Figure 8.4 illustrates how we could do this.

We have used two people on *Conduct interviews*, so the eight days' effort now only takes four elapsed days. Similarly, we have used a different analyst on each of *Analyse requirements*, *Investigate packages* and *Investigate hardware* but in this case we don't gain anything since the elapsed time becomes the eight days' effort of the longest of these activities, *Investigate hardware*. As a result we can now offer the customer the report in 17 elapsed days.

Although the feasibility study is a simple example, it does illustrate the approach that is used whatever the size of the project. An initial schedule is created and then it is adjusted and revised until the project manager is sure that it is realistic and provides a reasonable balance between the effective use of resources and the achievement of an acceptable end-date. There are, however, some other factors to consider in developing the project schedule.

8.2.3   Scheduling considerations

In our example, we have assumed that each of the tasks on our schedule can be partitioned and that, if we share an activity between two people, each will carry out exactly half of the work. While mathematically neat, neither of these assumptions is usually correct in practice. If we take an activity like digging a hole, then it is probably true that we can keep on partitioning it as many times as we have people available, the only constraint being the size of the hole and whether the people can all get down there without whacking each other with their shovels. Tasks on IS projects are more complex, however, and different considerations apply.

Let us suppose we have an activity for an analyst to produce a report comparing eight different relational databases. To do this, the analyst will:

- Study some background material and decide what evaluation criteria will be used.
- Read the technical literature about each of the eight databases and note how each performs against the evaluation criteria.
- Place the results of all the evaluations side by side on a table and compare them.
- Write a report documenting the findings.

If we partition this work between two analysts, then we find that not all of these sub-tasks can be divided neatly in half. Both analysts will have to study the same background material and it will probably take them longer to devise the evaluation criteria since there will inevitably be some discussion or argument about them. Each analyst can review four databases, so this sub-task can be partitioned, but documenting the evaluations may involve further discussion and even, if there is only one PC available, delays while one analyst waits for the other to finish. Finally, the report will be a shared effort and there will be additional work involved in ensuring that the style of the document is consistent. So if in this case we had estimated that it would take one analyst six days to do this job, two analysts would be more likely to take, say, four elapsed days than the three we might initially imagine.

In addition, there is another subtle feature of projects like IS development that involve considerable complexity. This is that the members of the team need to communicate with each other, to share information and to co-ordinate their efforts. The volume of this communication obviously increases with the size of the team. If, say, a person spends only one hour per week communicating with each team member, then in a two-person team, one hour will be spent thus by each person each week; but, in an eight-person team, more than a day a week for each person will be taken up with intra-team communication. There is also the question of the 'learning curve' to consider. However familiar someone is with a particular business or technical environment, there are unique features of each project that must be assimilated by each person involved in it. So, each person has to climb the learning curve before they become fully effective and the more people there are on a team, the more learning curves there are to climb.

The conclusion we may draw from all this, then, is that in developing our schedule we cannot necessarily take an activity of n days effort and divide it between two people to produce an elapsed time of $\frac{1}{2}n$. Be warned, too, that many project-planning packages do not seem aware of this fact and will happily divide a task simply by the number of resources declared for it – so you will have to assess carefully if the plan produced by your software has actually taken these complexities into account.

Another issue to consider is whether the activities we have identified in our product or work breakdown structure are all that need to go on the schedule. In our feasibility study, we have assumed that *Investigate packages* and *Investigate hardware* can both start as soon as the analysts are ready, when they have finished *Conduct interviews* and *Analyse other systems*. But actually, we would probably have had to write away for information on packages and hardware and we may well not yet have received the replies by the time we want to start our investigations. Similarly, on many projects, there is 'dead' time for the project team whilst the users review and comment on various products. Unless we allow for these things, our schedule will be impossibly tight and allow no margin for accommodating slight delays.

There is also the important question of resource availability. Our feasibility study project is quite short – two to six weeks – and so we might expect to know our staff's leave and training commitments and build them into our plan. But what about unplanned absence like sickness? In developing overall project plans, it is necessary to plan on less than 100 per cent availability for the staff. In Chapter 7, we showed how a 'full-time' person was available for around 18 days per month, calculated as follows:

Total working days per year (52 × 5):	260
Less holiday (say):	25
Less other non-working time (training, sickness etc):	15
Leaves:	220
Divided by 12 to give days per month:	18.33

This represents an average availability of about 85 per cent overall or 4.25 days per 5-day week. Allowing for other time-stealers like company meetings, appraisals and so forth, a good 'rule of thumb' for long-term scheduling is to assume that each person will be available four days per week. If we adjust the schedule in Fig 8.4 on this basis, we would get the more realistic plan shown in Fig 8.5.

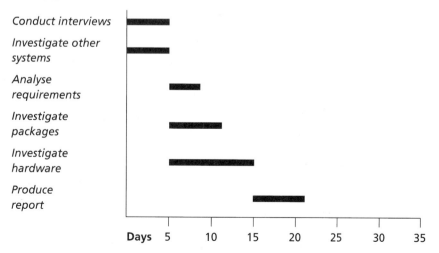

Fig 8.5   Schedule adjusted for four days per week availability

Here, we have multiplied each of our effort figures by 5/4 to give the elapsed time. Thus, for example, *Investigate other systems* – effort four days – gives an elapsed time of five days. Overall, we are now offering to complete the work in 21 elapsed days.

8.2.4 Project milestones

The schedule we have produced so far shows the sequence of activities that we shall need to carry out in order to complete our project. Completion will therefore mark an important *milestone* – the point at which our product is accepted by the customer or at which the customer will sign off our invoice for payment. However, we shall probably need to establish other milestones during the project, since:

- They provide useful control points, at which we can evaluate progress and adjust our plans for the rest of the project as necessary.
- They can be used to illustrate progress to the customer.
- There may be intermediate sign-offs or stage payments linked to the achievement of milestones.

Milestones should be chosen carefully. If there are too many, they become rather meaningless and lose their significance as major points in the project. If there are too few, then control is lost. Usually, it is best to establish milestones that coincide with a significant deliverable – for example, on completion of the specification or at the end of acceptance testing. Our example feasibility study project is probably too small to warrant inter-mediate milestones but, to illustrate the approach, we have modified our bar chart in Fig 8.6 to show milestones at the completion of the fact-finding, at

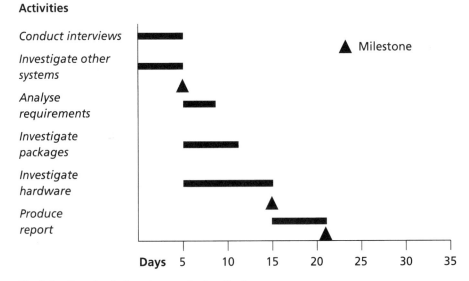

Fig 8.6   Bar chart showing project milestones

the conclusion of the hardware and package investigation and at the delivery of the final report.

8.2.5   Showing 'overhead' tasks on schedules

So far, the tasks we have shown on our schedule are reasonably 'discrete', that is they have definable start and end dates which we can model easily. But how do we show 'overhead' tasks like project management, administration – filling-in timesheets and the like – and things like regular team meetings? We *could* try to model each team meeting individually and show a small task every Friday afternoon for doing the timesheets but the schedule would become impossibly crowded and we couldn't then see the wood for the trees.

A better idea is to work out the average time that will be spent on each activity per week and then to spread this effort figure over the whole duration of the project as a continuous bar. Figure 8.7 shows the feasibility study with an extra line for project management added.

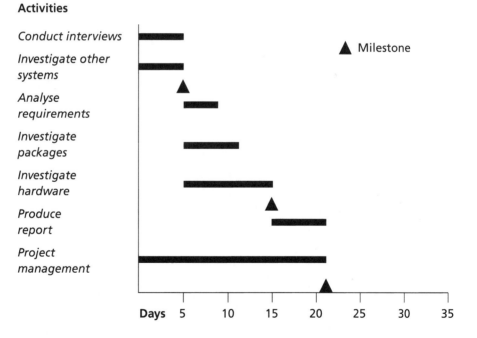

Fig 8.7   Bar chart showing project management as continuous activity over project

8.3 DEVELOPING RESOURCE PLANS

The resource plan is developed from, or alongside, the schedule and shows:

● How many of each type of resource will be required.

● When each resource will start and finish on the project.

'Resources' in an IS project usually refers to people but it could equally include hardware, special software or bought-in services such as data preparation. We need to know exactly what resources are required and when they are required so that we can put in motion the processes for obtaining them and work out what costs they will bring to bear on the project.

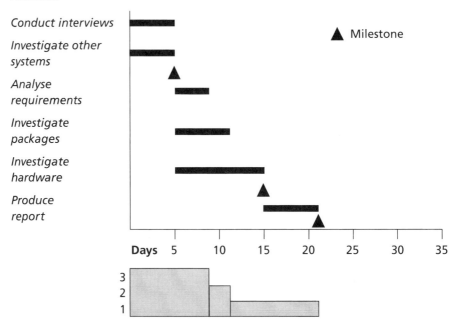

Activities

Conduct interviews

Investigate other systems

Analyse requirements

Investigate packages

Investigate hardware

Produce report

▲ Milestone

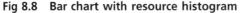

Fig 8.8   Bar chart with resource histogram

Figure 8.8 shows the bar chart for the feasibility study project and, underneath it, a **resource histogram** which shows the deployment of project resources – in this case, the analysts who will work on the study. It shows that, for the first nine elapsed days of the project, we need three analysts. The requirement then drops down to two analysts for two days and finally, we need one analyst only for the last ten days. This gives us a total of 41 analyst/days, worked out as follows:

Total number of analyst/days: $(9 \times 3) + (2 \times 2) + (10 \times 1) = 41$

But we have to remember that this is elapsed days, not effort days, which are 4/5 of the elapsed figure or 33 days. We can double-check this by comparing this figure with the sum of all activities shown on our network diagram in Fig 8.1.

If, say, our analysts are costed at £200 per day, we can now work out the staff costs of the project as 33 × £200 = £6,600.

We might also decide that, as the team are working on site, we shall need to hire a notebook PC for them to use, at a further cost of £50 per day. We shall need this for all 21 days of the project, so that will cost £1050. Thus, we can assess the total cost of the project as £7650.

It will be noticed, in Fig 8.8, that the use of resources over the duration of our project is not very even – three analysts for nine days, two for two days and one for ten days at the end. It may be possible to pick up people for the project and drop them again as indicated here but it is more likely that you would want a more stable team structure for the duration of the project. This would be the case if, for example, you were using contract staff who would probably have to be hired for complete weeks rather than odd days here and there. In this case, you will need to attempt some 'resource smoothing' to try to get a more even allocation of staff over the life of the project. Some software packages have automated facilities for resource smoothing but without them you'll have to adjust the schedule manually to achieve a better resource utilisation.

At the moment, we have produced our resource plans at a project level. On a small project like our feasibility study, the overall project plan would also be suitable for individual team members to see their tasks and when they are scheduled to take place. On a larger project, perhaps with hundreds of activities and dozens of team members, such an overall plan would be less useful at an individual level. We would want to extract parts of the overall plan to produce individual schedules and it is here that project planning software really comes into its own as most packages have the facility to produce selective reports in a variety of formats. Figure 8.9 represents a schedule for one of our analysts on the feasibility study project.

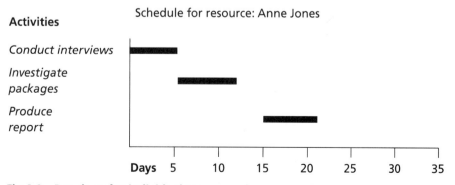

Fig 8.9   Bar chart for individual team member

There is, though, a danger in giving individuals copies of 'their' parts of the schedule. Remember that the schedule now shows elapsed time, rather than effort, and the team member may not appreciate this. In our example, Anne Jones might think she has five days' effort allocated for *Conduct interviews*, whereas in fact she has four days' effort spread over five elapsed days. Since, to some extent, estimates can become self-fulfilling prophecies, Ms Jones would then, in all likelihood, take five days over her four-day task. For this reason, many project managers prefer to give team members task specifications or work instructions showing the effort figure only, keeping the elapsed time plan under their own control. Quite a good incentive, though, is to share the dependency diagram with the team, so that everyone knows how their work will impact on their colleagues.

8.4 CONTINGENCY

So far, the plans we have developed have been *success-based*, that is they are founded on an assumption that things will go according to plan, with activities starting and finishing when they are supposed to and taking no longer than the estimates allow. We have allowed some margin in our elapsed time plan for foreseeable staff absence but otherwise we have not explicitly made any provision for things going wrong. Obviously, even in the best run project, things will inevitably go wrong and the prudent project manager will allow some additional margin, or *contingency*, in both the budget and schedule to deal with the effects of problems. The question, then, is how much contingency should we allow? There will be a different answer for every project based on a variety of factors such as:

- How tightly the requirement is defined and how much opportunity there is for growth in the scope of the work.
- The confidence we have in our estimates.
- The degree of innovation involved in the project.
- How confident we are of getting the resources we want, when we want them.
- Our knowledge of the customer and their likely commitment to the project.
- Our overall assessment of the risks involved in the project. These are discussed more fully in Chapter 13.
- And many other issues.

Contingency is usually expressed in two ways – as additional funds built into the project budget and as additional time built into the project schedule. The amount of the contingency will depend upon the project manager's assessment of the risk factors and, usually, upon a certain amount of haggling with senior management and the customer. There are two opposing dangers associated with contingency:

- No contingency is built into the plans – so there will be nothing in hand to deal with problems when they inevitably arise.

- Everyone concerned builds in contingency at each point – when assessing the tasks, producing the estimates and developing the schedules – so that contingency is piled upon contingency until the project becomes over-blown and uncompetitive.

So, it is important that reasonable contingency is allowed and also that it is only allowed once, preferably at project level. Contingency should be kept under the project manager's control and only the project manager should be able to authorise its use.

8.5   DOCUMENTING THE PLAN

We have now completed the actual work of planning the project. We have broken the project down into individual activities, analysed the dependencies between them, estimated the durations for the activities and developed real-istic schedules. To put the plan into effect, however, it must be documented in a way that is clear and accessible to all concerned in the project – to the team members, to the users, to senior customer staff and IT management. Development organisations will usually have standard formats for project plans but in this section we consider the subjects that should be included in a comprehensive plan. One issue to be decided in advance is whether the project plan should include the quality and risk management plans or whether these should be documents in their own right:

- Having one single document can avoid a lot of duplication – for example, all the plans mentioned would need some description of the project and this would only be needed once in a consolidated plan. In addition, having only one plan avoids a configuration management problem arising, whereby one plan is revised but the others are not and thereby get out of step.

- On the other hand, on a big project a consolidated document may be large and unwieldy and the different sections may be the responsibility of different people – the project manager, risk manager and quality manager, for instance. If this is so or if the circulation of the various plans is likely to be very different, then separate plans may be the best idea.

Needless to say, the plan should not be produced once at the start of the project and then forgotten. There are few things more useless than a project plan that no longer reflects what is actually going on in the project. So the plan must be revised whenever any significant changes are planned in the project and copies must be issued to all the interested parties highlighting the changes. This is a good reason for restricting the circulation as far as possible so that there is not a massive distribution job involved but, with some projects, this just may not be possible and a few trees may have to be sacrificed every time the plan is reissued! In the list of headings that follows, we have generally assumed the use of a consolidated plan. A comprehensive project plan should, at the minimum, contain the following:

1 **Introduction**

A description of the document and of the items covered by it.

2 **Authorisation and amendment record**

A description of the status of the document, information on its authorship and who has approved it and a history of its amendments.

3 **Distribution**

A list of the people who will receive the document.

4 **Related documents**

Cross-references to other documents – for example, to the risk management and quality plans if these are separate or to other relevant papers such as departmental standards to which the project must conform.

5 **Overview of project**

A brief description of the project and its objectives. If the plan relates only to one stage in a project, this section should also explain where and how the stage fits in to the overall programme of work.

6 **Products and deliverables**

The overall product breakdown structure, which was discussed in Chapter 6, should be described, perhaps using the PRINCE subdivision of management products, quality products and technical products. The products should be listed with a cross-reference to the place where they are defined more fully – either in an appendix to the project plan, in a separate product description document or in an external document of some sort; if SSADM is being used, the SSADM manuals provide descriptions of the default SSADM products.

7 **Milestones**

A statement of the principal milestones of the project, what they represent and when they occur.

8 **Organisation and responsibilities**

A description of the main roles and responsibilities in the project, including if useful an organisation chart showing the relationships of the roles involved.

9 **Monitoring and control**

A description and explanation of the methods that will be used to monitor progress on the project, together with the mechanism – for example, a weekly progress meeting – that will be used to exercise control over the work.

10 Quality control

This defines where quality control will be exercised and the form that it will take – for example, management reviews, formal inspections, walk-throughs and so on. The method to be used for categorising review comments and ensuring that they are cleared is also covered here. Quality control may be addressed in a separate quality plan.

11 Reporting

A description of the reporting mechanism – who will write the management reports, what they shall cover, how often they will be produced and who will receive them.

12 Review and approvals

This is related to quality control and sets out, probably in tabular form, who is responsible for producing, reviewing and authorising the various project products.

13 Risks to the project

This may be covered by a separate risk management plan and risk register; there is more about this in Chapter 13. Otherwise, this section will include a description of the principal risks, an assessment of their likelihood and possible impact and an outline of the envisaged avoidance and mitigation actions.

14 Project schedule

The network diagram and bar charts for the project.

15 Task descriptions

These are probably best placed in an appendix. For each task on the network and bar chart, there should be a description of:

- The objective of the task.
- The work to be carried out.
- The methods to be used.
- The standards to be followed.
- The effort allocated.
- The products, both deliverable and intermediate.
- The completion criteria – in other words, how we will know when the task has been finished satisfactorily.

These task descriptions can therefore serve as work instructions to individual team members, defining for them exactly what they are required to do and how.

8.6 PRINCE PLANS

The PRINCE structured project management method, as described in Chapter 6, defines a set of plans that seems at first sight slightly different to the project plan we have described so far. However, on closer examination, the PRINCE plans are seen to be quite compatible with our approach. PRINCE plans divide both by subject and hierarchically as shown in Fig 8.10.

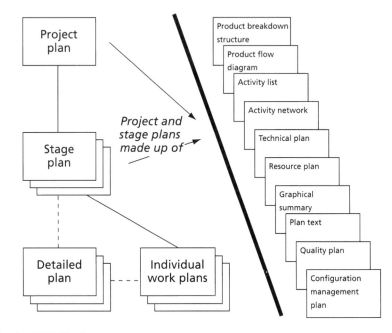

Fig 8.10 PRINCE plans

The **project plan** is produced at the start of the project and shows the main technical activities and the resources involved. Probably, the information will be shown at summary level here, to be broken down into more detail on lower-level plans. The project plan is one of the main inputs to the project initiation process. PRINCE projects are divided into one or more stages and, as each of these is reached, a **stage plan** is produced. This is more elaborate than the project plan and shows the detailed activities involved in carrying out the stage. If required, **detailed plans** may be produced to focus even more closely on individual aspects of a stage. Finally, **individual work plans** are produced, documenting individual team members' responsibilities under the stage plan. The project plan and stage plan are each made up of a number of components, as follows:

● The *product breakdown structure* and *product flow diagram* as described in Chapter 6 earlier.

- The *activity list* is the summary of tasks that we have discovered on the product flow diagram and which transform the products. The *activity network* shows the interdependency between these activities and the critical path through the project.

- The *technical plan* is the bar chart showing the sequence of activities against a timeline.

- The *resource plan* is a tabular summary of the resources and their costs required at each point in the project.

- The *resource plan graphical summary* is developed from the resource plan and shows the cumulative build-up of costs through the project. It also shows the status of the major products at each point. An illustration of a resource plan graphical summary for the feasibility study project is shown in Fig 8.11.

- *Plan text* is the written element of the plan – including a description of the plan, a list of the assumptions, constraints and external dependences and the reporting structure for the project or stage.

- *Quality plan* – documenting the methods and standards to be used.

- *Configuration management plan* – describing the configuration management methods, standards and tools to be used on the project.

We mentioned in Chapter 6 that PRINCE uses the concept of tolerances – that is, when authorised to go ahead, project and stage managers are also given tolerances, of time, cost and quality – within which they may vary their plan if necessary. If it becomes apparent that any of these tolerances is likely to be exceeded, the manager must prepare an **exception plan** to show the

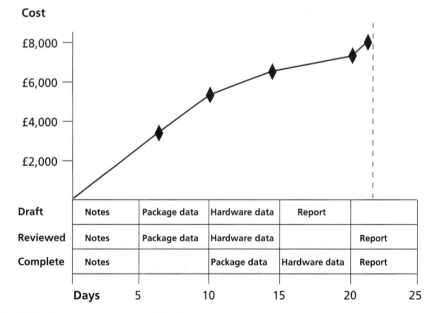

Fig 8.11   Resource plan graphical summary

effects of the variation and how the project or stage may proceed after taking it into account. If approved by the Project Board, the exception plan takes the place of the relevant project or stage plan for the remainder of the relevant stage or part of the project.

8.7 SUMMARY

It is important to distinguish between the effort on a project and the elapsed time it will take.

The schedule is developed iteratively from the network by trying various combinations of resources until a satisfactory balance is achieved between the effective and economical use of resources and meeting the required end dates.

Care must be taken in partitioning tasks so that adequate allowance is made for start-up activities, the 'learning curve' for individuals and so on.

Milestones should be added to the schedule to indicate significant points in the project.

Once the schedule is developed, resource plans can be derived from it and project costs calculated.

Adequate contingency must be allowed in the plan to cater for any problems that may arise and use of the contingency should be kept under the project manager's control.

The plan must be fully documented and kept up-to-date to reflect changes as the project proceeds.

PRINCE contains a standard set of planning products.

8.8 QUESTIONS

1 Explain the difference between *effort* and *elapsed time*. What is the significance of this difference for project planning purposes?

2 Scheduling a project involves understanding the degree to which project tasks can be *partitioned*. What is meant by this term and what effect does partitioning have on the scheduling process?

3 In long-term project planning, it is wise to assume that staff will be available for project work for less than 100 per cent of the total available time. What factors will reduce staff availability and what adjustments should be made for them?

4 What do you understand by the term *project milestone*? How would you decide how many milestones to show on your project plan?

5 The PRINCE project management method envisages a hierarchy of plans. Describe this hierarchy.

CHAPTER 9

Monitoring progress

9.1 INTRODUCTION

We have now covered planning the project – establishing what is to be done, by whom, by when, to what standards – and we have analysed the risks we face and devised measures to counter them. However, this is actually the easier part of project management. Much more difficult is the actual running of the project on a day-to-day basis, monitoring progress and making changes as necessary to ensure that it keeps on track for delivering its final objectives. We shall examine the continuing management of projects in the next two chapters. In this chapter, we shall discuss the mechanisms that the project manager will need to monitor progress, to see what is really going on; and in Chapter 10 we shall look at what can be done to exercise control when we spot that our project is not going quite as we planned it.

The project needs to be managed from three perspectives, those of the 'triple constraint' of time, cost and quality. Sometimes, the management decisions we make will involve a trade-off between these three elements – we might be able to deliver on time if we sacrifice some of the performance of the system or guarantee the quality if the costs can be allowed to rise. These decisions may be outside the project manager's control and the project manager may have to get involved with some hard bargaining with the Project Board or the customer, or his or her own senior management, before a revised approach can be agreed.

In this chapter, we shall consider monitoring techniques for each element of the triple constraint.

9.2 MONITORING EFFORT

To monitor progress, we need first some mechanism for collecting figures on the resources used. On IS projects, the major resource element is staff time but there are also costs to be considered for resources like machine usage and bought-in hardware and services.

To gather information on the effort expended, there really is no alternative but to get the team members to complete timesheets of some sort. Although this is pretty obvious, there can be political difficulties in the way. Staff, and sometimes trade unions, will see the completion of timesheets as 'Big Brother' spying on them, and others – perhaps the more senior or experienced people

Name:	DAVE SIMS	Project:	PERSONNEL 2000					Week ending: 19/05/96		
Code		Mon	Tue	Wed	Thu	Fri	Sat	Sun	Total	To go
A/01	CODE PROGRAM CV004	6.5	5.0	7.5					19.0	NIL
A/02	TEST PROGRAM CV004				7.5	3.0			10.5	NIL
A/07	CODE PROGRAM EN025					4.0			4.0	15.0
M/03	TEAM MEETING	1.0							1.0	
M/02	COMPLETE TIMESHEET					0.5			0.5	

Fig 9.1 Effort monitoring timesheet

– will resent having their work examined minutely in this way. In consultancy companies, the use of timesheets is quite usual as they support the billing process and the same is also true for in-house IT departments that operate as profit or cost centres. If you are working somewhere where timesheets are not the norm, then you will have to practise your diplomacy in explaining to your team why timesheets are so important and how vital they are to proper control of the project. If there really are problems in getting timesheets accepted, one possibility is to use a design that only records time spent on project work – in other words, you are not interested in time spent on non-project activities.

Figure 9.1 gives an idea of the sort of information that is needed on a timesheet:

● Identifiers for the team member, the project and the week being reported on.

● A code and title – taken from the project plan or bar chart – for each activity.

● The time spent on each activity each day and a total for the week.

● Very important – an estimate of the effort to go. We shall say some more about this shortly.

Strictly speaking, we are probably not very interested in the daily effort figure for each task but experience shows that we get a much more accurate record if people fill in their timesheets daily. We might want to add to this minimal data some additional features, for example:

● Somewhere for the person to qualify their 'to go' figure and comment upon any problems or delays encountered.

- A column to record the predicted end-date as well as the effort to go – remember, the former is related to elapsed time and the latter to effort.

- A place to record non-productive, but project-related, activities such as appraisals or progress meetings – though we may have assigned activity codes for this.

One of the most important pieces of information on the timesheet is the 'effort to go' figure. There is very little that can be done about the effort already expended, which is now so much water under the bridge, and the project manager's efforts need to be focused on the future and the work yet to be done. Because of this, it is essential that the 'effort to go' figure is properly estimated. It is not unknown for the figure to be arrived at by the following calculation:

[Original estimate] *less* **[Effort expended to date] = [Estimate to go]**

Now this, of course, is not an honest estimate at all but an expression of wishful thinking. Using this approach, activities will seem to be proceeding to schedule until they lurch disastrously into overrun. Team members must be encouraged to estimate their 'to go' figures as accurately as they can and the project manager can help here by the way in which she or he receives the bad news of a possible overrun. If the project manager always explodes, or otherwise reacts negatively, then team members will want to keep the bad news to themselves until the last minute – when it is probably too late to take any remedial action. Of course, the project manager has to look into the reasons for the predicted overrun but this must be done in a neutral way, simply finding out the facts, not as a 'witch hunt' to apportion blame.

The reasons for any departure from the planned timescale must be examined thoroughly since the remedial action to be taken will depend upon the result of the analysis. We shall have more to say on this in the next chapter but, for now, let us consider the situation where a programmer is expecting an estimated ten-day coding task to overrun by two days. There could be various causes of this including:

- The programmer's inexperience. In this case the program may have been too difficult and the project manager could consider reassigning work so that this programmer has simpler programs in future.

- Lack of clarity in the program specification. If this is so, the question to be asked is 'does the same apply to the other specifications?'. In other words, is this an isolated situation or is it likely to be reflected throughout the project so that all the programming estimates will be too low?

- Lack of access to the development machine. Here, the project manager can ease things for the team by obtaining greater access.

- The programmer is experienced and competent, the specification clear and there are no problems with access to the development machine. If this is so, then it suggests that the original estimate was too low and this might apply to other estimates also.

If the project manager is to take the right action to deal with the matter, it is necessary to know which of these problems – or any others – is at the root of the trouble.

Having collected information at an individual level, the next step is to summarise it at a project level to see the overall situation. Project planning packages usually have facilities to do this, although sometimes they are rather cumbrous to use. Alternatively, the project manager can set up a spreadsheet to do the same thing. For each activity, we need to know:

- Its current status – not started, in progress or completed.
- The original effort estimate.
- The original cost estimate (effort times daily rate).
- The original start date.
- The original end date.
- The actual start date.
- The effort booked to date.
- The cost booked to date (effort times daily rate).
- The effort estimated still to go.
- The cost estimated still to go (effort times daily rate).
- The current predicted total effort.
- The current predicted total cost (effort times daily rate).
- The current estimated end date.

Some of this information can be expressed graphically on a bar chart. Figure 9.2 is a development of the bar chart for the feasibility study project featured in Chapter 8.

This chart shows the situation at the end of the second week – shown by the vertical double line. *Conduct interviews* has taken two days longer than planned, due to the non-availability of some of the interviewees; this is shown by extending the time bar. As a result of this, the three activities that are dependent on *Conduct interviews* have started two days late. In addition, the analyst who will carry out *Investigate packages* has reported that the task will take three days longer than estimated due to some difficulties in getting to see the package vendors; this will not delay the project as a whole since the report cannot be started in any case until *Investigate hardware* has been completed. It will be noticed, too, that the first of our milestones has been missed – we show when it did actually occur, together with its originally-planned position. Similarly, we are predicting slippage in the second and third milestones.

This does, however, illustrate one of the deficiencies of a bar chart as a monitoring tool. We may *know* that *Analyse requirements*, *Investigate packages* and *Investigate hardware* can only start when *Conduct interviews* and *Investigate other systems* have both finished – but this is not necessarily evident from the chart itself. To find out the effects on other activities – and on the project as

Activities

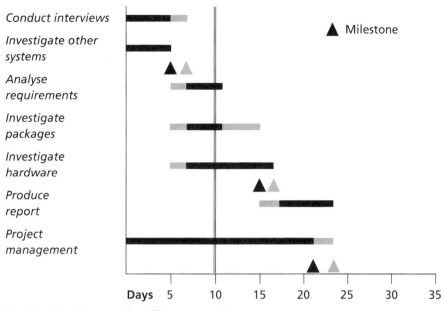

Fig 9.2   **Bar chart used to illustrate project progress**

a whole – it is necessary to consult the network chart and to re-calculate the critical path to take account of the slippage.

Returning to the bar chart for the moment, though, the slippage of *Analyse requirements* has also had other effects on the project, not immediately obvious. Originally, it was intended that the second analyst would start work on *Investigate packages* as soon as he or she had finished with *Investigate other systems*. However, a two-day delay has now been introduced, during which presumably the analyst will continue to book time to the project – so we have incurred an extra two days' costs as well. Similarly, the project manager's assignment will have to be extended for another two days, with further additional costs. This goes to show that an apparently small slippage can have more severe knock-on effects and that working out all the effects of a slippage involves very careful examination of the plans.

9.3   MONITORING OTHER COSTS

Labour costs are usually the main cost component of an IS project but there are other costs as well and all have to be kept under review. In this section, we consider how best to do this.

To start with, it is important to distinguish between the cost and the price of something. The *cost* is what we have to pay for the resource, be it staff salaries or a piece of hardware. The *price* is what we charge for the same thing and the difference between the two represents our profit, if we are out to make a profit. If you are working within an in-house IT department, you may not be intending to make a profit but you may still wish to add a mark-up to bought-in items to cover your administrative overheads.

Staff costs are best dealt with by establishing some sort of daily rate for each team member, probably based on their grade or classification. Staff costs do not just include the person's salary; on top of that, there will be additional costs such as contributions to the pension fund, the employer's National Insurance contributions, perhaps a private medical scheme or company car. And on top of *that*, there will be additional overheads to cover things like office space, heating, lighting and the provision of furniture and equipment. Different firms calculate these things in different ways and the advice of the finance or accounts department should be sought.

Where contract staff are being used, they will probably submit a weekly timesheet. Once signed off by the project manager, this will be used by their agency as the basis for an invoice. That will then be submitted for approval, after which it will get paid and posted to the project's accounts. The trouble with this arrangement, of course, is that there might be quite a time lag between the work being done and the costs appearing on the accounts. So our advice to project managers is to capture the information at the timesheet stage and to keep your own records of contractor costs – perhaps on a spreadsheet.

The same applies to the costs for other bought-in items. If you are buying a piece of hardware, or perhaps hiring some for the duration of the project, the suppliers' invoices will probably trail behind the actual goods by quite a period. This can be useful, of course, if you want to take advantage of a favourable cash flow, since you can probably bill your customer before you have been charged yourself and enjoy the use of the money until the supplier's invoice arrives.

There are other expenses that could, depending on your organisation's accounting practices, get chalked up to your project, for example:

- **Project-specific training.** Sometimes, costs for general developmental training are borne centrally – though reflected in the staff costs or charge-out rates – but training for a project task, like learning a specialised programming language, may fall on the project.
- **Specially-arranged accommodation.** If, for instance, your team is big enough to require a self-contained office, the rental of this space may get charged to the project.
- **Lodging and subsistence costs.** If project staff have to work away from base for any length of time, the project might have to pay for hotels, meals or perhaps the rental of apartments.
- **Travel costs.** Whether or not they have to stay away from home, staff may be entitled to reimbursement of travel costs over and above their normal journey to work. They may be entitled to travel *time* as well, usually at something like half the normal rate.

- **Consumables.** Such as stationery, diskettes, laser toner cartridges and other items that can add a surprising amount of cost to a project.

- **Insurance.** If special safety or other considerations apply, the organisation's normal public liability and similar insurance may not be adequate and special arrangements may have to be made and charged to the project.

As with other expenses, there will probably be some delay between the costs being incurred, being signed off and appearing in the accounts so prudent project managers will keep their own record of them.

9.4   MONITORING QUALITY

9.4.1   Establishing the climate for successful quality control

Chapter 12 discusses the basic approaches to monitoring quality – inspection versus testing, for example. Here, we review some techniques that may be employed to check on the quality of deliverables as they are produced.

It is important, first of all, for the project manager to create the right climate for quality control to work properly. It is often difficult for people to divorce themselves from their work, so that criticism of the work becomes criticism of them personally. It is probably a good thing that people do feel personally involved in what they are doing – otherwise why should they care whether it is done well or not? But this does mean that reviews and criticism must be handled sensitively. Some do's and don'ts are:

- All criticism should be non-personal – not 'you're doing this wrong' but 'this is wrong'.

- Criticism should be non-judgemental. Simply state the factual error or concern without appearing to cast doubt on the author's competence or commitment – or intelligence!

- Avoid comparisons with how you would have tackled the same task; other approaches, though different, may be equally valid and, as long as standards are followed, ought to be accommodated.

- Don't try to resolve problems during reviews. Identify the problem and leave it to the author or someone else to find a solution.

- But do use quality control reviews as an opportunity to coach more junior staff. If it is clear that an error has arisen because of inexperience or a lack of knowledge, grasp the chance to improve their skill or knowledge in that area.

- Don't aim for perfection. Excellence and conformance to requirement are not the same thing and if the customer only wants, or can only afford, a Mini you won't get any thanks for delivering a Rolls-Royce.

9.4.2 Timing of quality control checks

There are two major phases in the quality control process – checking or reviewing work as it is in progress and testing the finished product. Taking the review process first, it is important to apply checks at sensible points in the project's lifecycle. In general, it is not sensible to apply quality control to each item as it is produced, for example to each module of code – although in the 'total quality' climate we would expect the originators of work to be applying their own checks on a continuous basis. On the other hand, it is no use waiting until, say, a whole suite of programs has been developed before checking them and finding that there is some fundamental problem with all of them. Where there is a clearly defined project lifecycle, there should be checks at the end of each stage and before the project moves on to the next stage. Thus, one would review the analysis work before moving on to design and check the design before starting development.

However, there can sometimes be a case for checking smaller units of work. If, for example, a new design method is being used or the person doing the work is unfamiliar with the techniques or standards to be used, it would be wise to carry out a check as the first unit emerges from production before moving on to the rest of the work. As with many other aspects of project management, there are no hard and fast rules here but a checklist of decision points at which to apply quality control would include:

- Having checks at the project milestones defined in the project plan.
- Applying checks when moving from one development phase to the next.
- Checking the operation of new standards after their first application.
- Checking on work involving new techniques or methods.
- Checking the work of inexperienced staff or those newly recruited who may have worked to different standards elsewhere.

With regard to the testing of finished products, there is a fairly self-evident hierarchy of test to be followed:

- Individual components, programs or modules, for example, are tested to ensure that they meet their individual specifications.
- Components are linked together and integration tests check that they work satisfactorily in combination.
- The complete system is tested to ensure that all the components function together to deliver what the customer specified.
- The customers conduct an acceptance test to satisfy themselves that the product meets their requirements.

In addition to the above, there may be a need for other checks to ensure that the product can handle large volumes, or operate in adverse conditions of work reliably over a long period of time.

9.4.3 Methods for monitoring quality

Various methods exist for conducting quality control reviews, some rather informal and others highly structured. In choosing one, the guiding idea should be the usual touchstone of appropriateness. Whatever approach is taken, the review process must be planned. The reviewers must be clear about:

- The criteria to be applied.
- The definitions of pass or fail for the items reviewed.

Among the approaches you might consider are the following:

Self-checking   This really supports the 'total quality management' theme and relies on the author of the work having a good understanding of the requirement and also of the skills and techniques needed to meet it. The approach is best suited to more experienced team members who should, as with any other check, formally record their reviews. The big disadvantage with self-checking is, of course, that if someone has misunderstood something in, say, a design document, they will continue to labour under the same misapprehension during the checking process and the defect will not be discovered. For this reason, one of the other forms of check should be used in areas of known criticality and occasionally elsewhere to verify the self-checking procedure.

Team leader reviews   Here, a team member's supervisor is responsible for checking that work meets its specification and conforms to any requisite standards. If defects are identified, corrective work is undertaken and the work is then re-inspected as necessary. This method is very useful when reviews of work are to be linked to coaching – as will often be the case for junior staff. The problem is that it is only as effective as the supervisor's ability to spot problems and, of course, the team leader may not in fact be as skilled as the author in the particular discipline or technique involved. In addition, bottlenecks can occur with this method, as all checking has to be undertaken by one person; this is particularly the case with projects that are using fast programming methods where programmer productivity can outstrip the ability of the team leader to review the work.

Peer reviews   In principle, this is similar to a team leader review in that one person is checking the work of another. Team leader review and peer review can be used in tandem, with the team leader effectively sharing the review work with one of the more experienced team members. Peer review does, of course, rely on the ability of the reviewer to spot defects, and some people are rather better at this than others. There is a special danger for the project manager to watch for with peer reviews – that of rivalry or one-upmanship between the author and reviewer. They may need reminding that the objective is not to score points off each other but to produce a high-quality product. In a multi-disciplinary team, where the team leader does not have expertise in the area to be reviewed, peer review may be the only practical way of conducting quality control.

Walkthroughs This technique, which involves a review by a group of people, can prove very effective as the skills, knowledge and eyesight – for spotting errors! – of a number of people are brought to bear. Walkthroughs do, however, require good organisation so that everyone concerned is clear about their objectives and has the necessary documentation available early enough for proper study. In addition, to keep review meetings moving forward and to stop them straying from the point, good chairmanship is essential. It is particularly important in walkthroughs to stick to the identification of problems and to avoid trying to find solutions. Obviously, if a solution does emerge immediately, it would be silly to discard it; but since, in meetings, the length of time spent discussing things tends to rise exponentially with the numbers present, too many ideas for solutions will soon get the meeting completely bogged down. Finally, since reviewing is an intensive activity, meetings should be time-limited – say to a maximum of one or two hours. If the review cannot be completed in that time, it will be much more productive to adjourn and reconvene than to continue with the current meeting.

Fagan inspection These are a very formalised form of walkthrough, named after Michael Fagan who devised the technique for IBM. With this method, the author of a piece of work reports to the project manager that it is complete and ready for checking. This triggers a six-stage review process:

- *Planning.* A trained Fagan 'moderator' organises the inspection, nominating people for the roles of 'inspector', 'reader' and 'scribe' and defining the date, duration and purpose of the meeting.
- *Overview.* This optional meeting can be used to provide background information on the work or on the Fagan process or to assign particular inspection tasks to individuals.
- *Preparation.* Individuals prepare for the inspection by examining the material and developing their understanding prior to the review.
- *Meeting.* This is very structured and chaired by the moderator. The reader paraphrases the item; each inspector, including the author and moderator, reports defects in the item and these are recorded by the scribe.
- *Rework.* The author takes the list of defects and, having corrected them, categorises them by severity and type.
- *Follow-up* A reviewer, nominated by the moderator, checks that the rework is complete and that the defects have been categorised correctly. The data resulting from the inspection is recorded on a database and the moderator signs off the inspection.

The compilation of statistics is an important part of the Fagan process, since they can be used to:

- Measure the cost of the inspection.
- Produce defect rates for the project.
- Identify 'hot spots' in a project for more intensive management.
- Predict the effort required for quality management.

Disadvantages cited of the Fagan technique are that training is required in the various roles, especially those of moderator and inspector, and that inspections are time-consuming and expensive. While there is some truth in both of these claims, it must be remembered that the costs of not discovering problems early enough usually outweigh the costs of thorough checking.

External review   It may sometimes be a good idea to request a review of work from a body or individual outside the project team. This could be by a quality assurance department or simply from an expert in the work being undertaken. External reviews may be a requirement of the contract or they may be imposed as part of an ISO9001 conformance procedure – see Chapter 12 for more on this. The principal disadvantage of an external review is probably cost but, on a large project at least, the plans should allow some margin for it. There is an additional problem in that the reviewer will not have the same familiarity with the material as will members of the project team, so an external review is likely to take longer. The reverse of this, of course, is that the external person approaches the review without any preconceptions and the resultant objectivity should improve the effectiveness of the review.

9.4.4   Documenting quality control

Whatever methods are employed for the quality control exercises, it is very important that the process be properly documented. Standards such as ISO9001 require that it be possible to trace the quality control process from the discovery of a problem to its resolution. Even without this external discipline, how else can you be sure that everything has been covered and that you do not inadvertently go over the same ground more than once?

There are various ways of documenting the process and the precise documentation will depend to some extent on the method used – Fagan inspections for instance will generate reports in a particular format. However, a simple two-layer process which has proved effective is:

- A log is maintained of all checks carried out. For each review, the log shows the date, a brief description of the subject and a reference to the papers which detail the results of the check.
- For each check, a report sheet is compiled. This contains: the date of the review; details to identify the material reviewed; the identity of the reviewer; a description of each error or omission discovered; an assessment of the severity of the defect and space to record a satisfactory recheck of the material.

QUALITY CONTROL REVIEW FORM						
Object of review:						
Version:		*Reviewer:*				
Date:		*Signed:*			*Date:*	
Author:		*Approved:*			*Date:*	
Location Page Para				*Class*	*Fixed* Initials	*Recheck* Initials Date

Fig 9.3   Quality control review form

Figure 9.3 provides an example of a form used to document quality control reviews.

For each error found, there should be some assessment of its severity and of the remedial action required. The assessment will depend to some extent on the nature of the project; for example, the design of, say, some life-critical software for an aircraft command system may require the complete re-check of every defect found, no matter how trivial.

Two systems of classification that have been used in various types of project are:

A three-stage system

1 Severe defect, requiring considerable rework and re-inspection.

2 Less severe defect, requiring some rework and re-inspection.

3 Minor defect, requiring rework but no re-inspection by the reviewer.

A four-stage system

1 Minor non-conformance to requirement; can be approved by project manager.
2 More serious non-conformance which must be approved by the customer.
3 Major non-conformance, requiring rework and re-inspection.
4 Very severe non-conformance. Work must be scrapped and performed again.

9.5 OTHER MEASURES OF PROJECT PERFORMANCE

Before leaving the subject of monitoring progress, there are two other tools that can be used to illustrate and measure progress on a project. The first of these is the *milestone slip chart*, illustrated in Fig 9.4.

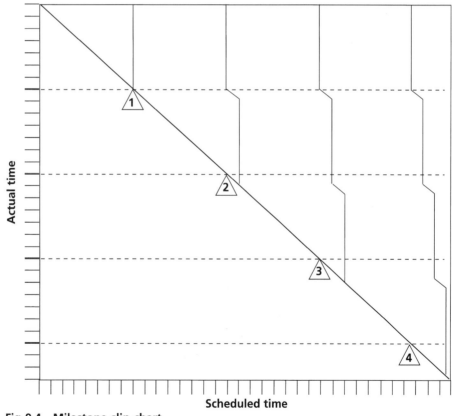

Fig 9.4 Milestone slip chart

In the milestone slip chart, the planned progress is shown on the X-axis and the actual progress on the Y-axis. The diagonal line shows where the project should be if it proceeds according to plan and four project milestones are superimposed. The first milestone was achieved on time and at that point it was predicted that the other milestones would be achieved also; these are shown by vertical lines. At milestone two, some slippage has occurred but we are predicting that there will be no further delays so the remaining milestones are displaced to the right by an equal amount. But actually, further delay occurs at milestone three and yet more before the final milestone is achieved. The milestone slip chart is a highly visual way of showing where in a project slippage has occurred and, more importantly, of illustrating what its final effects should be.

The other tool is known as *earned value analysis*. To use this, we need three important measures of the project's current status.

- **The Actual Cost of Work Performed (ACWP)** is the expenditure to date on the project. This may, of course, have been spent on scheduled or unscheduled activities and may include overruns on activities.

- **The Budgeted Cost of Work Scheduled (BCWS)** is the amount the plans say should have been spent at this point on scheduled activities.

- **The Budgeted Cost of Work Performed (BCWP)** is an analysis of the work actually done, scheduled or not, priced on the same basis as the scheduled work.

By subtracting the Actual Cost of Work Performed from the Budgeted Cost of Work Performed (BCWP–ACWP), we get the *cost variance* for the project. By subtracting the Budgeted Cost of Work Scheduled from the Budgeted Cost of Work Performed (BCWP–BCWS), we arrive at the *schedule variance*. These two variance figures provide a good measure of where the project is in terms of meeting its requirements against the planned cost and effort budgets.

9.6 SUMMARY

To monitor effort on a project, it is essential to have some sort of time recording system. For each activity, team members should record the time spent so far and make a fresh estimate of the time and effort left to come. With this information, the project manager can assess the likely out-turn of the project and identify where corrective actions may be needed on the project.

Other costs need to be monitored as well and, in view of the delay that often occurs between authorisation of an invoice and its appearance on the accounts, project managers will probably have to devise their own system to track costs.

There are various techniques available for monitoring quality methods and the technique must be chosen which is appropriate to the project. The results of quality control measure should be properly documented. Milestone slip charts provide a very visual way of illustrating project progress, and schedule and cost variances can be calculated to show the current status of a project against its planned progress.

9.7   QUESTIONS

1   How is effort monitored on a project? It is important that the effort to be spent on activities is reassessed on a regular basis – why is this so vital?

2   Staff time is usually the principal cost component of an IS project. Describe five other areas where project costs could arise.

3   Describe three methods than could be used to exercise quality control and explain the advantages and disadvantages of each.

4   In what circumstances might you consider increasing the volume and/or frequency of quality control checks? When might you decrease their volume or frequency?

5   Explain these terms: *Actual Cost of Work Performed* (ACWP); *Budgeted Cost of Work Performed* (BCWP); *Budgeted Cost of Work Scheduled* (BCWS).

CHAPTER 10

Exercising control

10.1 INTRODUCTION

In Chapter 9, we considered the various methods that you can use to monitor the progress of the project in terms of the triple constraint of time, cost and quality. But monitoring by itself isn't management and finding out how things are going is quite useless unless you are prepared to DO something to apply corrective action where it is needed. This may sound obvious but it is surprising how many project managers are happy to sit at their computers all day, lovingly capturing in immense detail the timesheet, financial and quality review data, whilst the project is careering crazily out of control. This has been described as 'management by spreadsheet' but, in reality, it represents the antithesis of management; it is merely book-keeping.

Exercising control really has four elements, illustrated in Fig 10.1.

The first stage is to evaluate the current situation – in other words what will happen if things continue as they are? The second is to consider various corrective measures that could be applied and to assess the pros and cons of adopting each alternative course of action. The third stage is to select and

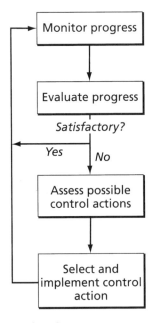

Fig 10.1   Monitoring and control cycle

implement one of the courses of action. And the fourth stage links back into the monitoring process since you need to check that the control action has had the desired corrective action on the project. We shall examine the first three stages in this chapter and, for stage four, you are recommended to re-read Chapter 9.

10.2   EVALUATING THE CURRENT SITUATION

The starting point for this is the information you have gathered through your monitoring processes, for example:

- Timesheet information showing the effort booked to date on a task, the effort still to go and the predicted end-date.
- The results of quality reviews showing whether the deliverables are meeting their defined quality criteria.
- Financial information showing costs accrued so far and expected in the future.

This information is compared with the various plans to find out if there is a problem and, if so, how big it is likely to be. For effort and timescale information, the important plan to examine is the network diagram. If a task has got – or is expected to get – behind schedule, is it on the critical path? If it isn't, is there sufficient 'float' or slack to accommodate it? Even if there is, this doesn't deal with the effort overrun, so can we afford the extra work that now seems to be involved? If the task *is* on the critical path, what will be the knock-on effects? For information on quality, will the defects discovered affect our ability to deliver a conformant product at the end? Do we need to rework the deliverables and, if so, have we the time and resources available to do so? Is the quality failure a one-off incident or does it indicate some deeper problem, like an overall lack of the necessary skills, or a too-tight timescale, or an imprecise specification? For cost information, is the project likely to come in over budget at the end? Can we compensate for some increased costs now by using cheaper or alternative materials or suppliers later?

In carrying out these evaluations, you need to consider what the balance is on this particular project between the triple constraints of time, cost and quality. Each project will be different and Fig 10.2 illustrates three extreme-case possibilities.

If the project's aim is to get a system in very quickly so that the customer can secure some competitive advantage, then time will tend to be the dominant factor. If, on the other hand, the project has safety-critical implications – an airliner's control system or a system to run a nuclear power station, for example – then quality will be most important. And if the customer wants something done as cheaply as possible, perhaps because of the pressure of legislation, then cost will predominate. This does not mean that the other

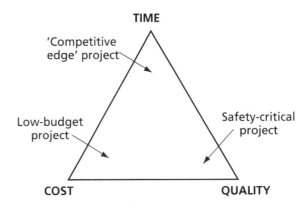

Fig 10.2 Time/cost/quality triangle for projects

constraints do not matter, just that one or two of them may be dominant in a particular situation. A knowledge of this balance is clearly vital in developing corrective actions since, for example, one response to a time problem is sometimes to throw resources – that is, money – at it; and quality can often be improved by taking more time over the work.

So, the question is, what will happen if I do nothing about this situation and does it matter? If it does, what will be the impact in terms of time, cost and quality? And, very importantly, what are the risks associated with the current course of action? It may be at this point that the project manager alone cannot decide how to act. It could well be appropriate to bring the customer into the discussion, to say quite frankly that this is the situation, these are the possible results and how do you view these outcomes? This is discussed further in Chapter 16 where customer management issues are covered in more detail. Before getting the customer involved, however, it is necessary to identify and evaluate the possible alternative courses of action that may be available.

10.3 POSSIBLE CORRECTIVE ACTIONS

It is clearly impossible within the scope of this or any other book to identify all of the possible corrective actions that might be considered during an IS project. The possibilities are literally endless, especially as typically we end up with some sort of composite solution. However, we present here some of the most common project management responses to problems encountered on IS projects. Incidentally, in trying to identify control actions, do not forget one of your most valuable sources of ideas – the project team members.

Doing nothing This option should always be considered first as it provides the benchmark against which to evaluate the other possibilities and it may even be the right answer. By doing nothing, we do not mean failing to act. We mean considering the alternatives and then deciding that allowing things to continue as they are is the best – or perhaps the least bad – option. There are two major dangers associated with the 'do nothing' option:

- An indecisive project manager may wish to disguise inactivity as a constructive act, thereby claiming that doing nothing is the best answer when, in fact, some more vigorous action is needed.

- The desire to be seen to be 'doing something' may cause the project manager to take an action which, in fact, makes the situation worse, whereas letting things continue on course for the time being might have been the correct response.

Avoiding these pitfalls requires that the project manager be rigorously honest with herself or himself and it also needs considerable 'ego strength' to withstand the pressure to be taking some visible action. It can be very helpful if a proper risk assessment is made of the various options, including doing nothing, so that the decision not to act can be seen to be based on a full analysis of the situation.

Adding more staff

If the problem is that an activity is getting behind schedule, then one possibility is to assign more staff to it. However, as we discussed in Chapter 8, this will only work if the task can really be partitioned since otherwise we shall get a situation of 'too many cooks spoil the broth'. Even if the task can be partitioned, the need for the additional staff to get up to speed on the work, the need for the existing staff to brief and guide the newcomers and the need for communication between the staff, will all mean that the overall productivity will be lowered to some extent. At the limit, adding more staff may actually make the task take *longer* than if we had plugged on with the original people.

Adding different skills

As an alternative to adding more staff, we could consider adding people with different, or greater skills. For example, if we are using an unfamiliar programming language and creating programs is taking an inordinate time, one possibility might be to get hold of a real expert in the language – perhaps an external consultant – and let him or her act as a technical 'guru' to advise and guide the rest of the team. Alternatively, if the problem is that the staff lack experience in the general sense, adding a few 'old hands' to the team could make all the difference. There is a noticeable difference in productivity between experienced staff and new trainees, so a sprinkling of experience could yield great improvements in overall team efficiency and effectiveness.

Using overtime

Overtime is often the cheapest way of buying additional effort. It is cheap since, although we pay an enhanced hourly rate for it, we do not have to pay additional overheads for National Insurance, pension, office space and so on. So, to meet a short-term crisis, overtime is a good answer. However, long-term or consistent use of overtime is a different proposition. If people are regularly working long hours, their overall productivity gradually reduces. Also, people come to rely on the income from overtime and therefore – whether consciously or not – may begin to spin out their tasks in order to guarantee the overtime payments. Finally, if a team is already working permanent overtime, what contingency is there left to deal with a real crisis when it develops? There is a cultural issue at work here too since, in the UK, performance is often judged by the hours one puts in rather than on the output produced; in Scandinavian countries, people who work regularly over their contracted hours are assumed to be inefficient!

Reassigning tasks

Without adding anyone new to the team, you can sometimes get better productivity, or better quality work, by switching the tasks around. For example, if you have someone who is extremely pedantic and thorough, they may be very slow in producing anything worthwhile – though it will be of very good quality once it appears. If this slowness is a problem, then why not use this person in a QC or reviewer role? Some people are very good at creative work, developing ideas from a blank sheet of paper but maybe not so good at following through into detailed designs. So use them for the up-front analysis tasks. You can use your knowledge of the characteristics of your team members to make sure that they are assigned to tasks that will exploit their strengths. There is more on this in Chapter 20.

Increasing individual supervision

A member of the team may be having productivity or quality problems with their work and this may only be coming to light when they deliver products. If so, consider partitioning the tasks and creating some smaller deliverables, so that quality control can be exercised more frequently. If you have an inexperienced or nervous person on the team, they will welcome the opportunity to share their difficulties and obtain guidance on a more regular basis.

Decreasing individual supervision

An opposite situation can arise with experienced personnel. They may resent being checked up on every five minutes and may, in the end, give up any personal interest in producing good quality work as it will only be combed through by someone else. You can increase job interest, motivation and productivity by giving experienced people greater individual responsibility for larger deliverables. There is another gain from this too, in that the work of the supervisor is reduced, thereby allowing more concentration of management effort on the less experienced team members.

Finding improved methods of working

As well as the work itself, you need to consider whether the methods adopted are the most suitable for the tasks in hand. For example, you may be involved in the analysis phase of the project and you find yourselves shuttling back and forth between different users trying to reconcile what seem to be mutually-exclusive requirements. The answer here might be to abandon the conventional analysis techniques and to adopt some sort of JAD (Joint Application Development, ©IBM) approach, staging workshops where all the users can come together with the analysts and thrash out their requirements.

Or you may be trying to make a fourth-generation language handle some complex algorithmic manipulation of data when you could more effectively commission a small amount of assembler code to do the job instead.

Streamlining the procedures

The procedures you have defined for tasks like quality control may prove to be bureaucratic and time-consuming. If, for instance, you have decided to use Fagan inspections and are finding a very low rate of errors, you might consider a less rigorous approach like peer review for most work, with the Fagan technique used only for the most critical areas.

Changing resource priorities

It is possible, though less common nowadays, that access to a development machine may be restricted. More likely, you will only have occasional access to a production environment – at weekends, say – for important testing. If this sort of thing is creating a bottleneck for your team, then you will have to try to negotiate increased access or perhaps find an alternative environment in which they can work. If this is not possible, examine the critical path for the project and use it to decide who should have first call on the time that *is* available.

Replanning the project

Your evaluation of the problems may reveal some fundamental flaws in the way the project has been planned. This is irritating, as planning is an intensive process and it is galling to find that the plan is not working out. However, there is no point in pretending that a plan is still viable if some of its assumptions have been proved invalid and the only recourse is to go back to square one – or at any rate, back far enough – and see whether a more realistic plan can be devised for the rest of the project. In particular, once the work has started, you may become aware of dependences between tasks that were unsuspected at the beginning. If so, you need to take them into account now in producing a new plan. In developing your new plan, remember that the old one gave rise to certain risks; the new plan may remove or mitigate these risks but it will almost certainly introduce new ones, so a reappraisal of the risks should form part of the replanning process. And in case you think it looks silly to go along to your management and the customer with a new plan, remember that you will look even sillier if you are later seen to have clung to the old plan long after it had been proved inadequate.

Changing the phasing of deliverables

Short of a complete revision of the plan, it may be possible to achieve a big improvement in effectiveness by changing the phasing of the deliverables. For example, the original plan may have shown the requirements specification as being delivered as one document but the initial analysis may show that the system can be partitioned into several more or less discrete elements. If so, some of these may have higher priority with the customer than others and it could be possible to consider some sort of phased delivery, with effort initially concentrated on the most urgent requirements. You may also decide to adopt some parallel working, for example with the design work overlapping the requirements analysis. There is always an element of risk in this approach – in that some design work may have to be repeated if the analysis turns up something unexpected – but accepting the risk may be justified if there is a pressing timescale for delivery. Again, proper risk analysis of the options will provide the best factual basis on which to make your decisions.

Decreasing the number of inspections

This could be considered as a response to falling behind the schedule but only if you are convinced that the inspections are uncovering an acceptably low number of defects. If the defect rate is high, then reducing inspections may improve delivery rates in the short term but the problems will come back to haunt you later during system or acceptance testing or as an excessive volume of warranty or maintenance work.

Increasing the number of inspections

If, on the other hand, you are getting a very high level of defects on completed large deliverables, a response could be to increase the number of inspections. This should ensure that errors are trapped earlier when they are more easily and quickly rectified.

Encouraging the team

Over a long project, something known as 'project fatigue' often sets in. This manifests itself in various ways: lowered productivity; increased absenteeism; resignations; more complaints about management and the users; and so on. If unchecked, this can have an increasingly corrosive effect, and things you might try to counteract it could include:

- Re-focusing on the team's achievements to date, to rekindle enthusiasm.
- Some sort of social event, ideally in company time, to bring the whole team together and engender a sense of team spirit.
- Re-distribution of work, to increase interest and give people opportunities for development.
- A team-building exercise of some sort.
- Reducing the size of deliverables. This is subtle as, in the later stages of a project, deliverables tend to get bigger. The benefit of reducing the size of deliverables is that it creates a series of small successes which is, in itself, motivating.

Introducing incentives

Depending on your organisation, you may or may not be able to offer financial incentives, like bonus payments, for improved performance. But you should be able to take someone out to lunch or give them an afternoon off for meeting or beating a deadline. Or you could introduce some form of recognition – like a 'programmer of the month' award, say, for exceptional achievement. If you have multiple teams working on a project, you could consider some sort of inter-team competition, always bearing in mind that you want all the teams still to be focused on the overall project and not just on beating each other!

Subcontracting parts of the work

You may find that, despite using all your tools and techniques of management, you are falling behind the schedule or not producing work of the required quality. If so, you could consider subcontracting some of the work to companies or organisations specialising in the skills or materials required. For example, small software houses that specialise in particular environments often have greater expertise per person than a larger, general purpose organisation. If you do subcontract the work, remember that you cannot subcontract the responsibility and you will have to make sure that the subcontractors work to the required standards. See Chapter 17 for more on supplier management issues.

Negotiating changes in the specification

If all else fails, you may have to go back to the customer and negotiate some change in the specification. It could be that the original objectives of the project have proved too ambitious for the time or money available but it may still be possible to deliver something that would achieve a large proportion of the hoped-for benefits. Alternatively, you could perhaps agree phased delivery, with the majority of important functions being delivered as originally planned, followed by incremental improvements until the full functionality is achieved. It has to be admitted that this sort of thing is not usually well received by customers but, on the other hand, you will probably get more credit for delivering something by the due date rather than a complete system six months late.

10.4 IMPLEMENTING CORRECTIVE ACTIONS

Whatever control actions you decide to take, there are two important things you must do:

● Make sure that everyone knows about the changes you are making and how they impact on the project as a whole. There is nothing more infuriating for team members, or wasteful of scarce resources, for someone to be left beavering away on a deliverable that is no longer wanted, or wanted in a different form, because of a change of plan.

● Evaluate, through your normal monitoring system, whether the changes have had the desired effect.

With regard to the first, copies of the revised plans and work instructions must be circulated to everyone affected and, if the changes are at all extensive, it is probably best to hold some meetings to present the revisions and discuss their implications.

The effects of the changes should be monitored closely to see whether they are working or not and, in particular, to see if the risks associated with them are coming to pass or not. It is very likely that you will have to make further adjustments and it is a sign of strength, not weakness, to make these when necessary. However, resist the temptation to keep 'fiddling' with the plan; if your control actions seem to be having broadly the desired results, leave things alone unless they are seen to be going adrift again.

10.5 CHANGE CONTROL

During the lifecycle of anything but the smallest IS project, change is more or less inevitable. Project changes can arise from many things:

- Change in the business environment in which the customer operates and to which they must respond – for example, the introduction of a new product or service by a competitor.
- New personnel coming into the customer organisation with different views from their predecessors, particularly if the sponsor of the project or leading users change.
- Revised user ideas of what the project should be about – perhaps triggered by the discussions that have occurred during detailed requirements analysis.
- Suggestions from the development team, based on an improving understanding of the users' requirements.
- The availability of new technology, offering different possible system solutions.
- New or revised legislation, imposing additional or different responsibilities on the customer.
- A straightforward change of mind by the users as to what they really want.

The chief problem with changes is that they are not always seen as such by all the parties involved. Quite often, the developers will classify something as a change which the users say is merely a clarification of a requirement that was always there. Disagreements of this sort have always bedevilled IS projects and seem to stem from the inability of users and developers to find a common means of communication. The use of structured analysis methods, like SSADM, can help somewhat in this area by replacing a reliance on written specifications with the use of diagrammatic techniques – it is rather less easy to commit sins of omission or ambiguity with pictures than with text. Nevertheless, there are still likely to be areas where different interpretations of the requirement are possible and it is more or less inevitable that the project manager will get drawn into discussion or even argument with the customer over whether something is a change or not. Chapter 16 offers some suggestions about how to handle this conflict.

One thing that often decides the intensity of the argument is the perceived cost of implementing the change. Generally speaking, the earlier the change is identified, the less will be the costs of incorporating it. If a change is noticed during analysis, then it is likely that the requirement specification will just be written a little differently. If it is identified during the acceptance test, however, then the design will have to be changed, the programs re-written and the various tests repeated. This is, incidentally, another argument for the use of structured analysis techniques, since their increased rigour reduces the likelihood of missing something out in the early stages of a project. Before a decision can be made on whether to implement a change, a thorough investigation needs to be conducted to discover:

- The total impact of the change on the development work – time, cost and quality.
- The effect of the change on the users – on their training and implementation requirements, for example.
- Any implications of the change on the proposed size or configuration of hardware or communications.
- The consequences of not implementing the change.
- The risks resulting from implementing, and from not implementing, the change.

All changes therefore need to be subjected to proper cost-benefit, impact and risk analysis. Once this information is available, the project manager and the customer can have an informed negotiation on the change and, hopefully, agree the way in which to handle it. This will almost certainly involve some change to the plan and quite possibly a variation to the contract as well.

A maxim that the project manager should bear in mind is that there is no such thing as an insignificant change – or at least there isn't until you have investigated it thoroughly. This may seem a rather sweeping assertion but a moment's reflection will reveal the truth in it. A change that seems at first sight trivial may, in fact, have very significant consequences. Moreover, the investigation of a change in itself incurs effort and takes time so that will have a small impact on the project if nothing else does. In view of this, the project manager should ensure that the mechanism for investigating and costing changes is explained to the customer at the start of the project and an early opportunity should be sought to put the mechanism into practice. If this can be done for a small change, for which it is decided ultimately not to charge the customer, then at least it establishes the principle of change control and the way changes will be handled.

One final thought on changes. It is not unknown for an external supplier to win a contract with a very competitive price on the basis of a very tight specification. Then, as soon as the customer makes the smallest change in the requirement, very tough change management is employed to drive up the value, and the profitability, of the project. This sort of approach is perhaps understandable in a highly competitive marketplace but it seldom leads to a successful project in that the customer and developer spend much of their time in contractual wrangles and part bitter enemies at the end.

The consequences for the development of a mutually-beneficial long-term business relationship can be imagined.

10.6 CHANGE CONTROL AND CONFIGURATION MANAGEMENT

Configuration management is discussed in Chapter 12 but it has been included here as there is often confusion between change control and configuration management. The basic distinction is this:

- *Change control* is the set of procedures that ensure that changes are made only after due consideration of their impact.
- *Configuration management* ensures that, if the changes are implemented, then amendments to each of the affected deliverables are properly controlled and recorded.

Configuration management is required in all projects, whether or not they ever have any changes imposed on them and the evaluation of the effects of a change will be greatly facilitated if there is a good configuration management regime in place.

10.7 SUMMARY

Exercising control involves evaluating the current situation, considering the pros and cons of potential corrective measures, selecting and implementing one of the options and checking that the control action has had the desired corrective effect.

In evaluating the current and optional situations, the project manager needs to consider the project's constraints of time, cost and quality/performance.

There are various control actions that could be applied and these will generally involve some sort of trade-off between the three constraints. Once a control action has been selected, it needs to be reflected in the plans and communicated to those involved and should then be monitored to check on its effectiveness.

Most projects involve changes and these should be properly evaluated and costed and agreed with the customer before implementation. A good configuration management regime will make it much easier to assess the effects of proposed changes.

10.8   QUESTIONS

1   What is meant by the term the *triple constraint*? What are the three elements of the triple constraint and why is an understanding of their relative weight important in exercising control over a project?

2   Your project is behind schedule and you are considering adding extra staff to the team. What would be the potential advantages and disadvantages of this approach?

3   In what circumstances might you (*a*) increase or (*b*) decrease the amount of supervision given to a team member?

4   Changes often bedevil IS projects. What steps are required to ensure that proper change control is exercised on a project?

5   Explain the difference between *change control* and *configuration management* and the relationship between them.

CHAPTER 11

Reporting progress

11.1   INTRODUCTION

In this chapter, we examine the ways in which progress is reported. Usually, when we talk of reporting progress, we are thinking about reporting upwards – to our immediate boss, to the board maybe, to the customer certainly. But for the project manager, there is another group of people who need to know how we are doing – the project team. You might imagine that team members would know how they are doing but it is surprising how often people feel in the dark about the overall progress of the project, the significance of their 'bit' and their own management's and customer's perception of their work.

Reporting progress to the team can often be a very motivating experience, as they can see the importance of their own contribution and the appreciation that others feel towards their efforts. Even when the news is 'bad', explaining the situation frankly to the team will help them understand why you may be putting more pressure on them and – who knows? – someone may just respond with a suggestion that will help you to put the project back on course. Project managers do not have a monopoly of good ideas! So remember to develop some mechanism for disseminating progress information to the team members as well.

11.2   RECIPIENTS OF PROGRESS REPORTS

Apart from the project team members, mentioned already, who is likely to want to receive reports on the progress of the project? The situation will differ from project to project, of course, but recipients are likely to include:

- *The project manager's immediate superior*. In an in-house IT department, this may be a systems development manager or IT manager/director. In a systems company, this is likely to be a business manager or, for a very large project, perhaps a board member. There may also, or instead of these, be a project controller or projects director – someone with overall responsibility for all project work.

- *The 'customer'*. Where the work is being carried out under some sort of contractual relationship, the customer will be the person who has commissioned, and will pay for the project, sometimes also known as the project 'sponsor'.

- *The 'users'* – who may well be different people from the sponsor. In some organisations, and on some projects, the 'users' may be a large and disparate group and generating the paperwork to keep them all informed may involve a regular assault on the world's trees!
- *The quality assurance department*, if there is one.

Each of these will have rather different reporting requirements. The users will be primarily interested in seeing when they are likely to get their system and when, perhaps, they will have to start preparing themselves for training or system implementation. The sponsor will also wish to know these things plus, if the work is being done on a time-and-materials basis, a summary of the costs to date and the likely overall cost. The IT manager will want to know when resources will be required for this project and when they will become available for other work. In the systems company, the business manager will require predictions on the current and predicted profitability of the project and will need to know when invoices should be raised for payments. And the quality assurance people will want to arrange quality audits at appropriate points in the project. So, depending on the actual organisation in which the project is taking place, the project manager may have to prepare a variety of reports, each with a slightly different slant. Clearly, the more open the organisational climate, or the contractual arrangements, the easier it will be for the project manager, since there will be less need to 'adjust' the information that is provided to the various stakeholders.

11.3   FREQUENCY OF REPORTING

Some judgement needs to be exercised in deciding how often to produce the various reports. If they are too frequent, then their production can become a full-time occupation to the detriment of other project management work – like actually controlling the project. On the other hand, if they are very infrequent, you lose the opportunity to raise important issues and to get decisions made and clarified. Possibly, the major reporting cycles will have been established at project initiation or mandated in the contract. For internal reporting, a monthly cycle is quite common, usually tied to the end of accounting periods.

Reports should, at the least, be prepared at the end of project phases or stages, or perhaps keyed to significant project milestones – like the sign-off of the requirements specification. This gives everyone an opportunity to take stock, review the project and decide if any changes of direction are needed. If the project has a very long stage – requirements specification often falls into this category – some mid-stage report may be advisable.

11.4 REPORT CONTENT AND FORMAT

11.4.1 Written reports

The reporting requirements should be established at the start of the project, when the contract is being agreed or the project plans are being developed. That way, the project manager can include effort for report preparation in the plans. In addition, the format and structure of the reports should be agreed and documented.

The usual recommendation is to aim for a system of reporting 'by exception'. What this means is that, instead of trotting out a long list of things which have gone according to plan, we highlight only – or at any rate, mainly – those activities that for some reason or other are not going according to plan. Assuming the project is running reasonably smoothly, this form of reporting should lessen the work involved for the project manager and enable everyone to concentrate on those areas that are not going quite so well and hence require more management attention. However, there is quite a significant drawback to exception reporting, especially if the project manager is trying to sustain the enthusiasm and commitment of sponsor and users. The snag is that exception reporting, by its very nature, tends to concentrate on failure – missed deadlines, cost overruns, staffing problems and so on. In turn, this can engender a rather negative view of how the project is doing. As an example of what we mean, when the Stock Exchange 'Big Bang' reorganisation took place in 1987, the national newspapers reported that some of the new computerised systems had not worked properly. Whilst this was true, Big Bang involved the co-ordination and interlinking of literally dozens of systems built for different clients by different developers. The wonder was not that a couple of systems did not work but that so many did; but the impression created by the press articles was overwhelmingly negative at the time. So, to create a more positive impression of project progress, the project manager needs to develop a formula that highlights problems but that also emphasises the project's achievements.

Reports are normally provided in writing, as this enables them to be circulated easily and gives the recipients time to read, analyse and digest the information. Often, though, the report will be supplemented by a progress meeting of some sort where the project manager will present a summary of the report and deal with any comments, queries or questions that arise from it.

The reports to the various parties will usually take the formats that follow.

Reports to the customer/sponsor

These will contain:

- A report identifier – project name, report sequence number, date of report.
- A short narrative review of progress since the last report.
- Milestones achieved, with dates and comparison with planned dates.

- Problems encountered – ideally with solutions used or proposed.
- Current predicted project end-date and dates for other significant events like system implementation.
- Change requests – details of new ones, status of existing ones.
- Costs to date and estimated outturn. However, if the project is being undertaken under a fixed-price contract, the internal costs of the project – though not the costs of agreed changes – are the business of the supplier only.

In addition to the above, the report may also contain an updated version of the project plan, perhaps at a high level – showing only the main phases of the project – and highlighting any variations from the previous version.

Reports to the users

The user report will contain:

- A report identifier – project name, report sequence number, date of report.
- A short narrative review of progress since the last report.
- Milestones achieved, with dates and comparison with planned dates.
- A revised schedule of user interface activities – such as review meetings, prototyping demonstrations, training and implementation dates.

In writing this report, the project manager needs to remember that one responsibility is to sustain the interest and commitment of the users and to ensure that they are able to play their full part in the project. So, without disguising or ignoring difficulties, an effort must be made to frame the report in a positive, upbeat way that emphasises the benefits that the users will ultimately derive from the system.

Reports to IT management or business management

These should include:

- A report identifier – project name, report sequence number, date of report.
- A short narrative review of progress since the last report.
- Milestones achieved, with dates and comparison with planned dates.
- Problems encountered – ideally with solutions used or proposed.
- Current predicted end-date and dates for other significant events such as system implementation.
- Change requests – details of new ones, status of existing ones.
- Costs to date and estimated out-turn.
- Significant customer interface issues encountered – for example, any disagreements over the scope or specification of the work.
- Opportunities for additional work or follow-on business.

This report should be completely frank and open and should be written to ensure that senior management is fully apprised of the real current state of the project. This frankness can sometimes create difficulties for project managers who work in closed cultures or where their management do not want to hear about problems. Project managers have to tread a fine line between keeping information to themselves, in which case they will probably take the sole blame for any subsequent disasters, or seeming to do nothing but report problems. The answer here is to present the problems but also the possible solutions with a recommendation on the best course of action. It is possible, though sometimes difficult, to present bad news in a positive way. It will be noticed, too, that we've included opportunities for further work in this report. The project manager, unlike, say, a sales manager, will have the benefit of close day-to-day contact with all sorts of people in the customer/user organisation and so will be in a very good position to identify opportunities. Whether the project manager personally follows these up will depend on his or her character and attitude – some people just don't like up-front selling – and on the organisation, which may want all sales opportunities handled by the sales force. Nonetheless, the project manager's input is invaluable both in spotting the business in the first place and in helping to decide the best way in which to exploit it. For more on the project manager's role in selling, see Chapter 15.

Reports to the quality assurance function

The QA personnel are generally regarded as either policemen to keep the project teams in order or valuable additional resources available to the project, depending on the attitude of the project manager and the way in which the QA people go about their business. Reports to QA should include:

- A report identifier – project name, report sequence number, date of report.
- A short narrative review of progress since the last report, focusing mainly on the project's quality control activities.
- Milestone achieved, with dates and comparison with planned dates.
- Quality problems encountered and solutions applied.
- Current predicted end-date and dates for significant quality events such as major reviews or stage-ends.

The objective of the report should be to enlist the help of the QA function in reviewing areas where quality problems have become evident and in suggesting better, more rigorous and perhaps less time-consuming methods of applying quality control.

Reports to the project team

These are usually less formal than the reports discussed already and it is actually probably better to stage a team meeting and deliver a verbal report, as discussed in the next section. However, on a large project, perhaps with the team dispersed over several sites, this may not be practical on a regular basis and some sort of written communication will be necessary. A more discursive, 'chatty' style may be appropriate for a team report and the aim should be to focus on the positive – the achievements to date, the quality of the work produced and the long-term benefits of the project both to the users and developers. If there have been, or still are, problems, mention them but also stress the way in which they are being overcome. There is no harm, either, in singling out individuals for praise but please make sure you do commend the right person; nothing is more annoying than seeing someone rewarded for another's achievements.

11.4.2   Report presentations

Quite often, the written report will be followed by some sort of presentation – to the project sponsor, to the project steering committee, to a user group, to senior IT management or to a team briefing. The presentation may be delivered round the table or at a larger forum. Although some people dislike speaking at such gatherings, they do provide an opportunity to inject some more animation into the reporting process and to rekindle the enthusiasm and commitment of the audience. So, the project manager needs to prepare carefully for the presentation.

The main thing *not* to do is to use the presentation to read through the written reports. This is a waste of an opportunity and insulting to the audience – after all, they can read for themselves, thank you very much. Instead, prepare a short, punchy presentation, ideally illustrated with slides or overheads, focusing on the main issues. These should include:

- The objectives of the project and its expected benefits. It is always worth restating these, especially when the project has been running for some time, everyone is up to their ears in its difficulties and interest is beginning to flag.
- The achievements to date. Starting here helps engender a positive view of the project, whatever comes next.
- The problems. Be frank and open, but don't seek to apportion blame. Problems happen and they need to be dealt with, so identify the possible solutions and engage the audience's commitment to getting the problems out of the way.
- The vision of the future – where the project is going and when it will get there.

This book is not about giving presentations, and there are many excellent publications and training videos on the subject; a companion book to this one, *Systems Analysis and Design* by Yeates, Shields and Helmy, published by Pitman Publishing, has some useful things to say. All the experts agree that the presenter must concentrate on impact and on getting a few simple messages across. So, don't put up lots of overheads with complex charts and tables and long bulleted lists of achievements. Use a very few slides with one or two points on each – made pictorially if possible.

If the project is not going too well – and, at times, most projects aren't going too well – the project manager can expect to suffer a fair amount of criticism at a meeting. Stoicism and an even temperament will help here and the main thing is not to be drawn into argument and recrimination. However much 'getting it off your chest' may make you feel better at the time, you will probably have antagonised someone in the process and their enmity will come back to haunt you later. So, take a deep breath, respond calmly and try to focus the discussion on nice, neutral facts. You may even gain in stature and authority for your ability to ride out a storm. There are some helpful ideas in Chapter 16 about dealing with these situations.

11.5   REPORTING IN PRINCE

The PRINCE project management method includes a set of control mechanisms which include reports at various levels. Some of these controls take the form of meetings and some of written reports only. The basic controls are:

Project Initiation   A project initiation meeting is held at which the plans for the project are presented and the objectives and scope of the project are agreed. This meeting gives approval for the first stage of the project to begin.

End Stage Assessment   At the end of each project stage, the project manager prepares a report on the stage and the Project Assurance Team provides a review of the project from the user, technical and quality perspectives. The plans for the next stage are presented and reviewed and, if acceptable, approval is given to move on to the next stage.

Mid-stage Assessment   This is optional in PRINCE and will usually occur in the following circumstances:

● If an Exception situation has arisen that will cause the stage to exceed the tolerances previously given to the project manager.

● If there are Requests for Change that need to be considered urgently and which cannot be accommodated within the tolerances of the current stage.

● If it is desired to start work on the next or another stage before this one is complete, thus overlapping the stages.

● At some point during a long stage, to review progress and to provide a confidence boost.

The format of the mid-stage assessment is similar to that of the end-stage assessment.

Highlight Report   This is PRINCE's main ongoing reporting mechanism, prepared regularly by the project manager and supplied to the Project Board, the Project Assurance Team and the stage manager, if this is a separate role from the project manager. The report should be short and include:

● Project identifier and date.

● The period covered by the report.

- The current budget and schedule status of the project.
- Products completed during the period.
- Problems either encountered or anticipated.
- Products scheduled to be completed during the next period.
- Total of Requests for Change approved.
- Budget and schedule impacts of the changes.

The frequency of highlight reports is agreed at project initiation and a monthly cycle is quite common.

Checkpoint   The checkpoint is the main internal control mechanism of a PRINCE project. Checkpoint meetings are held frequently, usually weekly or fortnightly, and are attended by the team leaders and team members and, optionally, by the stage manager and Project Assurance Team members. Progress is reviewed against individual work plans and a report is produced showing:

- The date of the meeting and the period covered.
- The follow-up of activities from previous reports.
- Activities during the period and products completed.
- Quality reviews performed during the period, with results.
- Problems encountered or anticipated and deviations from the plan.
- Work planned for next period.
- Products scheduled to be completed during the next period.

Project Closure   The project closure meeting is held at the end of the project and brings it to a formal conclusion. It is attended by the Project Board, Project Assurance Team, project manager and stage manager of the final stage. The objectives of the meeting are:

- To bring the project to an orderly close.
- To confirm that all the planned work has been carried out.
- To check that all Technical Exceptions and Quality Review actions have been closed off.
- To agree that all the documentation needed to maintain the delivered system is available.
- To confirm that the various acceptance letters have been signed off.
- To review any lessons learned from the project for future reference.

A report is prepared summarising the meeting and this is submitted to the Executive Committee.

11.6 SUMMARY

Various interested parties will wish to receive reports on the progress of the project. These include the customer, the users, senior IT management and members of the project team.

The reporting frequency needs to be set to ensure adequate control without imposing an undue bureaucratic overhead on the project manager.

The content and format of reports should be tailored to the needs of the recipients. Written reports may be supplemented by presentations.

The PRINCE method includes a series of reports at different levels and different stages in a project.

11.7 QUESTIONS

1 What factors would you consider when deciding on the frequency with which you would report progress to: (*a*) senior IS management; and (*b*) customer management?

2 What is meant by the term *exception reporting*? What are the benefits and the disadvantages of this type of reporting?

3 What are the benefits to the project manager in providing regular progress reports to the project team members?

4 Explain the following terms used in the PRINCE project management method:

Project Initiation;

End Stage Assessment;

Highlight Report;

Checkpoint.

CHAPTER 12

Quality

12.1 INTRODUCTION

Wherever you look nowadays, companies and their products use the term 'quality' as a differentiator, real or perceived, from their competition. Advertising and other publicity material, even company names, include the word 'quality' for additional impact. Why is this necessary? There are three main reasons. The first is that the word carries with it implications of excellence, value for money, superiority over the competition. The second is that the buying public, both private and commercial, recognises the fact that products and services have often fallen short of – however we define it – an acceptable level of performance. The third reason is that the Japanese have demonstrated that, by concentrating on quality, you can become world beaters from a standing start over a relatively short period of time.

The Information Technology industry is relatively new and rapidly changing. Issues of quality are different in a software development project from those on an automobile production line. Customer expectations, however, are much the same and it is for this reason that the national and international quality management system standards, ISO 9000, have been adopted equally for the IT industry as for all others.

In this chapter we'll discuss some of the issues around quality in IT projects.

12.2 QUALITY CONCEPTS

First of all, what is 'quality'? It's a word that has many definitions. 'I own a quality car'; 'I am pleased with the quality of my car'; 'My car has some interesting qualities' – all of these have different undertones with regard to the word 'quality'. It is essential therefore to ensure that everyone involved in a working 'quality' environment has the same understanding of the term.

In terms of delivered software and information technology services, the most commonly accepted definition of the term is *conformance to customer requirements*. In other words, a supplier and customer understand and agree what the customer wants; the supplier provides the product or service; and the customer acknowledges, in a formal way, that he or she has received what was expected. While purists may argue that quality is absolute and that the product or service either conforms to the stated requirements or does not, pragmatically customers prefer one supplier's quality to another's, however it is measured. Since buying decisions are most often made on non-quantitative or intangible or even emotional grounds, 'soft' quality issues are frequently more relevant than the more tangible ones. This is particularly true in the provision of a service where, for example, human factors such as friendliness, flexibility and helpfulness may play a large part in customer satisfaction.

Many organisations, both in product and in services businesses have evolved a reputation for quality. In many cases, this is confused with ultimate excellence such as with Rolls-Royce. In our terms, where quality means conformance to requirements, a Rolls-Royce is only a quality car for the person who has considerable funds, requires the capability to carry more than four passengers, etc. It is assumed that someone who is prepared to consider buying a Rolls-Royce will do so on its reputation alone. Mercedes-Benz, on the other hand, is reputed to have adopted a new approach to the development of its latest model range. Previously, the engineers provided a design which was subsequently sold by the marketing department. Now, the marketing people actually go and talk to potential customers to find out what the buying public wants. That information is then conveyed to the engineers, who produce a design which will satisfy those needs. Marks & Spencer, however, has cultivated relationships with both its suppliers and its customers. In this way, its suppliers understand the important quality issues with regard to Marks & Spencer and to Marks & Spencer's customers. And every one of Marks & Spencer's staff appreciates the importance of customer relationships to the success of the business. Most organisations these days include the word 'quality' in their mission statements, their publicity material and their recruitment advertisements. In other words, they address the three key dimensions of any business: customers, shareholders and staff. A generic mission statement might say:

Our mission is to deliver competitive advantage to our customers through the use of our high-quality products and services, a challenging and rewarding career to our staff, and a fair return for our shareholders.

Because the definition of quality is so imprecise and all-pervasive, techniques have emerged to formalise aspects of 'quality'. They are usually promoted by a highly persuasive champion, or 'guru'. Most of the quality gurus of the past 50 years have been concerned with the formalisation and improvement of the process:

- W Edwards Deming was trained as a statistician and based his ideas on statistical process control to separate 'special causes' of production variability from 'common causes'. He used this technique to promote a systematic and rigorous approach to quality improvement.

- Joseph Juran claimed that management is responsible for 85 per cent of failures within organisations. He emphasised that quality control should be an integral part of management control and that management should adopt a structured approach to company-wide quality planning.

- Philip Crosby promoted the 'four absolutes' of quality management:
  1 quality is defined as 'conformance to customer requirements';
  2 the system for implementing quality is prevention not inspection;
  3 the performance standard must be zero defects;
  4 the measurement of quality is the price of non-conformance.

- Michael Fagan developed inspection as the primary defect prevention tool. It involves a formal critique of one document against another that looks for and records inconsistencies, initiates rework as necessary, is led by an independent chairperson and makes use of checklists based on historical data.

The proliferation of techniques, initiatives and pilgrimages is gradually leading to a realisation that a holistic approach is the most likely solution to all the quality-related problems of an organisation. Thus Total Quality Management has begun to emerge as the most generally acceptable way forward.

12.3 TOTAL QUALITY MANAGEMENT

Although a well-controlled process is important in the delivery of a 'quality' product, it is not a guarantee of success. Once again, when we look at the example of Japanese industry, we see a culture in place which is far removed from the type of discipline engendered by the adherence to an international standard. This 'culture' has been established from early school days and is therefore ingrained into the attitudes and behaviour of the entire workforce. The visible effects of this are:

- The removal of hierarchical differentiators in the workplace: for example, the managing director of a manufacturing company wearing the same clothing as the person on the shop floor, or the provision of a single canteen for management and staff alike.

- The commitment of all staff to the organisation's mission: many companies are now publishing and issuing corporate vision and mission statements to their staff, often on small cards, so that they will be carried about, referred to and shown to customers.

- The application of appropriate resources: quality circles or quality improvement teams are being introduced to encourage staff to become involved in the identification and solution of problems at the point of issue.

- The continual striving for improvement: suggestion schemes and their associated rewards are becoming the norm rather than the exception.

All of these are parameters in what may be called a 'Total Quality' approach.

Table 12.1 Founder members of the EFQM

British Telecommunications plc	UK-based international telecommunications company
Robert Bosch GmbH	Electrical equipment company
Bull SA	Information technology company
Ciba–Geigy AG	Chemicals company
Dassault Aviation	Airplane manufacturers
AB Electrolux	Domestic appliance company
Fiat Auto SpA	Automobile manufacturers
KLM–Royal Dutch Airlines	Airline
Nestlé AG	Chocolate products manufacturer
Philips Electronics NV	Electronics company
Ing C Olivetti & C SpA	Italian electronics supplier
Renault	French automobile manufacturer
Gebr Sulzer AG	Engineering company
Volkswagen AG	Automobile manufacturer

Gradually, industries in the USA and in Europe are evolving methods of describing their aspirations in terms of business excellence and, equally importantly, of measuring their progress towards that excellence. In the USA, the Baldrige award was introduced to measure that progress and to motivate management and their companies to improve the overall quality of their organisations in a demonstrable way. More recently, in Europe, the European Foundation for Quality Management (EFQM), formed by an informal consortium of major organisations (see Table 12.1), developed a model, similar in concept to Baldrige, which would provide a means for quantitative evaluation of the key criteria for a total quality business.

The model, illustrated in Fig 12.1, shows the interrelationship between people, processes and results. In other words, the processes are the means by which an organisation harnesses and releases the talents of its people to produce results.

In essence, this tells us that Customer Satisfaction, People (employee) Satisfaction and Impact on Society are achieved through Leadership driving Policy and Strategy, People Management, Resources and Processes, leading ultimately to excellence in Business Results.

The nine elements shown in the model correspond to the criteria which are used to assess an organisation's progress towards excellence. For the purposes of quantitative assessment against the model, a relative value is

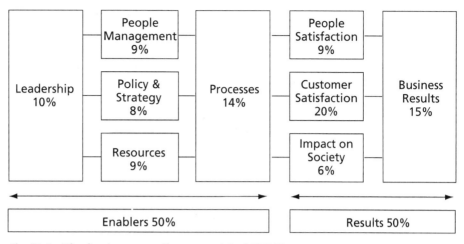

Fig 12.1 The business excellence model of EFQM

ascribed to each of the criteria. Enablers and Results each total 50 per cent. Within those totals, individual percentages, as shown in the diagram, reflect the relative importance attributed to each criterion.

The Enabler criteria are concerned with *how* the organisation approaches each of the criterion parts. Information is required on the excellence of the approach used and the extent of the deployment of the approach – vertically through all levels of the organisation and horizontally to all areas and activities.

The Results criteria are concerned with *what* the organisation has achieved and is achieving. The organisation being assessed should present numerical data including perception or direct feedback and predictor or relevant performance measures. Graphs showing trends over a period of years should also be presented.

For example, let us take a look at a 'typical' company Quality Services plc. It has always been proud of its staff recruitment, appraisal and training scheme, which it applies to all of its junior technical staff. The company has a five-year 'rolling' business strategy, which it uses to determine both the numbers and the skill profiles of the staff it needs to recruit. It operates a regular appraisal process, which determines the training needs and promotion potential for each member of staff.

Under the heading 'People Management', Quality Services plc might score well for its approach to human resource planning and improvement, although not so well for the deployment, since senior technical staff and administrative staff are not part of the scheme. Under both this criterion and also the result criterion 'People Satisfaction' the company might be marked down for not positively canvassing the views of its staff as to the effectiveness, from their point of view, of the scheme; for not establishing a quantitative measure of their satisfaction and of the evolution of that measure over time; and for not implementing the results of the feedback in order to improve the process.

Thus, out of the 18 per cent of the Total Quality measure assigned to the People criteria, Quality Services plc might achieve only 5 per cent. The comprehensive nature of the model, however, should enable Quality Services plc to address the areas in which they could make improvements, rather than feeling bad about a notional 'score'.

The British Quality Foundation (BQF) has now adopted this model as the basis for the UK Quality Award scheme, whose first winners in 1994 were Rover Group and TNT Express. The sole winners in 1995 were ICL High Performance Technology. The BQF also provide ample supporting documentation on the model, the self-assessment process and the award scheme.

By its nature, Total Quality Management applies to the entirety of an organisation and, where that larger unit operates a TQM policy, then it is natural that IS projects should also subscribe to the same approach. TQM, however, implies a significant, long-term commitment to a specific culture. If that is not in place within an organisation then it is most unlikely, if not impossible, for a single project manager to implement it within the constraints of a project. Nevertheless, all the techniques discussed later in this chapter that form part of a TQM approach and many of the ideas encapsulated within the model are worth considering for implementation in individual projects. For example:

- Is it clear who is the customer, internal or external, and exactly what that customer expects of the project in terms of timescale, cost, function, benefits?

- Are there agreed ways of carrying out the project and its sub-tasks and is everyone on the lookout for ways of improving those methods?

- Will the appropriate resources be available to carry out the project:

    are appropriate budgets available?

    do we have the technical skills?

    do we have the necessary effort?

    is there an adequate information flow?

    is there an appropriate technological infrastructure?

- Are staff suitably motivated for the project to succeed?

12.4 NATIONAL AND INTERNATIONAL INITIATIVES

12.4.1 European Software and Systems Initiative

ESSI, the European Software and Systems Initiative, is a technology transfer programme funded by the European Community. It aims to promote good practices in software engineering, and is specifically concerned with the later stages of the lifecycle. ESSI began with a pilot programme which ran for about 18 months from autumn 1993; this pilot programme supported two sorts of projects:

- Process Improvement Experiments (PIE) to fund software engineering to make new use of a method or tool that would not otherwise be considered. Each experiment would consist of a technology provider/consumer pair. Funding would be provided to the consumer, who would document the experiment.

- Dissemination Activities to spread information about experience with new methods and tools throughout the software engineering community via an on-line tool clearing house, an on-line consultancy service, or a register of practitioners.

An example of an ESSI project might be where a group of organisations which want to introduce a library of generic, reusable software components and to 'measure' the increased quality and maintainability achieved by the process of reuse. The 'primary' applicant would need to identify a pilot application project – one which would have been undertaken in any event – and all the additional tasks which would be needed to establish the new approach to analysis, design and development which would be required in order to achieve the objective of reusability. This could include employing a subcontractor to act as consultants, training staff in the concepts, purchasing software tools to implement a new library structure. This would form the process improvement part of the project. Once the project had been completed, a report would need to be presented with the results, formal presentations would be proposed and an on-going view of productivity gains might be suggested. This would form the dissemination commitment.

12.4.2   The European Software Institute

The European Software Institute (ESI) is an industrial initiative founded by fourteen leading European companies (Table 12.2). Its primary objective is to help to improve the competitiveness of European industry, by promoting and disseminating best practice in software engineering.

Table 12.2   Founding members of the European Software Institute

Bilbao Bizkaia Kutxa	Spain	Finsiel	Italy
Board Telecom Eirann	Ireland	Iberdrola	Spain
Bull SA	France	Lloyd's Register	UK
Cap Gemini Sogeti	France	Matra Marconi Space	France
Eritel	Spain	Olivetti SpA	Italy
ESB International Ltd	Ireland	Sema Group	UK
Etnoteam	Italy	Siemens–Nixdorf Informationssysteme	Germany

Based in Bilbao, in northern Spain, ESI is a user-driven, membership-based organisation, bringing together industry users and suppliers of software engineering practices. Focusing on the software process, with a goal of practice improvement, ESI provides improvement aids, training and education, publications and events.

12.4.3 The European Foundation for Quality Management

The European Foundation for Quality Management (EFQM) was founded in 1989, as a non-profit organisation. Today it is directed by the Presidents or CEOs of 20 member companies and supported by the European Commission. Its first activity was to sponsor the development of the TQM model described in section 12.3 above, and the European Quality Award, based upon that model. Amongst its other objectives are the pan-European co-ordination of benchmarking activities and the evolution of the TQM scheme to include small and medium-sized enterprises and public services.

12.4.4 The Software Engineering Institute

In the middle of the 1980s, the US federal government issued a request for a method of assessing the capability of its software contractors. In November 1986, in response to this request, the Software Engineering Institute of the Carnegie Mellon University, Pittsburgh, Pennsylvania, began developing a process maturity framework, to assist organisations in improving their software process.

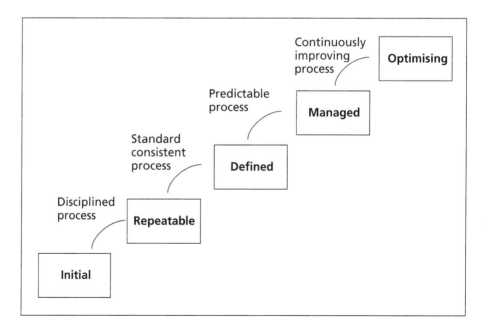

Fig 12.2 The five levels of software process maturity

In September 1987, the SEI released a brief description of the process maturity framework (Fig 12.2) and a maturity questionnaire. The SEI intended the maturity questionnaire to provide a simple tool for identifying areas where an organisation's software process needed improvement. Unfortunately, the questionnaire was too often regarded as 'the model' rather than as the vehicle for exploring process maturity issues.

After four years of experience with the software process maturity framework and the preliminary version of the maturity questionnaire, the SEI evolved the software process maturity framework into a fully defined model. This is now known as the Capability Maturity Model for Software (CMM).

12.4.5 Software Process Improvement Capability dEtermination

In 1993, the International Organisation for Standards (ISO) software engineering group started the Software Process Improvement Capability dEtermination (SPICE) project. Its objective was to develop a common, international standard for software process assessment. It aims to build on the best features of existing software assessment methods, such as the SEI CMM and the EFQM model mentioned above.

Essentially, SPICE addresses the three fundamental issues: how to identify the key processes; how to assess the efficiency of those processes; and how to go about improving them. Since it will be an international standard, SPICE is document-based. Nevertheless, it does include in its document set a guide to conducting assessments; the construction, selection and use of assessment instruments; and the qualification and training of assessors. The SPICE component set also includes: a concepts and introductory guide that describes how the other products fit together as well as technical guides relating to a model for process management; rating processes; guide for its use in process improvement; guide for use in determining supplier process capability; and a vocabulary.

A fast development route has been adopted for the SPICE standard. A key feature of the project, and one which distinguishes it from most other standardisation initiatives in software engineering, is the use of structured trials to test the proposed standard against a representative sample of organisations in different industry sectors, and to validate the documents before they become standards.

The trials aim to identify shortcomings in the document set and demonstrate that the SPICE-compliant assessment methods are valid and repeatable. A no less important aim is to collect data on the benefits obtained using SPICE in the field.

The ESI is Regional Trials Co-ordinator for the European component of these trials and so is responsible for collecting and analysing the data collected from trial participants.

12.5   QUALITY MANAGEMENT SYSTEMS

The international standards for a quality management system (QMS), ISO 9000, are generic in nature and represent maximum agreement across all sectors of industry. As a result the standards represent minimum not maximum best practice within any one sector. TickIT was an initiative, promoted by the UK Department of Trade and Industry, to establish the relevance of these standards to the production of software. Its objectives are:

● to harmonise QMS standards, through the common route of ISO 9000;

● to improve market confidence in third party certification of QMSs;

● to provide authoritative guidance material to help QMS implementors;

● to improve professional practice amongst software QMS auditors.

In addition, it has the objective of stimulating software developers to think about what quality really is and how it may be achieved.

A quality system brings together all the functions, objectives and activities which contribute to the consistent quality of a product or service. Writing down these policies and procedures demonstrates how each aspect of the quality system interacts to ensure the system's success in improving the efficiency, performance and cost-effectiveness of the entire operation. The term *quality management system* may be used, rather than the more limiting one of *quality system*, to reflect the additional management responsibilities. For example, where procedures from the conventional management system can affect quality, such as the recruitment programme, then they need to be part of the QMS.

The QMS is a snapshot of an organisation at an instant in time and is founded upon a statement of the organisation's objectives and policy for quality. These should correspond to the type and scope of product or service being offered. There must be a description of the responsibilities and the internal organisation for the QMS, to ensure that all quality practices are understood and are operated effectively. The structure of a typical QMS is shown in Fig 12.3.

Having established a QMS, the visible sign that the system is operational for a given project, product or service is the quality plan. The quality plan has a number of direct and indirect benefits:

● It is a formal definition of how the work is to be accomplished.

● It provides a discipline for the project manager, offering a framework around which all the issues in prospect for the work can be considered and addressed before and during the project.

● It provides a key reference point for project team members.

● It acts as a bridge between the customer and the supplier.

There is no generally accepted format for a quality plan. Indeed, the distinction between a project plan and a quality plan is becoming increasingly

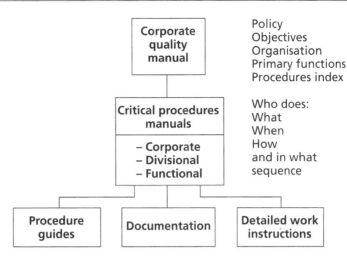

Fig 12.3 Quality management system structure

blurred. However, the presentation of the document should be standardised wherever possible. It should be easy to use by project staff, easy to update and should clearly demonstrate that it fulfils contractual or external requirements. The quality plan should call up, as necessary:

- Authorised procedures, referenced from the QMS.
- Project-related procedures, meeting the objectives of the standard procedures, but with specific issues highlighted.
- Purchaser procedures, as specified in the contract.

The supplier's quality plan should be a deliverable of the project at the earliest practicable time from its start. It must be produced by the project manager and the team, not imposed by the quality assurance function. Since an objective of producing a quality plan is to confront likely problems before they arise, it should not merely be a copy of a previous plan. The increasing use of electronic documentation makes it more and more tempting to do this.

In preparing a quality plan, or even in thinking about a standard for quality plans, it is important to place it in the context of the scope of work being carried out. For a large, complex, innovative project, it may be appropriate to address all the issues covered by the ISO 9000 standard, although many of these sections may just warrant a reference approach. For the supply of a standard product, or for a well-understood development, where the risk to customer and supplier is relatively small, a concise, 'report-by-exception' type of plan would be more effective. The key issues, in either case, are:

- What are the lifecycle stages of the project?
- What standards are to be used throughout that lifecycle?
- What controls are to be exercised by the project manager to ensure quality?
- What checks, independent of the project, are to be imposed?

12.6 THE COST OF POOR QUALITY

We are all aware of the costs of producing poor quality systems. We add to the work to be done to correct and re-test programs. We have to make design changes late in the lifecycle because we did not really identify or understand the user's real needs. For this reason the cost of the additional work is often referred to as 'the cost of poor quality', or the 'price of non-conformance'. The objective for a project is to minimise this price of non-conformance. Its measurement can be broken down into four elements:

- Prevention
- Appraisal
- Internal failure
- External failure.

The cost of prevention is the amount spent to ensure that the work will be done correctly. It includes risk reduction and error prevention, for example ensuring the design is right before beginning production. Examples of prevention costs are supplier evaluation and the training and development of staff. Figure 12.4 shows that, if we allocate resources early in the development lifecycle to prevent poor quality – by training people thoroughly, for example – the incidence of defects and the costs of rectifying them will fall.

Appraisal costs are those associated with inspection and testing of both the company's own products and products received from suppliers. On software projects, we might have the appraisal costs of testing, walkthroughs, Fagan inspections and design reviews. As with prevention, we should make appraisal cost investments early in the development lifecycle. Figure 12.4 illustrates how, by dedicating more resources to appraisal, the number of defects in the end product is drastically reduced. For example, the more design reviews carried out during system design – an increased investment in appraisal – the greater the chance of spotting and correcting defects before resources are wasted programming those incorrect designs.

The cost of internal failure is the cost of rectifying everything that is discovered to be wrong while the product or service is still under our control and before it is delivered to a customer. An example of an internal failure would be part of a software system having to be scrapped and then designed and coded again, as a result of a major problem being unearthed during integration testing. One of the key strengths of the Japanese quality approach is that they have been able to reduce the costs of internal failure to almost zero, because they are orientated around defect prevention and process improvement – in other words, solve the problem, not the symptom.

External failure costs are incurred by a company because defects are only detected after delivery to customers. These costs are typically incurred under a warranty agreement, or in handling customer complaints. In the latter category, however, are the unseen costs of lost repeat orders and a damaged reputation. On average, it costs five times as much to win new customers as

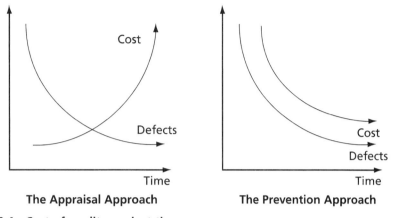

Fig 12.4   Cost of quality against time

it does to keep existing ones. According to one survey, if you buy a product and are happy about it, you tell, on average, eight other people about it. If, on the other hand, you are unhappy about a product you have bought, you will make your dissatisfaction known to 22 other people.

This puts into perspective both the indirect costs of quality and also the need to prevent errors occurring late in the cycle.

12.7   INSPECTION VERSUS TESTING

The software quality problem may be defined to be the result of defects in code and documentation causing failure to satisfy user requirements. For the purposes of this discussion we shall define a 'defect' to be an instance in which a requirement is not satisfied; and a 'requirement' is anything agreed on commitment – either a recognisable, external product requirement, or an internal development requirement.

Examples of such internal requirements are a test plan that completely verifies that the product meets the agreed needs of the user, or that the code of a program must be complete before it is submitted for testing. Whilst defects become manifest in the end product documentation or code, most of them are actually present while the functional aspects of the product and its quality attributes are being created during the development of the requirements or the design or coding or by insertion of changes.

How can this software quality problem be eliminated?

The attributes of software quality may be evaluated by two principal methods: testing and inspection. Both methods are aimed at the detection and elimination of defects during the lifecycle of a project. The principal difference, however, is the frame of reference for that detection process. Figure 12.5 shows the software development lifecycle model and the scope of inspection and testing within the components of the model.

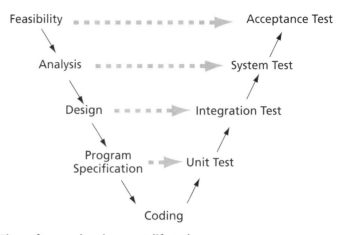

Fig 12.5   The software development lifecycle

The solid lines show the progression through the stages in the lifecycle. Inspection takes place at each stage, using the information available at the tail of the line for verification of the information created at the head of that line. Testing uses the information at the tail of the dotted lines to verify the information at the head of those lines. For example, the unit test has to ensure that the program specification has been satisfied, whilst the system test is used to verify that the requirements specified in the analysis phase have been met.

Most, if not all, development environments require a combination of both types of defect detection. It can be seen from the diagram though that the later in the process detection occurs, the further back you will have to go and the more far reaching will be the implications of correcting defects. For example, an error detected in unit testing will require recoding, whilst an error discovered as late as the acceptance test may require a rework of all the specification stages and all the testing phases.

Inspections are intended to minimise the number of issues, defects, or errors propagated to the next level of the lifecycle. In this way they help to overcome the known cost escalation of finding and correcting errors. Inspections are document-based and people-intensive and consequently their use must be carefully controlled if they are to be cost-effective.

The objectives of each inspection in the software development environment are:

● to find and record issues – checking for discrepancies between the document under inspection and any source documents used to create it;

● to instigate rework as necessary and verify that corrective action is complete.

Additional objectives include the improvement of the software development process by identifying recurring sources of defects, or potential for the creation of defects, and the improvement of the inspection process itself.

Inspections, if they are to be used, are a normal part of the lifecycle of a project. Normally, this means that their use is identified within a specific project plan. When considering whether it is worthwhile conducting an inspection, the key decision criteria are:

- The importance of the document to be inspected, within the context of the project.
- The cost-effectiveness of the inspection process.
- The complexity of the document.
- The impact on other areas of the project.

Having decided that an inspection is worthwhile, the appropriate, trained resources must be committed to it. This means, they must be assigned; briefed; and available to give the necessary time and effort, both before and during the inspection.

Authors of documents may often feel threatened by the very idea of an inspection but enlightened authors are grateful for the defects found during an inspection, since it avoids a less friendly person finding them later!

12.8   THE MANAGEMENT OF SOFTWARE TESTING

Software testing is an important part of any quality plan; in fact, the interpretation of ISO 9000 for software development stresses the significance of planning, reviewing and authorising a test environment as a key part of the quality planning process. In addition, the results of each test must be recorded and the problems identified must be tracked. Following the standard therefore ensures, at least, that some testing will be done in a well-documented fashion. The problem with software, though, is that it is virtually certain that you will never find all the errors. Projects often seem to be pouring time and resources into a black hole called 'testing' and even after this has been done, the end customer will always find too many errors himself.

The project manager's problem is to optimise the return on the effort put into the testing exercise. Inspection, as discussed in the previous section, is part of that equation, the use of test techniques gives a more effective process, and the use of tools may make the test process more efficient. We've seen that in the software development lifecycle shown in Fig 12.5 several levels of testing are required and that the specification of those sets of tests is carried out in the reverse order of their execution with unit tests being the first to run. A key factor in the optimisation process is to plan the tests early in the lifecycle, even though the execution will not take place until later on. Also, the recognition that each type of test is different in nature, in objective and in execution will help the members of the project team to clarify the different issues addressed by the testing process as a whole.

Testing can be performed manually, or using software tools. The decision about whether to use tools depends upon the size and complexity of the project, the size and complexity of the task, the monotony of the manual task, the relevance of the tools and the quality of the tools – in every sense of the word 'quality'. For each of the types of test the number of individual tasks is significant and includes the following:

- Planning of the entire test – the identification and scheduling of tasks and assignment of resources.
- Designing the test conditions.
- Specifying test case.
- Preparing test data.
- The formal setting-out of the expected outcome of each of the tests planned.
- Running of the software with the chosen input data.
- Comparing the actual results against the expected results.
- Identifying and correcting errors in the software, the design, the analysis and the requirement.
- Monitoring the progress of the tests.
- Improving the testing process – a continuous search for enhancements to all aspects of the test process.
- Using volume tests and performance issues to ensure that the hardware and software configuration can cope with operational extremes.
- Evaluating the non-functional aspects, such as user friendliness of the system, maintainability of the code.
- Finally, regression testing, to show that corrections to the software as a result of the detection of errors have not had knock-on effects elsewhere.
- A statistical assessment of the completeness of the testing undertaken.

It is easy to be misled into believing that in a world of sophisticated software, there must be a software tool to carry out these tasks. But bear in mind that the errors have been put there by one or more human beings and the delivered system is to be used by human beings. Only through significant intervention by human beings will quality be delivered. For example, if a software tool were able to generate the expected results from a given set of input data, then that tool would be doing what the developed software is required to do – but correctly. Why not just use the tool instead of developing new software!

Nevertheless, there are several useful software tools under the CAST (Computer Aided Software Testing) banner, which will be worth considering. Most of the market research organisations have produced reports, which are updated on a regular basis, evaluating and comparing the available products and their suppliers.

12.9 METRICS AND STATISTICAL QUALITY CONTROL

It is very tempting to measure 'everything that moves' on a project in the belief that by measuring you are in control. Part of the quality planning activity will be to identify those aspects of the project which are key to the control, evaluation and improvement of the software development process and to the quality of the service or product delivered to the customer in the context of the current project.

As the project manager, you need to 'have a feel' for how the project is going. You'll need to recognise where individual team members are falling behind with their work:

● where external events are having an impact on the progress of the project;
● where initial assumptions may have been optimistic, or wrong;
● where risks were calculated at the start of the project.

Intuition, or experience can count for a lot, but concrete, statistical evidence is easier to demonstrate to people outside of the project and also makes remedial action easier to quantify and to justify.

The most apparent measures for project management control are time, effort and money. Before the start of any project, estimates will have been drawn up of the total elapsed time for the project, of the manpower effort required to deliver the work and of the cost of the various elements of the project. Often the person drawing up the estimates is not the same as the person having to live with them! It is essential therefore that, in conjunction with those estimates, there is a clear statement setting out the reasoning behind the estimates, the assumptions upon which they were based and the commercial decisions taken. During the course of the project, the project manager should report the above measures in terms of spend-to-date and spend-to-go: budget and actual.

History – and collected data – tells us that for programs, or documents of a certain size, novelty and complexity, we can expect certain levels of error. The calibration of such measures for your own development environment provides an invaluable platform for estimating and controlling projects. The key issue is to determine which are to be the metrics on which to establish the statistical baseline.

If you decide to use inspections as a standard technique, then establish a database showing the size of document, number of defects per page, severity of those errors, and the time it takes to inspect each page. If you use function point analysis or lines of code (LOC), establish a measure of development effort per function point or thousands of lines of code (KLOC). Then, at the system test stage, measure the number of errors detected per unit of the system and their origin whether from analysis, design or coding.

In this manner, you can quickly tell whether there are issues related to particular parts of a system; to particular programmers, or teams; or to this project as a whole, which are causing it to be more or less defect-prone than normal. Once such an evaluation has been made, decisions can be taken as to whether to make fundamental changes to the estimates, or to the team, in order to achieve the project's objectives.

Project managers often have a view that they and their projects are unique: no one has ever done anything like them before and no one will ever do anything similar in the future. For those reasons it is not worth exploring historical data, nor is it beneficial to 'waste time' recording data for posterity. The prophecy is often self-fulfilling. It is usually the role of an installation quality manager to establish a culture of continuous improvement, often through the use of such statistics. On large projects, where project managers will see the benefits of statistics within the lifecycle of their own work, this is not difficult.

The key to the successful implementation of a useful, statistically based project management and quality improvement environment is to make the statistics easy to understand and, more important, easy to collect. To the latter end, the collection of statistics should be a part of the project management process and, if possible, should be automatic. Thus, for example, if project management is normally carried out using an electronic tool, whether a specific project management package, or a word processing or spreadsheet package, templates should be built in which can prompt for, or calculate directly, the information required, with the minimum of additional effort on the part of the project manager.

12.10 SUPPORTING ACTIVITIES

ISO 9000 identifies a number of activities within the quality management system as being of a supportive nature – outside of the software development lifecycle itself. This section addresses the key issues for project managers in these areas, which are not dealt with elsewhere.

'Documentation,' said Dick Brandon, the pioneer of computing standards, 'is like sex. When it's good, it's very, very good; and when it's bad, it's better than nothing.'

As part of the quality planning process, the project manager is responsible for identifying the key documents which will form the framework for the project. These will include documents outside the manager's control – such as installation or customer standards – and project-specific documents – such as local standards, planning documents and project lifecycle documents, from phase inputs and outputs, to operational and user guides. For those latter documents, which are the responsibility of the project, there must be mechanisms in place to control their preparation, approval, release, change, access and removal. This will go a long way towards eliminating the errors which so often happen when information about documents is taken for granted. For paper documents such controls are relatively straightforward to envisage and to implement. Increasingly, however, technology is enabling project managers to introduce electronic documents as the norm. Similar disciplines are available and must be enforced, through password protection, electronic signature and time stamping.

The purpose of quality records is to demonstrate the achievement of the required quality and the effective operation of the quality system. This is another area for optimisation of effort in order to achieve the desired result. It is often tempting to flood the project with paperwork, just to impress an auditor. The quality plan should however have identified the key processes, responsibilities, communication mechanisms, and process improvement opportunities. Evidence is needed that these issues have been addressed, through minutes, action planning and follow-up, debriefs and, where appropriate, supporting statistical information.

In all aspects of project management there are software tools and well-tried techniques to support you. The ISO 9000 standard identifies the fact that project managers must be aware and make use of such tools and techniques *where they are appropriate.*

In this context, the tools will be used by the project manager for project management purposes; and also by the project team for product development in order to support and make more effective the quality management system. These are discussed under the separate sub-sections to which they apply.

Every issue which we have dealt with in this book requires some element of training, experiential self-study, or formal classroom work. Part of the planning activity will require the project manager to identify the skills required to address the tasks involved in the project and to match those against the resources available.

It is always tempting to try to 'gain time' by assigning people to tasks as soon as they are available. This temptation must be resisted in favour of providing the necessary training for a task before its launch. ISO 9000 requires records to be maintained of training received, both for the benefit of an individual's career progression and also for the sake of future task assignment.

12.11 CONFIGURATION MANAGEMENT

British Standard BS8488:1984 defines configuration management as:

> *The discipline of identifying the components of a continuously evolving system (taking into account relevant system interfaces) for the purposes of controlling changes to these components and maintaining integrity and traceability throughout the system lifecycle.*

This definition means knowing where you are at any given time with regard to the components of a system – hardware, software and documentation – and being able to say with certainty what the status of each item is, both on its own and in relation to other items.

The importance of configuration management is best appreciated by considering what happens when it is not properly addressed:

- No one can be certain which version of a component is the current one, so for example, time and effort may be wasted by working from an obsolete version of the specification.
- Individual items, such a program specifications, the completed code and the test specification, are mutually incompatible.
- The release of products is not controlled, so that no one can be sure which version of a program is running; which version of system software is currently is use; or which combination of hardware items is relevant.
- Changes to the environment – program, system software, or hardware – are applied in an uncontrolled manner, without proper analysis of their impact.
- If a catastrophe occurs, no one can be sure what the current state of the project should be, or how to regenerate it.

The larger and more complex the project, therefore, the more relevant will be a configuration management system to support it. Configuration management includes:

- *Version and variant control,* recording the history of items and records during development.
- *Configuration control,* the orchestration of processes for maintaining the visibility of the software parts of the system during the development life-cycle.
- *Change control,* the management of changes through suitable evaluation and authorisation.

A configuration management environment should be established during the quality planning stage of a development project. Any later, and the system, by its nature, is liable to be 'chasing its own tail'. Procedures should be flexible enough to control all items, whatever their origin, within the same framework. An item will normally come under configuration control when it reaches a relatively stable state and has been reviewed and approved. Points of reference should be established for each item at each stage of the project, giving the reference, author and approver. Equally, there must be a readily available reference point for the whole system and provision for keeping a history of changes. In this manner, the system is traceable through its life, and the release of products, both internally and externally, can be easily controlled.

The project manager should consider whether to instigate regular audits, or spot checks, to ensure that the configuration management procedures are being followed properly.

12.12 MANAGING QUALITY WITH PRINCE

Projects in Controlled Environments (PRINCE) is a structured method for project management consisting of a set of procedures designed specifically for managing and controlling the planning, progress and quality of IS projects.

In PRINCE a project is regarded as having a defined and unique set of products, a set of activities to construct the products, appropriate resources to undertake the activities and a finite lifespan. PRINCE also requires an organisational structure with defined responsibilities. Within the context of the software development lifecycle, PRINCE is typically used to control activities or the sub-activities which make them up, from feasibility study through production and installation. PRINCE does not specify the activities that a project should embrace. Thus more than one activity, such as design through production, may be controlled as one PRINCE project.

Other activities within the lifecycle, such as operation, do not fall within the PRINCE definition of a project and are not controlled using PRINCE. However, many of the PRINCE procedures are relevant to the control of such activities but need to be supplemented by further documented procedures and standards. These further procedures and standards often already exist within an organisation and their introduction merely involves formally specifying and documenting them.

PRINCE was not designed to be a comprehensive quality system. However, three of its constituents contribute to a significant part of such a system. These are:

● Quality controls which are clearly defined technical and management procedures

● Product-based planning and the product descriptions which define the product quality criteria

● The PRINCE organisation.

Because PRINCE is not in itself a quality system, its use does not automatically produce conformance to ISO 9000. In fact, PRINCE itself may need tailoring to meet the specific needs of the organisation. Further procedures and standards which are required to satisfy ISO 9000 and which PRINCE does not cover, in the context of project management, include:

● The availability of procedures for verification and use of automated tools

● Procedures must be defined and documented for the distribution of replicated systems, such as software products

● Procedures should be defined and documented for reviewing and updating the quality system

● Procedures must be defined and documented which provide records demonstrating the effectiveness of the quality system. These records should include:

- – internal and external quality audit documentation
- – results of customer satisfaction surveys
- – quality system change control documentation
- Audit procedures and schedules must be defined and documented
- All issues relevant to staff training and to measurement and statistics need to be addressed.

12.13 SUMMARY

In this chapter we have introduced the use and misuse of the term 'quality'. We've noted the many new aspects and initiatives which have evolved in recent years and which are so important to project managers. We've discussed the benefits of the formal approach to quality and the cost of not adopting such an approach. We've also shown how project managers need to be aware of the areas closely related to quality management which form an integral part of the management task.

12.14 QUESTIONS

1 How could the quality culture behaviours described in section 12.3 be applied in a hospital?

2 Why do you suppose there are an increasing number of organisations concerned with the development of quality practices for IS development?

3 Consider the model shown in Fig 12.4, the Software Process Maturity Model. How could it be applied to the training or personnel processes in a large bank?

4 Do you agree with what Dick Brandon said about sex in section 12.10? Do not take this question too seriously!

CHAPTER 13

Risk management

13.1 INTRODUCTION

All projects involve risk of some sort. This may stem from the nature of the work – for example if there is a lot of innovation involved – from the type of resources available, from the contractual relationship which is in place or from political factors which influence the project. It is usually not practicable to eliminate risks altogether – indeed, this would not be desirable since it would inhibit innovation and stifle creativity. But it is possible to manage projects in a way that recognises the existence of the risks and prepares, in advance, methods of dealing with them if they occur.s

In recent years, the subject of risk management has become increasingly important. This is partly because the use of project organisations, with associated project management techniques, is now often seen as a means of achieving some desired change in an organisation and is used more widely than in traditional areas such as the development of information systems. In addition, projects are assuming ever greater levels of complexity, with many different skills and technologies being employed and the resulting inter-dependencies leading to a higher degree of uncertainty in the project's outcome.

13.2 OUTLINE OF THE RISK MANAGEMENT PROCESS

The risk management process is illustrated in Fig 13.1. Reduced to its essentials, risk management requires:

- The establishment of mechanisms to keep risks under review and to make sure they are being addressed.
- A means of identifying the potential risks to the project.
- An assessment of the likelihood of each risk materialising.
- An assessment of the probable impact of each risk.
- The formulation of measures to avoid each risk occurring.
- The development of fallback measures to mitigate the risks if avoidance actions fail.
- The determination of the urgency of the risk and of taking appropriate countermeasures.

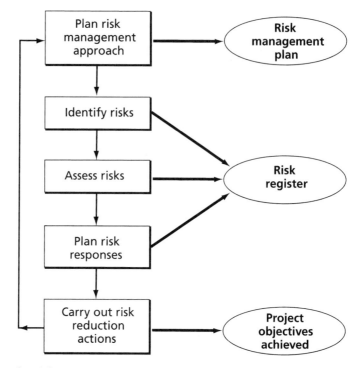

Fig 13.1   The risk management process

Also key to successful risk management is the issue of 'ownership' – that someone should be responsible for each risk. Each of these issues is addressed in the sections that follow.

13.3   RISK IDENTIFICATION

Clearly, the first step involved in managing risks is to discover what they are but this is more easily said than done. To some extent, each project is unique and its risks will arise from the interdependencies between factors that may not have been seen in this combination before. Nevertheless, there are some broad areas in which to look for potential risks and some of these are considered below. It is clear that there are a lot of areas in which risk could arise and it is difficult for the project manager to be sure that all of the possible risks have been identified. It is often valuable to get a second, or third, opinion from experienced project managers who may have encountered similar projects in the past. The most important thing, though, is for the project manager to be rigorously honest about the risks. All known risks *must* be highlighted, even if some of them are politically unpopular, as sweeping them under the carpet does not make them go away – it just makes it harder to manage them.

Once the risks have been identified, they need to be described succinctly so that it is clear exactly what each risk is about. For example, 'poor contractor performance' is obviously risky but described thus it will be very difficult to decide what can be done about it. This risk might be better broken down into three more specific risks, thus:

- Contract staff do not work at the pace assumed in preparing the estimates.
- Contract staff do not grasp and conform to the developer's programming standards.
- Contract staff are difficult to manage with inexperienced team leaders.

Once we have a fairly precise description of the risk, we are in a better position to describe its impacts and what needs to be done to counter it.

The following list, though by no means exhaustive, provides a starting point for the identification of risk in an IS project. In each case, the nature of the risk is described and some approaches to avoiding the risk are outlined.

The commercial background

The business case for the project may be unsound or the funding may not have been approved. There may be more than one customer, or several suppliers, involved and the commercial relationships between them may be unclear. The contract type may be inappropriate for the type of work – for example, a fixed-price contract for a research project. It may be a new business area in which the supplier has little experience. There may be immovable end-dates or price ceilings.

The best way to avoid these risks is to have some sort of pre-project review procedure where commercial issues are considered along with the technical problems the project will face. If any commercial risks are identified, these should be reflected in the way the project is set up, including the contract terms that are agreed.

The contract

The biggest risk here is that the scope of work is ill-defined or not agreed between the parties. There may be very onerous penalty clauses for delay or under-performance. The payment schedule may be unclear or not linked to tangible milestones. If there are prime contractor or subcontract arrangements in place, the contracts may not be 'back to back', with similar terms reflected through all the levels of contract, leaving one of the parties exposed. Finally, there may be no signed contract, with work proceeding on the basis of more informal arrangements.

If areas of the contract are ill-defined, then a wise policy is to document any assumptions and ask the customer to approve them; even if they do not, the resultant discussion provides an opportunity to remove the uncertainties. An experienced commercial manager, or contract lawyer, should be asked to review all of the contracts to check that the interests of the various parties are adequately protected.

The customer

The customer management structure may be unclear. Access to important customer staff may be difficult and it could be hard to get decisions made. There may be internal political difficulties in the customer's organisation, with no mechanism for resolving them. There may, indeed, be not one customer but several, each with a different perspective on the project and with varying levels of commitment to it.

If problems with the customer are anticipated, then the project manager – and perhaps also the salesperson – should make early efforts to get to know the various parties and to get them 'onside' with the project. If there are internal political squabbles, then the project manager must make sure that the most important players – those with the most 'clout' in the organisation – are supportive of the project and willing to use their authority as necessary to see it progress.

The users

The users may not be committed to the project or be able to devote sufficient time to it. They may be unfamiliar with the technology and require additional training. There may be an unwillingness to change working practices to fit in with the new system. There may be a very different view between the customer's senior management and the actual users as to what the system is supposed to do. The new system may threaten the jobs of many users.

Every effort must be made to involve the users in the project and this may involve providing training or familiarisation to enable them to play their parts effectively. If senior customer management is unwilling to involve the users, the project manager must try to persuade them into a more constructive approach.

Acceptance

The acceptance criteria, and the acceptance mechanisms, may not have been defined in the contract. The acceptance criteria may have been drawn very vaguely and not linked to specific, measurable demonstrations of performance. There may be other aspects of the project that could delay the customer carrying out the acceptance tests. The customer may have discretion over the acceptability of some or all of the system.

Acceptance is best handled as an incremental process. First, the test plan is agreed, then the test specifications, then the individual tests and then the whole system. This way, you avoid a big dispute towards the end of the project and lead the customer gradually towards acceptance of the total product. It is important, too, that the functional specification is tight enough to provide a conclusive yes/no answer as to whether the system meets a particular requirement.

The functional requirement

The requirement may not have been formally signed off before development proceeds. The requirement may not be complete or suffer from varying levels of detail or internal inconsistency. It may have been defined at too high a level, making it difficult to implement and operate change control procedures. The requirement may have been defined in more than one document, with the risk of inconsistencies and ambiguity between them. There may be a mismatch between the developer's and the customer's understanding of the requirement.

The functional requirement should be reviewed independently by someone not involved in the project – it is too easy otherwise to read what should be there, or is supposed to be there, rather than what is actually documented. A rigorous configuration management system is needed to ensure that documentation is consistent. A formal review technique – like a walkthrough – will help to identify differences between the customer's and the developer's expectations of the system.

The technical requirement

The system may be very complex technically or require a high degree of innovation. It may require the use of tools, techniques or hardware not familiar to the developer. The system design may make testing difficult, particularly if phased deliveries are involved. There may be a need to interface with other systems and to test these interfaces through simulation.

If the project team does not have sufficient technical expertise – and there's more about this later – then expertise must be obtained from elsewhere to at least define a suitable approach to the technical issues. A complete overall design should be in place before proceeding to the detailed design of the components.

Performance, reliability, availability and maintainability

There may be very stringent performance requirements for the system. A high degree of reliability or availability may be required. It may be difficult to test the system using realistic numbers of transactions or users. There may be no way to simulate performance in advance of system testing.

The contract should be examined very closely for challenging performance requirements and the project manager must ensure that the precise conditions and manner of measurement are defined. It could be advisable to build prototypes of critical functions and to test them early in the project so as to identify areas where additional effort will be required.

The project plan

The project manager may not have been involved in the bid phase and so not have contributed to the initial plan. The project may have very tight timescales. The project itself may be very large and require a rapid build-up of staff. The plan may not take into account the need to revisit work from previous phases. The estimates may not be based on solid metrics. Sufficient contingency may not have been added, or it may have been bargained away during the bidding process. There may be excessive reliance on a few key staff. Milestones may be too far apart, deliverables may not have been defined tightly enough or work packages may be too large for effective control.

If not involved in the bid phase, then the project manager should revisit the plans as soon as possible and flag up any concerns, inconsistencies or possible risks. Project managers need to assume that if anything can go wrong it will – and allow contingency accordingly.

The developer's skills

Key staff – for example, the project manager or team leaders – may be new to their role. The team as a whole may be very inexperienced in the business area or technology or both and there may be a lot of training required. The analysis or design work may have been performed by people with little experience in this work. Senior technical staff may be pursuing interesting, but unproven, methods or technologies.

If any of these risks are thought to be present, then the project manager should re-examine the estimates and consider on what basis they were prepared. If necessary, the plans should be adjusted to model the effects of using less experienced staff. If the project manager considers there is a dangerous weakness in some area – perhaps a critical technical skill – then they must lobby very hard for additional, perhaps consultancy, support.

Project staffing

Staff may not be available when required, or may have to join the project too early, when there is little for them to do. Staff may have other commitments that could divert them from the project. There may be too many junior or inexperienced staff, leading to effort overruns, or too many senior staff, leading to cost overruns. There may be unproven customer or contract staff involved. The project may coincide with a period of high staff turnover.

In general, the project manager should aim to take staff on board just when they are wanted. If they must join the team early, they should be kept away from the people already in place or they will distract them from their work. If staff must be shared with another project, the project manager must negotiate with the manager concerned the exact terms of the share and when they will be available to each team.

The development environment

The environment may be new to the developer. The development environment may not match the live environment closely enough and there may be restricted access to it. It may not be possible to get out-of-hours access in contingency situations. Access to the development environment may be via remote links and it may not be under the developer's control. The hardware may be unreliable or poorly documented.

If the environment is new to the developers, proper training must be provided. It is wasteful and inefficient to learn by 'trial and error' and the quality of software developed like this will be very poor. If necessary, arrange for access to a technical 'guru' to resolve difficult problems. The project manager may have to negotiate very hard with the operations people to get adequate access to the development environment.

System software

This may be new or unproven or not yet available. It may be unfamiliar to the developer and technical support may not be readily available. There may be excessive performance overheads. The version may be unstable and likely to change during the project. There may be several different elements to the system software, perhaps provided by different suppliers and not used in this combination before.

Proper training should be provided so that the development team understand the advantages and limitations of the system software. Consultancy support – perhaps from the vendors of the software – can prove cost-beneficial in the long run in terms of time saved and the most efficient exploitation of the software.

Tools and methods

The programming languages may be unfamiliar to the developers. It may be unsuited to the particular project requirements. If using a 4GL, there may be the need for some lower-level code to meet performance pinch-points. The standards and methods may be new either to the development staff or to the customers who will review deliverables. There may not be adequate tools for such matters as configuration management, project planning, testing and so on.

Training and familiarisation must be provided as required. If necessary, it may be advisable to use a small area of the project as a 'pilot' to gain experience of the tools that can be passed on to the rest of the development team. If tools are not available for, for example, configuration management, the project manager will have to develop them; spreadsheet packages are found to be very useful in these areas!

The target architecture

The hardware may be new or unproven, or not used before for this purpose. Some of the hardware may be custom-built and perhaps not available until late in the development. There may be doubts about the capacity of the hardware, for storage or performance or both. There may be many different pieces of hardware, from various suppliers, to be integrated.

Testing on the target environment should be scheduled as early as possible, to allow time to highlight and rectify any problems. If the equipment selected is near the top of its range, then examine the sizing calculations very closely and very pessimistically as the cost of a mistake could be very large if it became necessary to switch to a totally different platform.

Bought-in items

If third-party products – hardware or software – are required, there could be little experience of the suppliers. Or poor previous experience. The suppliers may be in a poor financial condition and at risk of going out of business. There may be difficulty in establishing tests for bought-in items.

The technical and financial credibility of potential suppliers should be examined very closely. In general using 'open', as opposed to proprietary, solutions should make is possible to switch suppliers if things get difficult. The developers should make sure that they are protected contractually if a supplier goes out of business:

- By having a copy of the software placed in 'escrow' – held with a third party to be released in certain specified events, including bankruptcy.
- By having a 'force majeure' clause in their own contract with their customer whereby they are released from their obligations if they are hit by events outside their control.

13.4 RISK ASSESSMENT

With the various risks identified and described, it is next necessary to make an assessment of their *impact* and *likelihood*. This is so that management attention can be focused on those risks with the greatest probability of occurring and/or those that will most damage the project if they do happen. For a given risk, there may of course be more than one possible impact. Continuing with one of our contract staff examples, the impacts of slowness could include:

- Failure to produce unit-tested code by the planned date.
- Inability to begin system test on time.
- The need to reschedule system test to work around modules not yet available.
- A switch of effort to other staff.

and perhaps others too.

The seriousness of these impacts will depend on what proportion of the programming work is being undertaken by contract staff. If, as is increasingly the case, a lot of contract staff are being used, then the impact will be severe. If contractors make up only a small proportion of the programming team, then the impact will be less. It is sometimes necessary to try to assess the impact very scientifically – perhaps by calculating the actual likely delay as a proportion of project effort. Usually, though, an assessment that an impact is large, moderate or small will suffice. This assessment could be related to the time/cost/quality criteria like this:

- *Large impact*   could extend project by more than 10%
- *Moderate impact*   could extend project by 5%–10%
- *Small impact*   could extend project by less than 5%

or using some other scale that is appropriate to the project concerned.

The other factor to consider is the likelihood, or probability, of the risk materialising. To continue with our example, the risk might be high if it were known that contract staff with the required skills were very rare, if the developers had no previous experience of the contractors concerned and if there were no independent way of verifying the claimed experience on their CVs. If, on the other hand, the plan was to use people who had been hired before, and on whom there were favourable reports, then the likelihood of the risk materialising could be assessed as low. As with impact, it is possible to try to estimate the probability mathematically but, for practical purposes, a simple scale of high, medium or low will be adequate. The likelihood could be given a rough numerical value like this:

- *High probability*   greater than 30%
- *Medium probability* 10%–30%
- *Low probability*   less than 10%

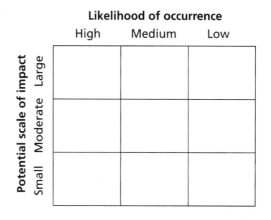

Fig 13.2   Risk map

We are now able to compare the risks with each other to decide which ones need the closest management attention. Obviously, the most important ones are those with a large impact and a high probability of occurrence. At the other extreme, we need be less concerned about those with a low probability and small impact. In between, there are various graduations of severity we can consider.

A useful way of highlighting the important risks is to use a **risk map**, illustrated in Fig 13.2. This plots the impacts of each risk down one axis and their likelihood along the other. The risks shown in the top left-hand corner are those with the highest impact and probability and therefore, probably, the ones that need the closest management attention.

One other factor to think about, however, is the **urgency** of the risk. This has two aspects:

● The urgency with which the risk is likely to materialise.

● The urgency with which we need to take avoidance or amelioration actions.

It may be, for example, that in comparing two risks one is found to be somewhat more severe than the other overall. But, for the less severe risk, there may be an immediate need to take the identified avoidance action. In this case, this risk might be addressed with more urgency than its absolute severity might indicate.

13.5   RISK ACTIONS

So far, we have identified the risks and quantified their effects. However, this is rather useless unless some actions are taken to deal with the risks. These actions are of two types:

- **Avoidance actions** – things we can do to try to prevent the risks from occurring (in other words, dealing with the likelihood).
- **Mitigation actions** – steps we can take to reduce the impact of the risks if they occur (in other words, dealing with the impact).

In practice, we need to consider both types of action, since avoidance measures may fail and we may need to recover from the risks' occurrence.

If we go back to our example of the risk associated with employing contract staff, we might decide that an avoidance action is to use only full-time, employed staff. That might, however, not work if competition from other projects means that enough staff are not available. So, we could identify various mitigation actions such as:

- Ensuring that we only use contractors of whom we have previous experience.
- Setting prospective contractors a short test to assess their speed of work.
- Conducting very searching interviews to discover their attitude to standards.

None of these measures would eliminate the risk entirely but they should go some way to reducing its likelihood and/or effect.

In identifying the countermeasures, we need to be aware of the creation of *secondary risks*. For example, if we decided that we would under no circumstances use contract staff, then a secondary risk might be that we could not get enough people to work on the project, leading to delay in delivery. If the secondary risks are serious enough, they should be treated like other risks and subjected to the full risk assessment process.

Once we have identified the actions, we can determine the urgency of taking the actions and act accordingly.

13.6 RISK MANAGEMENT PLANNING AND CONTROL

The initial identification of risks and their countermeasures is only part of risk management. As a project proceeds, the nature of risk changes:

- Some of the predicted risks materialise and have to be managed like other project issues – hopefully using the mitigation actions previously identified.
- Some of the predicted risks disappear, having been overtaken by events.
- New risks appear, not anticipated at the start of the project.

Risk management is therefore an ongoing process. There needs to be a procedure to revisit the risk register regularly and to reassess the status of each risk. There also needs to be a forum where the risk 'owners' – discussed later – can meet and discuss the steps they have taken to deal with their risks. On many projects, the review of risks is undertaken at regular progress meetings. Probably, only the major risks are reviewed here, with others being dealt with individually outside the meeting. On very large projects, with a large number of complex risks, there might be a specific risk review meeting. Whatever the approach taken, it should be documented in a **risk management plan**. This, depending on the project, might form part of the project plan or it might be a document in its own right. The risk management plan should set out:

- A statement of the *scope and intensity* of the risk management to be applied to the project. Risk management, like other project management tasks, must be tailored to the size, value and complexity of the individual project.

- An explanation of the *risk management cycle* to be used on the project, showing how and when risk reviews will be carried out and whether they will be a separate process or part of the ongoing project monitoring work.

- *Roles and responsibilities*. Who will be in charge of the risk management process and the mechanism by which risks will be reviewed and controlled.

- A description of the *products* of risk management – for example, a regular risk assessment report prepared for senior management.

13.7 THE RISK REGISTER

Another important document in the risk management process is the *risk register*. This could take various forms – loose-leaf register, word-processor file, spreadsheet or database – and will act as a central repository for the information gained on each risk. Specifically, you need to record:

- A *reference* – each risk needs a unique identifier, perhaps keyed to the phase, task or product on which it impacts.

- A *title and description* – of the risk.

- The *current status* of the risk – for example, candidate (identified but not yet quantified), live, or closed.

- *Potential impacts* – there may be more than one of these and, for each, you need to record a description and assessment of its likelihood and scale of impact.

- *Risk owner* – the person who will be responsible for carrying out the identified risk actions (see below).

- *Actions* – the avoidance and/or mitigation actions that have been identified.

- *Action log* – a record of the progress made in discharging the risk actions.

The storage medium for the risk register will depend on the scale of the project and on the volatility of the risks identified. For a small project with a few fairly long-term risks, a paper-based system would be quite adequate; for a larger project, with many changeable risks, a computerised system of some sort would clearly be advantageous.

13.8 RISK OWNERSHIP

We have mentioned risk ownership elsewhere and it is now time to explain the concept in more detail. Essentially, part of the process of risk identification is to decide who should be the *owner* of each risk. The owner should be someone who:

- has sufficient information concerning the risk
- has the necessary resources, and
- possesses the authority

to do something about the risk.

It is a common mistake to attribute the ownership of the risk to someone at too low a level in the organisation. Such a person might well have a very good understanding of the risk and its impacts but may lack the resources and authority to do much about it. Likewise, assigning ownership at too high a level can mean that the owner has the resources and authority but does not regard dealing with the risk as a main priority.

On some projects, risk ownership has been placed on the person who will suffer its impact. Whilst this undoubtedly gives the owner an incentive to do something about it, it does not follow that they have the necessary resources or authority and so they may not in fact be the best people to own a risk.

13.9 OTHER RISK CONCEPTS

In this chapter, we have considered risk management at a fairly simple level. However, on large projects, much more sophisticated techniques may be employed. For example, it is possible to use information in the risk register and elsewhere to construct a 'risk network'. This is rather similar to a dependency network or PERT chart except that it is the interdependency of risks that is being modelled. The model is then used to address 'what if?' questions such as 'If the contract staff do prove to be too slow, and we apply the countermeasure of reassigning work to our own staff, what will be the impact on the project outcome?' Sampling and simulation techniques can be employed. These involve the use of probability theory to model various project outcomes depending on the likelihood, impact and interaction of the various risks. If more than simple risk management methods are to be used, it is advisable to involve specialists, with the right statistical background, to provide consultancy on the construction and interpretation of the various models.

13.10 SUMMARY

IS projects are becoming increasingly complex and are subject to various risks. Risks cannot be avoided altogether but they can be managed in such a way that they are recognised and their impacts either avoided or mitigated. There are a number of areas where project risk can arise, from business, commercial and contractual risks to technical risks. The basic sequence for risk management is identification, assessment and the formulation and implementation of risk reduction actions. The approach to managing risk on a project should be documented in a formal risk management plan.

13.11 QUESTIONS

1 Why is the use of risk management techniques becoming increasingly important in IS projects?

2 Describe a five-stage process for project risk management.

3 Three factors that need to be assessed when considering risks are *likelihood*, *impact* and *urgency*. Explain what is meant by each of these terms and show how each might be assessed.

4 Risk actions are of two types: *avoidance actions* and *mitigation actions*. Describe the relationship between these types of risk action and where each might be employed.

5 Describe the characteristics needed in a *risk owner*.

CHAPTER 14

Value engineering and value management

14.1 INTRODUCTION

This chapter presents a very brief introduction to the topics of value engineering and value management. It is brief since these techniques have not, to date, been widely applied to the information systems field. Where they have been used, mainly in the building-construction and motor-engineering industries, they have been found to yield significant benefits in terms of projects meeting their objectives and producing viable returns on investment. The concept of stakeholders in a new systems project and the ideas of value management also additionally offer some new opportunities for project managers to explore when dealing with cost/benefit issues.

Value engineering dates back to the 1940s and is concerned with the achievements of a project's functional objectives at minimum cost, whilst ensuring that the constraints of time, quality, performance and reliability are met. The basic concept is that, for a given problem or requirement, there are alternative possible solutions that can be evaluated and compared on the basis of their costs. With the achievement of the functional objectives being a constant requirement for all viable solutions, the one that is adopted will be the one that costs less – in other words, the one that offers the maximum value. Value engineering is a disciplined process that follows a definite life-cycle. This is shown in Fig 14.1.

The process starts with a definition of the problem, or a specification of the requirement that is to be met. Then, alternative design solutions are generated and these are evaluated on the basis of whether or not they will meet the requirement. Those that are most feasible are developed further, with the emphasis on finding approaches that meet the requirement at minimum cost. Finally, again on the basis of cost, one of the approaches is selected as *the* design solution.

Value engineering can be applied to the whole of a project – to the design of a complete motor-car, for example – or to the design of individual components. In a sense, it is easier to apply at the component level, since the specification of the component in terms of its size, materials and performance will have been defined quite explicitly and the designers can concentrate on how to meet the specification at minimum cost. As an example of value engineering, consider the case of motor vehicle heating systems where the

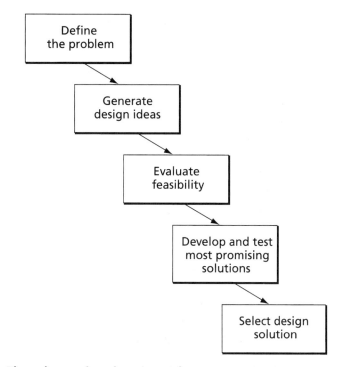

Fig 14.1 The value engineering approach

hoses always used to be secured with screw-operated 'Jubilee' clips. These are quite expensive, so some manufacturers decided that an acceptable performance could be achieved by using simpler spring-wire clips instead. Although this represents a small saving in itself, the application of the same regime throughout the design of the vehicle can produce a considerable reduction in the overall costs of manufacture.

Once the original design has been subjected to the value engineering discipline, the management of the project is constrained by the same regime with changes, for example, being evaluated on the basis of their cost compared to the value of altered objectives. Value engineering is also often used in trying to 'rescue' a project that is facing unacceptable cost overruns. Here, a rigorous examination is made of each aspect of the project to see if anything can be done more cheaply and still meet the project's objectives in terms of time, cost and quality. An underlying assumption of value engineering is therefore that there is agreement among the various stakeholders on the project's functional objectives.

Value management is a more recent development on the value engineering theme and recognises the common problem that – at least in its early stages – there may not be general agreement on the project's functional objectives. In this case, it is not possible simply to compare alternative solutions solely in terms of the cost of carrying them out – they also need to be evaluated in terms of the value of functionality that they each offer.

To appreciate the difference between these approaches, consider the following case study. An organisation wishes to introduce a new payroll system. The stakeholders are the organisation's finance director, payrolls manager and IT manager and they agree that the new system should offer the same facilities as the old one but require fewer staff to operate it. In this case, the functional objectives are clear enough and the possible solutions – for example, in-house development, contracting the work to a consultancy, buying a ready-made package – can readily be compared in terms of cost. Traditional value engineering would support this comparison. However, consider what would happen if the stakeholders actually had different objectives, for example:

● The finance director wishes to reduce the overall cost of payroll processing. With this objective, one option might be to outsource the whole payroll operation.

● The payrolls manager wishes to expand the scope of her operation and therefore wants a new system that will, as well as just payrolls, also cover personnel and pension administration systems.

● The IT manager is pursuing an 'open systems' strategy and so is mainly interested in technical solutions that support this approach.

Unless these objectives can be reconciled in some way, it will not be possible to define a set of functional objectives against which the various solutions can be compared in cost terms. Value management techniques can be used to develop and agree a set of defined objectives – with, perhaps, different 'weights' being given to the various requirements – as well as for carrying out the necessary comparison of costs with benefits.

Value management can thus be seen to be most useful to the project manager at the start of a project, when the objectives may be ill-defined and where there are many possible solutions. However, it can also be used as the project develops to help refine and select between the various options that will arise.

14.2 AN APPROACH TO VALUE MANAGEMENT IN PROJECTS

The basic approach of value management is illustrated in Fig 14.2. It can be seen at once that this is a more complex model than that for value engineering and this reflects the fact that, because it is trying to deal with uncertainty, value management necessarily requires an iterative approach. And, although we have shown iteration only between consecutive stages, there could well be other iterations as well; the evaluation of solutions may, for example, cause you to revisit the 'value tree'. In addition, of course, value management is concerned with identifying the value, as well as the cost, of the different design approaches.

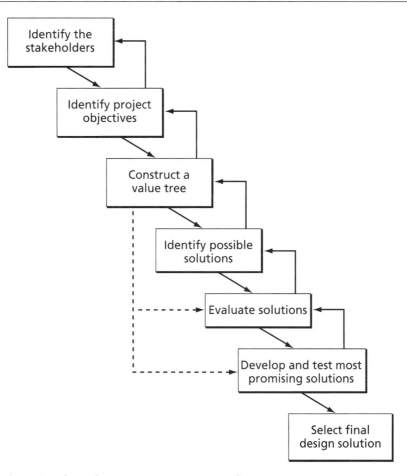

Fig 14.2   The value management approach

The starting point for value management is the identification of the stake-holders in the project. To continue with our payroll system scenario, we have already identified that the finance director, payrolls manager and IT manager will be stakeholders but there might be others interested in the project as well. For example, there may be a personnel director who will want to ensure that no industrial relations problems will result from changes to the way the payroll is processed. There could be staff bodies, works councils or trade unions who will be concerned at the employment implications of the change. There could be a telecommunications manager, interested in the infrastructures needed to support a different sort of system. The point is that, unless all of the stakeholders are identified and brought into the discussions at an early stage, the project's objectives will be incompletely defined and this is almost bound to invalidate, to some extent, the decisions made. This reinforces what we said earlier in the book about the importance of proper organisation for project management.

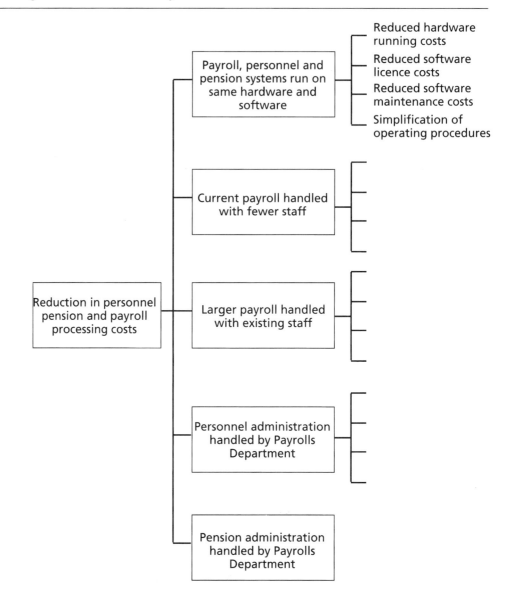

Fig 14.3 Value tree

With the stakeholders identified, they are next asked to define and discuss their objectives for the project. The best environment for this is probably some sort of workshop session, but this will have to be facilitated very skilfully to be most effective. With the list of 'raw' objectives on the table, agreement next needs to be reached on the overall objective of the entire project. Agreeing this will probably require a lot of discussion, even argument, but it is vital that this objective is identified. Once it is, the overall objective can be broken down into sub-objectives which can be represented as a 'value tree'. This is somewhat like a work breakdown structure or product breakdown structure, discussed elsewhere in Chapter 6, and an example is shown in Fig 14.3.

In this example, we have assumed that the various stakeholders in our payrolls project example have agreed that the overall objective of the project should be reduced costs for running the payroll, personnel and pensions systems. Subsidiary objectives of this include the ability to handle the current payroll with fewer staff, or a larger payroll with the same staff, and the ability to run all of the systems on the same hardware and software. Each of these can be broken down further and we have identified sub-sub-objectives for the IS elements.

Next, the list of objectives is reviewed and evaluated and each is subjected to the question 'how can it be addressed?' Combining the solutions to each objective produces an initial list of possible overall designs, which are then evaluated to get an initial idea of the costs and benefits of each. Once the outline costs are available, the value tree is revisited to see how well each proposal meets each objective. To do this, we need to decide how the various objectives compare with each other in terms of priority; some will be essential, others useful and others just nice to have. The best way of dealing with this is to assign some sort of value to each objective, for example a rating on a scale of 1–10. Then, each proposal is scored against each objective, perhaps in percentage terms. These two assessments, the relative 'weight' of the objective and its percentage achievement, are then used to rate the proposals against each other and decide which ones best meet the objectives set for the project. Finally, with the effectiveness of each option assessed on a comparable basis, the costs of each option are also compared to get a final cost/benefit comparison which can be used to make a shortlist of options to be developed in more detail.

The value management cycle is then repeated once the shortlisted designs have been developed further. The objectives will not have to be created all over again, but they should be revisited to check that they are still valid and that, for example, none of the stakeholders has changed their minds. The development of each design will produce a more definitive view of its features so that it will now be possible to say with more certainty how well each of the original objectives is likely to be met. In addition, with the designs more clearly defined, a more accurate assessment can be made of the likely costs of proceeding with each. The costs and benefits of each solution are then compared and a final decision is made on which way to proceed.

There are two main benefits claimed for the use of value management. The first, and perhaps most important, is that the technique of involving all of the stakeholders in the definition and quantification of the project's objectives means that there is greater consensus about the goals of the project and greater 'buy in' from the participants. This, of course, greatly improves the project's chances of meeting the stakeholders' expectations. The second benefit is that the selection of the solution has been based upon as rigorous an assessment as possible of the possibilities so that there is an improved likelihood that the right solution has been chosen.

Once the project is under way, value management offers other opportunities. The techniques used for the identification and quantification of objectives, and for the evaluation of alternative solutions, can also be applied to potential changes. Here, the aim would be to build consensus on whether the changes are really required and, if they are, what value should be placed on them. A clear advantage of this is that the project's original goals, in terms of producing value for the business, can be kept in mind and can provide a useful check on the possibility of uncontrolled – and perhaps unjustified – expansion of the project's scope.

Value management clearly has something to offer the IS practitioner. Most IS projects suffer from some initial uncertainty as to their precise objectives and the value management technique provides a vehicle for securing consensus on those objectives. It also provides a disciplined structure for evaluating and selecting between alternative approaches. Once the objectives have been defined, the value engineering approach can be applied to rigorously scrutinise each component of the project to ensure that it meets its requirements most cost-effectively.

14.3 SUMMARY

Both value management and value engineering are concerned with the achievement of the project's functional objectives – expressed in terms of timescale, quality, performance and reliability – at the least cost. Traditional value engineering is predicated on the assumption that there is consensus on the project's objectives and that the only variable is the cost at which the objectives can be met. Value management recognises the greater complexity of projects and the fact that there will almost certainly be multiple stakeholders with differing perspectives on the project's objectives. Value management therefore offers an approach to the development of agreed objectives and the selection of project solutions that most cost-effectively can meet those objectives.

14.4 QUESTIONS

1 Explain the difference between *value management* and *value engineering*.

2 What is meant by the term *value tree*?

3 How can value management be used to compare different possible design solutions?

4 Once a project is under way, how can value management be used to evaluate proposed changes?

CHAPTER 15

Selling the project

15.1 INTRODUCTION

This chapter is not intended to try to turn you into a salesperson. If you want to be one you should take some sort of assessment and, if it shows that you have the personal characteristics that make it likely that you'd succeed, then you should be properly trained in sales skills. The purpose of this chapter and the one that follows is to give you some understanding about why people buy, about what made them decide to have you manage their system project, and having begun the project how you can manage the customers to create a helpful and profitable environment for your project. We'll examine three things in this chapter. They are:

- Why people buy; how buyers make purchasing decisions; the different kinds of buyers.

- The selling process and how to make proposals that are persuasive.

- Negotiating and how to reach an agreement that works for both parties.

Why are these three things important for project managers? Let us look at some of the 'sales' situations you could find yourself in.

- At one extreme, you are a project manager working for a supplier of professional services of some kind, such as consultancy, project management, software development, outsourcing or software products. Your company is bidding to a prospect to supply its services. You're involved – as a project manager – for several reasons. Firstly, many bid teams find it useful to have the potential delivery project manager as part of the team. It helps to avoid an over-enthusiastic sales approach resulting in the promise of unachievable goals in terms of cost, delivery dates or functionality if delivery people are involved in the sale. Secondly, if your company wins the bid, it will partly be the result of you and the prospect hitting it off on a personal basis; you don't have to like each other but you do need mutual respect. Also your experience of running this kind of project before will influence the offering; you know the pitfalls. The prospect will get something extra from your company, namely your battle experience of having been through it before. So, you're not leading the sale but you have an important part to play in it. You contribute to the achievement of winning the sale.

- Now the project is under way. You and your team are probably spending a lot of time with the client and meeting people at all levels throughout the organisation. Soon you know far more about what really happens in the client's business than your sales team does. By luck or skilful exploration you uncover some new potential opportunities. Who is best placed to scope this potential new business? You are; knowing something about the sales process will be invaluable. This is true whether you're from an external services supplier or from the central, internal IS department. The ability to explore new opportunities and to firmly establish needs in the users' minds will be valuable to you as a project manager.

- All projects are subject to changes in requirements. The common mistake is to regard these as problems rather than opportunities. Every change opens the door to an opportunity to be creative, technically and commercially, and to explore with the user how better to deliver to their real needs. Project managers face the danger of identifying too closely with the work that's already been done – and may now need to be changed; with the technical solutions already reached – that may now need to be discarded; with the efforts of their team – that may now be wasted. This is natural. The project manager is, after all, a team manager responsible for maintaining the spirit of the team; experiencing the team's hopes and frustrations is part of this team maintenance. This inward-looking approach needs to be balanced by an outward view that recognises the need to meet changing user requirements and to take advantage of them to win benefits, tangible and intangible, for the project and for the team.

Let's now see this sales process through the customer's or user's eyes. Effective selling begins with an understanding of how people buy.

15.2   BUYING AND BUYERS

It's easy to believe that every project is different and that the buying decisions people make for your project are unique. This is a convenient excuse when things go wrong, but research shows that all buyers go through clearly identified stages when they buy. This buying cycle applies irrespective of what is being bought. Think about how you make important purchasing decisions yourself. Let's imagine you're going to buy a car. What went through your mind before you decided to replace your existing car? Perhaps you had some problems or difficulties with it. It let you down occasionally. Sometimes it caused you serious problems; you were late for meetings or social events; you were stranded in dangerous areas, such as the side of a motorway or in isolated countryside. Eventually you decide that you need to do something. Your options include substantial repairs to the car, buying a newer used model, leasing a car or buying a new one. After you've determined which option to take, you still have some residual worries; can you trust the dealer's warranty, what will family and colleagues think of your choice? The stages you go through in buying a car are essentially the same as those made by buyers of professional services. As buying decisions become more complex and the cost of the service to be purchased rises, more time is taken before a final decision is reached. Let's look at these stages.

We begin with a recognition of needs. The customer recognises that there are problems and imperfections with the current situation. The existing systems don't work properly, they don't deliver what is needed, business needs have changed. During this stage, buyers assess their current problems and their severity. They begin to specify their new needs and a decision is taken to solve the problem. This is where you have the opportunity to help the customer to identify problems, clarify them and develop them into clearly stated and recognisably important needs. Now the buyer begins to evaluate what options there are to finding an acceptable solution. During this time buyers measure different solutions, using formal and informal means, against the decision criteria they've established. They're looking for the best fit between their view of their requirements and the solutions they are offered. Eventually a choice is made. This follows a final resolution of concerns by the buyer: 'Now, can you be quite sure that the team will include project manager A and chief designer B?', and perhaps some final negotiation. So a decision is made and implementation begins. This is where the project manager plays the main part. The buyer is still worried about whether or not the right choice has been made and hopes never to have to say 'Well, they were clearly the best choice when we had to decide. I can't understand why it's all going so wrong now'. The project manager is the key person in ensuring that the buyer's decision is always the right one. This activity is so important that the next chapter is devoted to it. Finally no solution remains perfect forever. New dissatisfactions arise, new needs are identified and the whole process begins again. This cycle is shown in Fig 15.1.

So far in this section we've talked about 'the customer' or 'the buyer' as if it was one person, but many systems development projects are usually substantial, expensive, risky and have far-reaching consequences. In these circumstances it is unlikely that the decision to buy will be made by one person. Many buying decisions are made by committees that don't march evenly in step through the buying cycle. For example:

- Some may see no need for what you're offering.
- Some may think that the problems need a different solution.
- Some will be concerned at the expense involved.
- Some may be concerned about the implementation and the management of change.
- There may be internal politics between certain of the decision makers.

Often there are four influences at work:

- Firstly, there will be one person who has the final responsibility for making the decision. We can call this person the economic decision maker, since

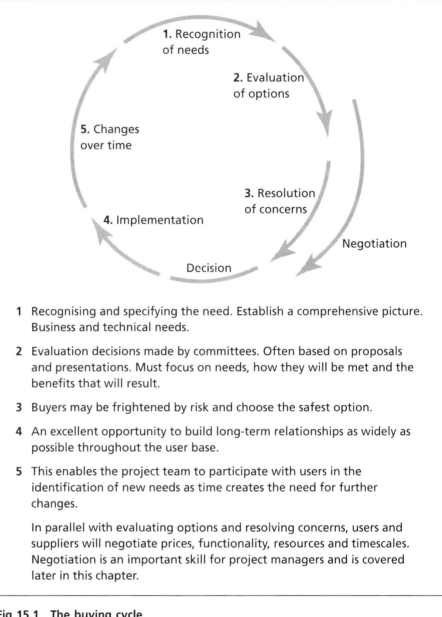

1 Recognising and specifying the need. Establish a comprehensive picture. Business and technical needs.

2 Evaluation decisions made by committees. Often based on proposals and presentations. Must focus on needs, how they will be met and the benefits that will result.

3 Buyers may be frightened by risk and choose the safest option.

4 An excellent opportunity to build long-term relationships as widely as possible throughout the user base.

5 This enables the project team to participate with users in the identification of new needs as time creates the need for further changes.

In parallel with evaluating options and resolving concerns, users and suppliers will negotiate prices, functionality, resources and timescales. Negotiation is an important skill for project managers and is covered later in this chapter.

Fig 15.1 The buying cycle

they have the authority to spend the budget, to commit finances to solving this problem. This individual will almost certainly take advice from others but in the end he or she eventually pays for the solution, for the new system that you will be managing into production. The economic buyer is concerned with costs and benefits.

● Secondly, there are technical experts who explore the technical merits of your solution, the skills and experience that you bring. They may of course be IT specialists but could equally be application area specialists, personnel people or accountants. The technical buyer is concerned with functionality.

- Thirdly, there are the users of the system that you will deliver. They have an indirect influence on the decision to buy. Solutions proposed or ways of developing solutions should be presented in their terms and follow implementation plans that fit into their business cycle. The end users are concerned about how it will affect them.

- Finally, there is a buyer who supports you and helps you to propose a winning solution. Often called the champion or coach, he or she is on your side and wants your solution to be chosen. Perhaps your solution accords with theirs, perhaps you've worked together successfully before, perhaps your solution will result in greater status or influence for the coach. Few competitive bids are won without at least one inside coach or champion.

15.3   THE SELLING PROCESS

In the lifetime of a project there will be many opportunities to sell. We're not talking here of big new investments in new projects, but of small additional features to the system or changes to the way that the project is being run so that it suits the customer better. The principles are the same for each kind of sale, small, large or in-between. It is tempting to think of selling as a 'telling process'. The seller tells the potential buyer about the wonderful features of the product or service. It's tempting but wrong. Selling is an asking process. People who are most successful in selling systems development projects or consultancy assignments are those who ask lots of questions. They ask questions about:

- *The customer's situation.* What happens now and how it works. 'Could you describe for me how you record the orders when they come in and how these records generate the invoices at the end of the month?'

- *The customer's problems.* 'So sometimes then, the invoices are wrong because there have been mistakes when the orders were taken.'

- *The implications of the problems.* 'If the invoices are wrong then you have to raise credit notes then re-invoice.' There must be a cost of doing this? How badly does it affect the cash flow? Is there an impact on customer satisfaction? Does it also mean that you supply the wrong product? What's the impact of this on production and stocks? . . . and so on.

- *The payoff or benefit from meeting the needs.* 'Suppose then that the order-taking system was reliable, how would that benefit you?' 'If orders could be analysed by customer, how could that help to increase sales?' . . . and so on.

In short, the seller seeks to explore all aspects of the problem and aims to encourage the buyer to identify all the problems of the present situation, the implications of those problems and their financial impact, in order to establish that there is a clear value in having a solution developed for the buyer. Steadily and progressively the seller seeks to build up in the mind of the buyer a greater and greater need for a solution. From what you've read earlier in this chapter you'll remember that there isn't just one single buyer. There are economic buyers, technical buyers and so on. Different needs must be built up for the different buyers, so the kinds of questions asked will be different.

The whole approach behind 'selling by asking questions' is built on the realisation that when we identify a problem ourselves, explore all its aspects, its implications and the consequences, we build up a powerful need for something, or someone, to solve the problem for us. Couple this with the fact that we have been taken through this process by a skilled diagnostician and it is easy to see how we are ready to accept ideas for a solution. It's obvious really, isn't it – just as your suggestions, solutions or ideas can be if you follow this approach. A reference at the end of the book gives you more information about where to go to learn more about this approach.

Eventually, the point is reached where the potential buyer says something like 'That's very interesting. Could you send me a proposal along those lines? I'd like to take it further'. If your proposal is for a new television franchise then you'll need a luggage trolley to deliver it; if it's to change the time of the weekly project team meeting you'll need one sheet of A4. Let's use as our model here a proposal from the project team that additional work needs to be done to more fully explore some aspect of the business and to re-examine the conclusions about it. At first sight, this will involve additional work and increase the cost, but it could lead to a reduction in rework later and to an improved solution that will better meet user needs. It's not a big additional task but it is significant enough to require authorisation from the user for the extra work. A proposal is required. The foundations of an effective proposal are:

- Appearance
- Content
- Structure

and we need to use each of these foundations to help us to secure our goal.

The appearance of the proposal can do a lot to make it look professional and interesting. Pictures, graphics and diagrams can break a lengthy text and emphasise points for the reader. Good presentation makes the proposal attractive to the eye, helps the reader to retain the content and helps to make the content accessible. It is however of much less importance than the content in helping to make the sale. The content may be intended to inform or persuade. If we are concerned with the simple reporting of facts following an investigation then we are principally concerned with informing. In our example here, however, we are trying to persuade the reader to authorise some new work.

In a 'persuading' document we'll talk primarily about the interests of the reader and will show an understanding of the readers' concerns and of the implications of those concerns. It will demonstrate how the adoption of the proposed solution will help to solve the difficulties or dangers identified and it will explore the benefits accruing from making the decision. The key to a persuasive proposal is to relate it as much as possible to what the reader has already said. For our example we might structure our proposal into:

- **The customer situation**

  Keep it brief. Describing in detail everything everyone already knows is very tedious, and turns the reader off! Something along the lines of: 'We studied the X department procedure relating to Y. We found that . . . and the conclusions were . . . on that basis it was agreed that . . . changed business circumstances now seem to show . . . consequently some of the agreed conclusions may be invalid.'

- **Potential problems**

  Here is where you deal with the problems that will arise if the project continues as planned when we now know that earlier work may be invalid and need to be redone. What are the implications? What are the possible future costs if the changed business circumstances do show up new needs and we have to do rework later? Remember that you'll have discussed all of this with key users so you won't be building up a fragile case. The situation and the problems will be understood and will have been articulated by the user.

- **The needs as stated by the customer**

  This will state the needs for a solution and the resolution of the present uncertainty.

- **A proposed solution**

  By this stage it should be clear that a solution is needed and the present circumstances cannot be allowed to continue. It's best to concentrate on those aspects of the solution that fit most closely to the users' needs. Summarise the solution by restating how the solution solves current problems and brings future benefits. State the cost of doing the work.

To assess your proposal, work with a colleague to determine whether your proposal:

• recaps more or less terms of reference	*or*	shows an understanding of customers' concerns and their implications
• emphasises the technical details of the solution	*or*	emphasises how the proposed solution will resolve the customer's concerns

- emphasises advantage
  statements

  or   explores the benefits resulting
  from going ahead with the change

- addresses only one reader

  or   addresses all the different
  readers/buyers

- has few charts or diagrams

  or   has clear diagrams that show the
  solution clearly

- offers little or no navigation
  help to the reader

  or   provides clear cross-references
  and navigation aids

- gives a full and detailed
  breakdown of costs

  or   gives a clear 'table d'hôte'
  statement of costs and does not
  offer an 'à la carte' selection

- has no executive summary

  or   summarises the issues and the
  good news

Needless to say, your proposal should be close to the criteria in the right-hand column!

The content and structure of a persuasive proposal should follow the outline and be rated according to the list above. It will be a summary of work that has been done beforehand and should therefore contain no surprises. The content should be matched to the users' interests and concerns.

When advising professional staff about how their clients or users behave David Maister wrote:

> 'There is an old joke about doctors that they get fascinated with the disease, but couldn't care less about the patient. Unfortunately, this attitude and behaviour is all too prevalent in a wide array of professions. Too many professionals get overly focussed on technical matters, and lose sight of the essential relationship nature of professional transactions. This doesn't mean that technical skill is irrelevant – of course it is critical. But having technical skills is only a necessary condition for success, not a critical one. Above all else, what I, the client, am looking for, is that rare professional who has both technical skill and a *sincere desire to be helpful*, to work with both me and my problem. The key is empathy – the ability to enter my world and see it through my eyes.'

15.4   NEGOTIATION

Project managers negotiate all the time; with their team members; with their back-up people – accountants, technical experts, support people generally; and with their customers. The negotiation might be about money; more money to do more work or more money to do the originally specified work. The negotiation might be about time; more time before a deliverable can be ready, or for a delivery date that has not yet been agreed. The negotiation might be about who will do a piece of work, Fred or Jill – both project team members, the team or the user, the team or a contractor. In this section we'll be concerned with a model for negotiations in general and, because people so often raise the issue, we'll review the use of power in negotiations.

A negotiation is a meeting between two sides and the objective is to reach an agreement. The kind of agreement that interests us is one that is good for both parties. It is a win/win agreement where both sides win and neither side feels that it has lost. To reach this desirable outcome requires both sides to be creative about moving from their starting points to an agreed finishing point. There's a typical process that leads from start to finish, but before we examine it there are some preliminaries to consider.

There is always a climate to a negotiation. It may be a harsh climate that will create tough negotiations; a low-key climate may create long-winded negotiations that grind on and on; a creative and friendly environment may lead to new solutions and the establishment of good long-term relationships. Since the climate has such an influence on negotiation, how is it created and what can be done to build a helpful climate? Project managers will often be negotiating with people they know and with whom they have regular contact – the project team, user staff and so on. Sometimes, then, the climate will have been created by what has already happened, but there is still much that can be done in the opening moments to influence the climate. What happens now can be more powerful than what happened in the past. Other negotiations will be with people they don't know – suppliers, customer or user staff they've not met before. In these circumstances, the first few minutes of the meeting can set the climate. We're concerned here about building rapport and there are many things that contribute to this feeling of 'comfortableness' between people. Negotiation is an interaction between people and can be affected not only by what we say and how we say it, but by our non-verbal behaviour. The non-verbal behaviours are often grouped under the general heading of 'body language', and, whether or not we consciously recognise the different behaviours individually, we take in a lot of information in the opening moments, during the rapport-building time. We notice:

- *How the other person looks at us.* Do they look us in the eye? How long do they maintain eye contact? Do they avoid eye contact? What else is happening with their face, do they smile?
- *What kind of contact is made?* Here we really mean 'the handshake'. We're not trying to demonstrate that we have the grip of a body builder, but nor do we want to offer a 'limp fish' for the other person to grasp. How do I feel if the other person grasps my hand with both of theirs, or holds my upper arm whilst shaking my hand?
- *The overall appearance.* My overall appearance has an impact too. Is my posture confident and relaxed? Am I dressed appropriately? Am I neat and tidy?

We also need a few minutes for introductions and social chat; for ice breaking. Just as fact-finding interviews need time for the interviewer and the interviewee to settle down together, a similar process is needed at the beginning of a negotiation. Through this opening behaviour, we're trying to create a CCBB climate; a climate that Bill Scott in *The Skills of Negotiation* calls:

- cordial
- collaborative
- brisk
- business like

Eventually, with the preliminaries over, the negotiation begins. Face to face, we discuss, propose and bargain and before any of this we'll have prepared. Without thorough preparation it is easy, in the heat of the moment, to make decisions and arrive at agreements that are subsequently regretted. Personal preparation:

- establishes your objectives, what you want to achieve
- identifies problems that may arise
- identifies the advantages of your position
- gives you a path to follow
- helps you to feel confident.

It helps during this stage to separate out the essential objectives that you must achieve and the ones you'd like to have as well, but can manage without.

Fully prepared and having built a rapport with the other side we can begin the next stage in the negotiation process – discussion. Here both parties explore the other's position and create an agenda of what really needs to be negotiated. 'So Fred, you want to do this particular piece of work because it would be developmental for you and give you the opportunity to use the new software. On the other hand, I think that Jill should do it because she already knows the new software and she'd catch up some time for us.' For Fred then, the issue is about learning some new things and developing some new skill. It is not really that he wants to do *this* task. During the discussion stage it helps if we reduce tension, get the issues clearly stated and begin to think about how the two positions could be moved closer together. Perhaps there are other development opportunities for Fred, for example.

We now begin to propose some solutions, some offers, some claims. We get offers made to us and we make counter offers. It shouldn't be like a tennis match, however, with the ball of the offer and counter offer being whacked backwards and forwards over the net. It helps to explain, to refer back to the original objectives, to clarify and summarise and to reflect. Finally a bargain is reached and we agree what has been agreed. So we've prepared, discussed, proposed and agreed and in a very simple negotiation perhaps we've gone through those stages in a linear fashion. It's more likely, however, that we've been negotiating a deal that has linked components and we've had to trade off time versus money, for example. In this case we'd have prepared, discussed and proposed within a more complex framework and cycled through the stages of discuss, propose and bargain several times.

Where does power fit in all of this? Power means the capacity to dominate, it's what gives you competitive advantage, it's the activity to get things done your way. Power is either:

- Personal, coming from your personal characteristics, what you know, your interpersonal skills, your mental agility and your skill in the use of power behaviours.
- Positional, coming from your position, your authority, the organisation you work for or from some dominance in the situation.

Typically people make assumptions about where power lies. Sellers are thought to have less power than buyers, and small companies to have less power than big ones. But this clearly isn't always the case. If yours is the only supplier in the territory for a particular application package, or if your staff are fully assigned for the next *n* months, then as a seller you will behave differently than if your people were coming to the end of a big project without future work ready for them. Whatever your assumption about which side has the relative power in a negotiation, there are some power behaviours that you can use:

- *Be prepared.* If you know you've a weakness or want to hide an area that the other side might probe, have your answers ready and make them powerful ones. 'Yes, I agree with you, this system change does need to be made. I'll look at people's work schedules and see when it can best be fitted in' is much more powerful than 'All right, we'll do it straight away. Roy's not busy next week'.
- *Have some creative option.* This is other side of the 'be prepared' coin. By having ready some new, creative and perhaps unusual options to offer you give out a strong message of 'we've put a lot of thought into this'.
- *Maintain control.* The person asking the questions is the one setting the agenda and moving the discussion in his or her preferred direction.
- *Summarise.* People in charge summarise. Chairpersons of meetings do it, it's associated with power and status and is another aspect of maintaining control.

Developing your own negotiating style is something only you can do. You can adopt a massive power play and kill off the other party who'll never do business with you again, or you can build up a long-term collaborative relationship. Whatever do you, being prepared is essential.

15.5 SUMMARY

Project managers 'sell' all the time. They influence buyers to buy and they build the reputation of their project through their commercial skills. In this chapter we've considered the buying cycle and the importance of 'selling by questions' has been emphasised, as has the importance of building up a clearly identified and urgent need with all of the different buyers.

We've examined the appearance, structure and content of proposals and suggested a framework for you to use when evaluating your own proposals.

Finally we considered negotiation and emphasised the need for preparation and the use of power behaviours, and described a simple negotiating process.

15.6 QUESTIONS

1 How would you assess the importance of sales skills to a project manager? Are they, in your view, increasing or decreasing in importance? Why do you think there is this change? Is it more important to understand selling or buying?

2 Persuading someone to buy is a complex process. Why is this? Is the process inherently complex, or is it because so many people are involved?

3 If selling is an 'asking process', how could you use it to help you sell some extra functionality to a system under development?

4 How would you prepare for a negotiation with your boss to spend £2000 on some training for you?

CHAPTER 16

Client management issues

16.1 INTRODUCTION

Throughout this book we've explored the full extent of the project manager's job, from the need to understand something about business strategy to the need to select and develop the project team. In this chapter we'll deal with client management issues – how one best 'manages the customer' so that everyone has realistic expectations, feels successful at the end of the project and maintains enough sanity and goodwill to see the benefit in working together again. Initially, we explore the question 'who is the customer?' Once that is defined, it is possible to deal with the customer's expectations, how to handle the customer relations issues around changes and variations to a project, the need to manage conflict and the importance of networking. All of this becomes theoretical, however, unless you have the skills you need so we also consider some practical interpersonal skills such as establishing rapport, listening, maintaining a neutral emotion and communicating.

16.2 WHO IS THE CUSTOMER?

This could appear to be an obvious question. However, in many projects it becomes clear that there will be a variety of customers you need to manage; after all there are many buyers as we saw in the previous chapter, and earlier when discussing the organisation of a project it was clear that there are many interested parties. Their needs will differ and so will their demands. For example:

● *You may be working on a project where the customer is another organisation – an external customer.* They agree a contract with your company that defines the scope of work and how they will pay the bills. You may personally have some contact with them or it may be through other people in your organisation.

● *You may work for an 'internal customer'.* This might be your own information systems manager who has given you a part of a contract to complete. In turn your IS manager may have a contract, or service level agreement, to supply services to the rest or other parts of the organisation. You will be part of that delivery team. Therefore, there may be several layers of 'customers'. Another type of internal customer may be another department or division or team in your organisation that needs your support. For example, a sales or marketing team may rely on your support in order to make a bid for some work. They will depend on your expertise and advice in order to win new business.

- *Your customer may be the end-user.* You need to be sensitive to all of the trials and tribulations, concerns and gripes that come from using systems in a practical, everyday way. Think of yourself and your demands when you buy a new piece of software or appliance for your home. You want the product to work with a minimum of effort and you want the maximum amount of support should the thing go wrong! End-users often feel that senior managers are insensitive to their needs and the problems they face. They believe that managers are divorced from the 'coal face'. Those with direct customer contact often need to be handled with extra sensitivity and given practical, but realistic solutions. They can feel like neglected stepchildren, but neglect them at your peril – they are usually the key in implementing a successful project.

At the beginning of any project it is useful to establish:

- Who are the customers?
- Are there any others who have a stake in the success or failure of this project?
- What does each stand to gain?
- What does each stand to lose?
- Where can you get this information?
- Do you have a plan for each of them?

Establishing the correct organisational structure, as discussed in Chapter 3, can help in this initial customer identification stage.

16.3 MANAGING EXPECTATIONS

Each customer is different in their expectations from you, the project manager. Those expectations are based on rational or irrational notions. For example, the customer may have worked with you before, had a good or bad experience and will expect more of the same this time. You or the company you work for may have a certain reputation in your field which might be based on word of mouth, personal experience or facts and figures which support your place in the market. You may be the only show in town and have a monopoly on what the customer needs – they may resent you for your price and their lack of choice! Customers approach you and you approach the customer with many unspoken expectations which colour the ways in which you deal with one another. Assumptions may be perilous. There are many examples of assumptions and expectations that have not been discussed and clarified early in a project that have come back to haunt it later on. If they're not dealt with openly, unrealistic expectations may break down what otherwise could have been a highly successful project.

Expectations are created by things that can be controlled and things that are uncontrollable. Together they equal customer expectations. We can divide controllable expectations into short-term and long-term expectations. Short-term controllable expectations can include such things as:

- *Sales promises* – the salesperson or your IS manager has agreed that the system will be able to do this function and that function and the customer expects that it will!

- *Marketing* – perhaps there has been an advertising campaign and your product or service has been portrayed as all singing, all-dancing and one that can be installed overnight.

- *The nature of your products and services* – are they the state of the art or relatively conservative?

- *First impressions* – you look professional, have good references and say that you can deliver.

Long-term controllable expectations include:

- *Innovation in products and services* – stick with us and we will give you the benefit of our research and development, our ability to keep up to date with new developments in technology and the fact that we intend always to stay a step ahead.

- *Marketing efforts* – that promote a growing involvement in your customer's sector.

- *Long-term quality standards* – these demonstrate a commitment to quality which must have a proven track record, but also support the need for good procedures which give the customer confidence.

In truth it may be difficult for a customer to change suppliers because of a high level of sophistication and past commitment from the supplier. Initial agreements were seen as long term and significant investment was made with that in mind. That long-term view will colour the customer's expectations. As project manager, you will need to be doubly sure that the relationship is not jeopardised over petty issues that might cloud these longer-term objectives.

Uncontrollable expectations may be more driven by the market and might be created by competitors who are interested in taking the customer away from you. They may go to great lengths to do that by marketing, advertising and positioning themselves with the customer in a more advantageous relationship. By word of mouth, individuals may say positive or negative things about you: there may be other satisfied customers who will sing your praises; they may be ex-employees who were made redundant, found incompetent, missed out on a bonus and hence wish to run you down; or a friend of a friend who thinks you are terrific, and so on.

The customer may lie behind most of the fundamental problems that develop in many projects. Expectations should be clearly defined at the start of a project and should be revisited at regular, formal and informal points throughout the project. The risk of misunderstanding, confusion and conflict run high if this is not done.

Managing Directors also have preferences and think that the system should 'just work a certain way'. They have it in their head that it will be done in a certain manner and haven't really checked whether or not this is reasonable. This can be a real problem if there is a gap between the customer's expectation and the reality that you will deliver. This gap ultimately reflects the level of customer satisfaction. So, how do you go about managing the customer's expectations so that these expectations and the reality that you'll deliver are the same? Customer satisfaction is often measured through:

- Meeting frequently with the customer to discuss what is working well and what could be better. The project plan should have established a mechanism for these meetings.
- Customer satisfaction surveys. Although it is unusual to use these during a development project, they can nevertheless prove very useful. An outsourcing project should regularly survey the customers to determine their level of satisfaction with the service.
- The number of escalations up through the management chain before issues are resolved.
- The number of disputes or complaints.

Essentially, there are four steps in managing customer expectations:

1 Define what customer satisfaction means in this case.
2 Discover the source of the expectation. Why is this the expectation?
3 Calibrate where you are – find out how well or poorly you're doing.
4 Create an action plan.

Define customer satisfaction

The project will have been defined in terms of time, cost and quality. These definitions need to be specific and measurable. Customer satisfaction should also be defined: what does it need to look like at the end in order for the customer to be satisfied? Are there named individuals in the organisation whose statements of satisfaction you need? What will ensure that the customer returns to you for future business? – if this is, indeed, one of your goals. Lastly what are the customer's business goals and how far are you going to meet them? By the same token, what are *your* business goals and how will a satisfactory outcome look to you and how will it meet your objectives? Be certain that you are clear what your organisation stands to gain from this project and what your role will be in making that happen.

Discover the source of the expectations

What is the source of your customer's expectations? Perhaps he/she has decided to outsource all of the computer department as a result of government legislation or in a drive to save overheads. Does he/she expect this to save x million pounds over five years? Do you think that is realistic? Have you a certain reputation in the marketplace? Are you on the leading edge? Has this customer worked with you or individuals in your organisation before? If so, what do others in your organisation have to say about your relationship with the customer and what might you expect? What are the implications for you in doing this project? Do you have the resources, the time, the staffing, the power to make this happen? What if you do not? Who do you need to talk to in your company to get what you need? What is the customer's position – in their own market, in terms of the pressures on them to deliver to others and to keep up with competition? Where do they stand now and how will your help manage to change or maintain that position? What is your position in relation to these same questions and how will this impact on your business objectives? Your customer needs to know where you stand in order to be realistic about what and how you can deliver the agreed outcome.

Calibrate where you are

To calibrate where you are, you must judge where you each stand in relation to one another and how matched or mismatched your expectations may be. You do this by each establishing what you:

- Need.
- Want.
- View as a 'wish list'.
- See as a political agenda.
- See as a personal agenda.

The last two are obviously not aired publicly. You will wish to discover as much as possible and factor these in for yourself when determining what is realistic within the context and what the motivators may be for each party – yourself included! Promotions, bonuses, perception and personal achievements within the organisation may play a far greater role than any of the issues that are discussed openly.

Create action plan

Now you are ready to plan what really needs to happen and to make your project successful. The action plan is where you record how you will manage the customer's expectations along the way. You can't afford to get lazy or sloppy as things eventually catch up with you and are invariably more difficult to deal with the longer they are ignored. Creating an action plan is in itself the first step in managing expectations since it leads the customer to be very specific about how their expectations are defined. The first thing to do is to establish realistic boundaries that you both find acceptable. Then set out the mechanisms that will be used to keep the customer satisfied. Some can be stated explicitly and agreed with the customer but others will be part of your plan for managing the customer which they need to experience but not necessarily know about beforehand.

Managing the customer's expectations is at the heart of customer management. Failure to manage expectations lies behind most of the fundamental problems that develop in many projects. Expectations should be clearly defined at the start of a project and should be revisited at regular formal and informal points throughout the project. The risk of misunderstanding, confusion and conflict run high if this is not done.

16.4 MANAGING CHANGE

One of the key expectations that should be managed with the customer is the inevitability of changed requirements or changes to plan. No project is without them and part of your success as a project manager will be your ability to handle these changes swiftly and effectively. Ignoring them or procrastinating may have an impact on the overall project and could affect how you are viewed by the customer in the long run. The sources of change are almost as great as the number of individuals involved in a project and are probably as unpredictable. However, they can usually be broken down into the following broad categories:

- *Failure to manage expectations* (you have already been warned!).
- *The learning process.* As the project develops, the customer will think of ways in which the original requirement could have been better expressed and will learn more about the technologies involved. Similarly, the project team will come up with new and improved ideas which they may wish to offer to the customer.
- *Internal forces* – suddenly your customer has other priorities which may come from real business pressures or be the result of internal politics.
- *External forces* – from your competitors closing in on your market or your customer and your need to keep ahead of the game. Or, perhaps, there could be changes in the customer's marketplace, or to legislation, to which the customer must respond.

A six-stage process you can use to help you to manage changes is:

1 Identify the initiator.
2 Define the desired outcome.
3 Initiate the change control process.
4 Discover the extent of the change.
5 Assess the impact of the change.
6 Develop an action plan.

Identify the initiator

What – or who – has initiated the change or variation? Who has decided that the change or variation should happen? It tends to be either the customer or you. However, it might be the result of government legislation or competitive forces in the marketplace or perhaps a bank loan that needs to be repaid. It is important to be clear where the change is coming from so that you know who needs to be happy with the outcome. Otherwise, you could be wasting your time trying to satisfy the wrong person and could end up with an expectation that's gone all wrong.

Define the desired outcome

Whatever the benefits of the change, you still need to remember to bring the project in to time, cost and quality. The customer's satisfaction in meeting their business goals is, of course, very important, but you need to attain your own business goals too. These should be spelled out so that you will recognise whether or not you have achieved your outcome. Often you need to consider minor variations. It might seem to be a waste to spend time being specific about what you expect to see at the end, but it is important to consider doing this for every change. It can help you to avoid potential conflict as these things have a tendency to build up and grow in significance. It's hard to know which one will generate a critical incident so for each one you must document what you hope to see as an outcome no matter how small.

Initiate the change control process

There are three steps to this phase. First, you and the customer must both agree that you are actually initiating a change. Until you do, one of you will resist tackling the problem and its implications and someone will end up being frustrated. Acknowledging this initiation process happens by sitting down and saying 'We've hit a point that was not in the original brief/agreement/proposal/contract and we need to sort it out'. You must both recognise that it was not spelled out originally, but is important now. Quite often, it is difficult to get agreement that you are in a change situation. The customer may insist that the 'change' was in the specification all along; you just failed to notice the requirement or appreciate its significance. Having a clear and detailed specification will help here but, even then, you are likely to have to use all your patience and negotiating skills to secure agreement. The second step is to initiate a change evaluation process. This means that you both accept that this is a variation to the original agreement and that it will need to be handled somehow separately from your other ongoing work on the project. This may have resource and time implications. Thirdly, you need to decide who will pay for the change. No variation is without a cost of some kind. It doesn't always mean that the customer – whether internal or external – needs to pay, but you must not ignore that there is a cost attached, even if only for investigating the change. This cost should be acknowledged, even if it is just in the form of goodwill and an understanding of flexibility on your part. Make sure that it is stated and noted.

Discover the extent of the change

Often the first reaction to a change requirement is resistance, anger and making excuses. That's why finding out why the change is being requested is so important. Think about the times when you have had to make a change to existing plans. Perhaps you had to postpone a holiday by a day or couldn't deliver a report or paper on the assigned day. Most likely there was a very logical explanation. If you weren't given the chance to explain why, you might have ended up exasperated with your holiday partner, tutor or boss. If you have the chance to explain why the change occurred, you stand a much better chance of getting what you need – goodwill on the holiday delay, an extension on the deadline – and still stay on good terms with one another. It works just the same when you have a change to a project. Allow the customer to give the background to the change, explain how he defines the problem, propose some solutions and describe the implications to the rest of the project. By allowing the customer to do this first, you have taken some of the anger out of the situation. Otherwise you run a risk of taking on that responsibility yourself, which also means you will get saddled with the blame when or if something goes wrong. Of course, you as project manager need to be there to offer advice and to help solve the problem, but the best rule of thumb is: let the person who brings the change be the one to start out by defining it and looking for possible solutions. Remember that you may be the one initiating the change, so having a neutral process will help you as well.

Assess the impact of the change When changes occur they have different impacts on different groups. It is useful to consider each when planning how to respond. Each more than likely has their own agenda and you may need to involve technical people, systems people, managers, users of the system who need it in their day-to-day work, and business or commercial people. Personal agendas with each of these parties may also come into play. A change to the project could be a very effective and simple way for someone to put a spanner in the works, or could be someone else's path to glory, especially if the proposed timescale were cut in half!

Develop an action plan Whatever you decide to do, you still need a plan. Your options are:

- Initiate the change or variation within the project without any charge.
- Initiate the sales process. It may be that the change or variation that is proposed sends you back to people within your organisation who need to draw up further plans for work for this client. It may not be as simple as agreeing to do the work, and instead needs to include a wider group to help with a longer-range solution.
- Abandon the change. It may not be appropriate, you may find another way round the problem; logistics or cost may make it impossible.
- The change escalates into a conflict. This is obviously not the desired outcome, but it does happen sometimes. If you cannot resolve how to handle the change, who will pay for it, who is responsible, etc. it may escalate and you will need to call in your procedures for handling a conflict. A lot can be done however before it gets to this point.

Change and variations come from a variety of sources. They are inevitable when working on any project. If you fear them, you will get caught out and caught up by them. Confront them directly, deal with them quickly and with honesty and they should become a natural part of the project rather than an unnecessary interruption. Change is part of learning. Change in a project shows that there is growth and adaptation, not failure. In addition, changes do have benefits. They enable the customer to improve the original requirement to take advantage of new markets or improved technologies. They give the developers the opportunity to add value for their customer by suggesting and implementing additional facilities. And, in a commercial context, they enable the suppliers to grow the value of the project as a piece of business.

16.5 MANAGING CONFLICT

Why is it that handling conflict is sometimes part of a project manager's job? You thought you'd done everything possible to avoid it, and suddenly you're in the midst of a situation that feels out of control and irretrievable. It generally isn't, but there are moments or hours or days even where it feels hopeless and endlessly frustrating. One of the main reasons that conflicts occur is that the smaller issues have not been confronted earlier. It often feels easier at the time to let them slide, assuming that time will sort things out or perhaps you're too busy to put in the effort to sort out 'that minor issue'. Sometimes, though, life is just too messy and the conflict occurs. We have to accept this fact, so let's look at where conflicts come from and suggest some ways of dealing with them.

Really, conflicts can come from anywhere, at any point in the life of a project. Sometimes they arise from practical matters, sometimes they are a result of personalities and personal agendas. Some you can avoid, others you cannot. Some of the more recognisable sources of conflict are:

- Different expectations – usually centred around timescales, costs or the range of facilities to be provided.

- Interruptions and the inability to keep to the original timescale.

- Lack of understanding of each other's position – this may be for technical, commercial, or personal reasons.

- Issues that have been left unresolved or avoided come back at a critical point and can no longer be ignored.

- Physical distances, proximity and culture. These may play a role, particularly if you need to be working on the customer's site. You may feel alienated from your own company and get caught in some cross-fire between your company and the customer.

Generally, conflict is about differences in perspective and the confusion that results from seeing a situation from different angles with differing motivations. The way out of this is to remove yourselffrom your entrenched position and to try and see the circumstances from a neutral viewpoint. This is easier said than done and demands a considerable degree of self-awareness. Try role playing the situation with a colleague to bring out the different perspectives. Having recognised how conflict can arise, what about resolving it? A process that has been found effective is:

1   Know your desired outcome.
2   Triage the conflict.
3   Agree a process.
4   Confirm the positions.
5   Take action.

Know your desired outcome

You need to know what you will accept as your 'bottom line'. Resolving a conflict involves negotiating and you need to know where you can no longer compromise. It is best to have this objective clearly in your mind; discuss it with others, write it down. If the client is saying that the project must now be completed in six months rather than the 12 months that was originally agreed, you need to be clear whether or not that is possible. If it is, what are the implications in terms of cost, and quality? If it is not possible, could you do it in nine months and what are the implications of that? Don't consider a discussion with the client without this outcome very clear in your mind and be sure that everyone in your team sings the same song!

Triage the conflict

To 'triage' is to sort according to quality. Hospital casualty departments triage incoming patients into those that need immediate treatment to survive, those who will survive without treatment and those who will die whatever the treatment. In our context, it is important to sort through the issues surrounding a conflict to decide which are critical and which may be peripheral. The idea is to find the root cause of the conflict. Here, it is a good idea to look at the different groups that may have a stake in the outcome of the project. Decide what each has to gain and to lose and where the power may lie. The idea is to determine, in order of priority, which are the most important issues to deal with – which are the conflicts that are essential to resolve – and in which order you will do that. Who are the people you need to involve and are they aware of the parts they will play?

Agree a process

You and the customer need to first agree that there is a conflict. With any luck, you will have established at the start of the project what might happen in the event of a conflict and it is now time to invoke that procedure. Even if only one side thinks that there is a conflict, then there is one. A good idea is to form a team that will work to sort out the conflict, because by doing so you broaden the discussion, dilute any personal disagreements and help to take some of the heat out of the situation. The process itself creates the need to behave correctly with one another. Instead of having just you and the customer it might make sense to have an independent third party involved as well. Finally, agree how you will resolve any impasse so that you have at least contemplated what happens if you reach the point of no return. It often helps you both to put this conflict into perspective. People rarely want to forfeit a whole project for a sake of an individual conflict. Too much has already been invested, egos and reputations are at stake, not to mention time, money and resources.

Confirm the positions

When the different sides in a conflict meet, they first need to establish their positions. In addition, the implications for each position should be put on the table and there should be an openness to resolve the situation. Naturally, this is the ideal situation, but anything less will probably result in the conflict taking longer to resolve.

Take action

Once both sides have agreed that they want to get through this conflict, there can be some progress. It is important that you and the customer share the same objectives, for example that the project has to be completed in a shorter timescale, that you both know there may be consequences in doing that, but you will achieve the overall project goals.

Together you can:

- Generate alternatives to what you are doing at present.
- Evaluate the alternatives.
- Rate the alternatives.
- Agree a plan of action.
- Escalate it outside of the team if that is appropriate.
- Make it happen.

There can be a great deal of creativity coming into the process at this point and the structure should not inhibit that at all. In fact it may be that better working relationships result from resolving a conflict.

Conclusion

Conflicts will arise in a project. There should always be a provision for them, if nothing else, to act as an insurance policy. Should they occur, try to deal with them clinically, with detachment and swiftly. Letting them linger can only make them worse. As the issues are rarely just about machines and procedures, the delicate business of dealing with people and their feelings make handling conflicts thorny at best. When through to the other side, you will probably have learned a great many lessons for the next time you work on a project – the same type of conflicts keep on reappearing.

16.6 CUSTOMER MANAGEMENT SKILLS

Managing your customer will stay highly theoretical unless you also think about, practise and incorporate the skills needed to make you successful at it. These may well take far longer to feel comfortable with than many of the technical skills but they are applicable in many other situations, in or out of work. Knowing how to listen and communicate, as well as not becoming overly emotional are helpful in most relationships. Perhaps one of the hardest things for people who are new to work or have had to move away from purely technical jobs is the very unpredictable and messy business of dealing with people. People do not behave consistently, they do very odd things for seemingly irrational reasons – if any reasons at all – and do not always do what you think is best. Unlike machines, they talk back, they sulk and they can make your life amazingly difficult. Having a few techniques or skills in dealing with them may make it a bit easier. Some of these issues have been addressed elsewhere in this book – in the chapter on leadership, for example and in the chapters dealing with team issues – but as you will appreciate by now, the relationship with a customer brings added dimensions of complexity. Customers need to be handled carefully, with respect but also with confidence and assertion. You don't have too many chances to get it right and it is worthwhile practising the skills in a situation where not that much is at stake, such as with friends, family and colleagues you can trust before you test it out where it counts.

Social and professional relationships

Let's look first of all at how we develop relationships with people in general. There is a distinction of course between social and professional relationships. Each has its own rules of behaviour. Life can become very tricky and unnecessarily complicated if the two are confused, particularly when it comes to dealing with a customer.

Our social relationships are developed very early in life. We acquire the rules when we are children, initially at home. We learn to say 'please' and 'thank you', not to interrupt, to accept our place in a group of other children or adults and so on. Many of the rules that we learn at home are then reinforced at school, where knowing how to listen and pay attention, as well as accepting authority are stressed. Most of these rules are then reinforced by our peer group, which can often be very powerful shapers of behaviour. For example, just think of the conformity of teenagers and the almost unspoken ways that they modify each other's behaviour. They can be very direct and very effective in their remarks to one another. As we get older, there are rules for behaving in social situations, such as at dinner parties, football matches and with boy- or girl-friends. These are, for the most part, unspoken ways in which we know how to and how not to behave with one another. We know what it acceptable and what is out of bounds.

Professional relationships are different from social ones. They may at times overlap when you socialise with people you work with, but for the most part they exist on a slightly different plane from your out-of-work friendships. Often we never acquire the rules for dealing with these relationships. We have to pick them up along the way. They are based on a different ethic. Whereas you may have social relationships with people who are similar to you in background and values and you have chosen one another, it may be the complete opposite with a professional relationship. The only thing you may have in common is the work you both need to do. The ground rules for dealing with one another are often quite pragmatic in nature, might appear to be inconsistent with social rules and may only last for as long as the project or your time on a particular job. It can feel quite hurtful when you return to an office where you have worked for years to realise that 'your best friends' no longer know what to say to you – or you to them – and what seemed to be such close friendships were really much more fleeting and based on what was going on in the office when you worked there – and it wasn't any deeper than that!

The confusion between social and professional relationships can sometimes make it difficult for you as a project manager to do your job. For example, when you are managing the customer, or trying to utilise a sales opportunity, there will inevitably be some manipulation involved on your part. Our 'social' ethics tell us that it is wrong to manipulate people, so we feel uncomfortable when we are being a little manipulative in a business situation. Similarly, when we consciously employ techniques for building rapport – covered in the next section – we may feel somewhat devious in doing so. There is no simple way to come to terms with this but an idea which may help is to think of yourself as an actor in a professional situation, acting out the part of 'project manager' or 'salesperson'. In this way you can put a mental barrier between your social and professional self which may help you to adopt different behaviours in each situation.

Establishing rapport

It is important to establish rapport with people you work with and specifically with your customer. Rapport is when you have high levels of trust and confidence between two people. You've probably observed people who have personal rapport with one another. Sometimes in a pub or at a restaurant you may see a couple, deep in conversation, oblivious to the outside world. They will be leaning in towards one another and, unconsciously, when one moves forward, so does the other – the same when they lean back. Also, they may 'mirror' one another's speech; using similar words or phrases. This all helps to establish or maintain rapport.

When you feel confident with someone and you are 'tuned in' to what is being said, your body and your words help you to have rapport. You can try to do this, in small ways when you are first meeting with a customer or someone in your organisation. Listen, nod, don't obviously mimic their body language, but try not to contradict what they are doing. If someone is leaning forward, looking you in the eyes and being open with their gestures, don't sit back with folded arms and look like you have closed the shutters to anything that is being said. Look them in the eyes, smile, nod when you agree and you will start to create some common ground. Discuss topics, inside or outside of work where you might have had similar experiences. Slowly, you will develop rapport. It doesn't happen overnight, just as friendships take a while, but with rapport you are looking to establish trust and confidence which will grow as you create the situations where you can prove to one another that you can be trusted.

Active listening

Few of us are ever taught how to listen. It is actually very hard to do it well. Listening well to your customers and your colleagues will go far in helping you to understand their needs. Unfortunately, it takes a lot of concentration, can be extremely tiring and there aren't obvious and immediate rewards. Active listening means that you are really hearing what someone else has to say, questioning, reflecting back and checking that you really understand what is being said. Don't assume anything! Even when you look as if you are listening, your mind can really be somewhere else. You may be framing your response, worried about if you know the answer or playing amateur psychologist. We've listed below some of the ways in which we all block effective listening. Tick those things you do and then try your best to overcome them. It takes a lot of practice to break a bad habit. Highlight any listening barriers where you think you have a problem and concentrate on them:

- *Advising:* You are listening, but only to be able to offer advice afterwards. 'I know what that's like, here's what I would do . . .'

- *Being right:* You listen to the information, but only so that you can win a point. Instead of listening well, you twist the facts, start raising your voice, making excuses or accusations and revisit past sins. At all costs, you do not want to be wrong.

- *Comparing:* You focus on who suffered more or who is the bigger victim. You might look for evidence as to why you're better than the speaker. For example, someone tells you about a rotten plane journey they've had. Rather than ask them more, you come back with your own even longer story which, of course, is far worse!

- *Derailing:* In order to eliminate discomfort or anxiety, you completely change the subject mid-stream or 'joke it off'.

- *Dreaming:* 'The lights are on, but nobody's home.' You have drifted away somewhere else, perhaps because you are uncomfortable, uncertain or just bored.

- *Filtering:* You are looking for specific pieces of information that support the plan that you already have in mind. When you're satisfied that you have the information you need, you stop listening.

- *Identifying:* You keep yourself as the centre of focus rather than the speaker. You refer most things back to your experience and not theirs, and cut in whenever possible about how what they're saying relates to you or something you know.

- *Judging:* In order to maintain your feelings of superiority, you only hear what fits in to what you have already judged to be correct. You might be filled with preconceptions.
- *Mind Reading:* You're working out 'what the other person really means is . . .'. You pay less attention to the words and more attention to the way they are being said. This can be a self-defence mechanism. Why aren't you concentrating on the message?
- *Rehearsing:* When you're rehearsing your reply, you're not able to listen much beyond the first thing someone says. You look interested, but your mind is busy elsewhere.
- *Placating:* In order to be perceived as nice, pleasant, supportive or whatever, you agree with everything. This can feel quite patronising if overdone.
- *Sparring:* Conversation is viewed as a glove sport because you enjoy an argument and will seek one out. This allows you to maintain control at all costs, but can feel like a put-down to someone else. They didn't engage you in conversation because they wanted a fight.

Neutral emotion   Managing a customer demands that you can take a step back and view a situation with an open mind. This can be very hard to do. You often have a lot at stake – personally, professionally and politically. There are times when the best option for you is to be dispassionate and divorce yourself from the heat of the moment. That means that you put yourself into a 'neutral emotional state'. By dissociating yourself from the situation you are able to deal with the real issues, deal with criticism and deal with objections.

A neutral emotional state allows you to approach problems productively and to reach better quality solutions. If you are dealing with someone who is angry, then wait and, eventually, they will run out of steam and calm down. By removing yourself from the situation and taking on much more of the role of an observer, you eliminate for the moment your personal investment and therefore move things along positively rather than being part of the problem yourself. It might help if you think of a time when you have felt very sure of yourself, very confident and in control. Summon up this state of mind in helping you to feel the confidence you will need to put yourself in a neutral state. Try it out first when you are not in a high-risk situation – become an 'observer' at a party, a family gathering or a meeting. See how it feels and begin to learn how you can pull yourself back if you need to.

Communication   Ideas need to be communicated from one person to another from the customer to you and from you to the customer. This is simple enough, but we all know that there are a myriad of ways in which messages can become confused, misunderstood and misinterpreted along the way. We're lucky if someone understands what we say or write in the way in which we intended. Understanding where and how things can go wrong may help you to avoid poor communication. For example:

- Person A wishes to communicate to B. A then takes that thought and turns it into written or spoken language, i.e. A has then *'encoded'* the message. Before it is encoded it passes through A's *filter* which will put A's own perspective on the message. This filter will include such things as A's cultural background, experience, education and values. It will colour the language that's used as well as the assumptions made about the listener. In addition, there might be words that denote urgency or importance which may have different meanings in different cultures. 'As soon as possible' may mean 'within the next day' in one setting and may mean 'when I get to it' somewhere else.

- The message then reaches *transmission*. This can be clear and easy to listen to or read, or there may be considerable *noise* such as in a meeting that is held in a busy hotel reception area where there are many distractions, an office where the phone keeps ringing or even a crackly phone line.

- B (the receiver) now has a chance to *decode* the message. In addition to all of the difficulties listed above that can interfere with understanding a message in the spirit in which it is sent, there are the problems already identified in being a good active listener. Poor listening habits can easily distort and edit a message.

- Finally, with some luck, B has received A's communication. It is hard to believe with so many opportunities for things to go wrong that we ever manage to understand one another!

Knowing the high potential for things to go wrong when communicating means that you need to take extra care when dealing with your customers. You will need to check and recheck your understanding, ask the client to state what in their opinion has been agreed and never lose your vigilance or patience for communicating well. It is a very good policy, at the end of a meeting or discussion, just to summarise what has been said and your understanding of the conclusions that have been reached, so that everyone leaves the meeting clear about the outcome.

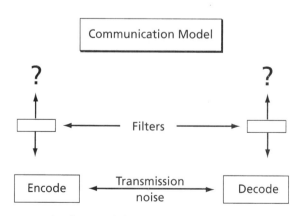

Fig 16.1 The communication model

Considerable skills are required when dealing with your customers. They are not different from the skills that you need in other aspects of your life. Watching those people who you think handle customers well is a good place to start. Notice what they do, and when. If you develop the art of being a good listener, you will have mastered the hardest part, because the other skills can follow on. Without hearing what is being said, questioning and probing so that you are sure what your client needs, expects and desires, you might be second-guessing and making assumptions at every turning. Start by observing and questioning those you can trust. In order to be successful you will need to develop these skills, but most importantly, don't be impatient. Learning new skills and breaking bad habits can take a long time.

16.7   NETWORKING

Networking is a very useful technique in managing customer relations. It is a complex business to find your way around not only the customer organisation but your own as well. Networking is the skill of knowing which people inside and outside of an organisation can help you. Because traditional lines of management hierarchies are fast disappearing, it helps to know people at different levels and in different departments. Networking is the system for 'plugging in' to those people and tapping into their expertise when you need it. In addition, there are those people in the organisation who have powerful roles within a network. Their power may have little to do with their status in the organisation and may instead rest with them for many other reasons, such as their expertise, whom they know, their political influence, their out-of-work social activities and so on. When first assigned to a project, try to determine how the decisions will be made and by whom. The people you typically need to identify are:

- **The decision maker:** An individual or the most influential member of the decision-making group.

- **The gatekeeper:** The person who controls your access to higher authority. Sometimes this could be the managing director's secretary or the decision maker's secretary who can make it difficult to meet the person with the influence. Be wise and cultivate the gatekeepers. Also, get to know the receptionist and the support staff – they are often the ones who know the most and can be your best allies!

- **The influencer:** Someone who advises the decision-maker. Influencers are not always easy to find and you may only become aware of their existence when your perfectly argued proposition is turned down for some obscure reason. For this reason, it pays to do the research needed to find out who the influencers are and how they are likely to act.

- **The end-user:** The person or people who will use or are directly affected by your product or service. These people are critical in your success. They will help to make the system or project work and will give you powerful feedback for future improvements. Once over the initial resistance they may put up, you will find that it is in their interest to have the project succeed, because they will have to use your product or service.

- **The champion:** This is someone within the customer's organisation who is sympathetic to what you are trying to achieve and may be prepared to argue your case for you.

Effective managers have always established informal networks within organisations. As a project manager, you will want to create both informal and formal networks for getting things done. You should consider doing this both within your organisation and within the customer organisation. The wider and deeper your contacts, the more effective you will be. You will be perceived as knowing your way around; as being independent and productive. It demands a certain amount of getting out and about, chatting to people, handling the small-talk side of conversations as well as getting down to business and delivering at the right times and for the right people. It is hard to imagine a successful project manager who has not established a wide and effective network.

16.8 SUMMARY

With today's unquestioning focus on the customer, it has become essential to feel comfortable with the different aspects of managing the customer relationship and the related issues. Models can help in looking at managing the processes of expectations, change and conflict, but they will not be directly applicable to all of the variables you will encounter. That is because both you and the customer are complex human beings with your own sets of values, preconceptions, expectations and desires. They may at times be matched, but they will also clash. The skill is in handling these moments as they arise, keeping your cool and maintaining the focus of the project. No two projects and no two customers will ever be the same. Rather than bemoaning that fact, it is both realistic and productive to look forward to the differences.

16.9 QUESTIONS

1   What is meant by the term *managing expectations*? Why is expectation management an important part of the project manager's job? What influences a customer's expectations?

2   What are the common origins of change in an IS project? A project is well into the design stage when a user raises with the project manager the possibility of an additional requirement. The information being

produced by the system could perhaps be manipulated to produce additional useful information for another department. How should the project manager handle this request?

3 Explain the differences between professional and social relationships and show how these differences may influence your approach to customer management. What are the practical things that project managers can do every day to manage their customers? Refer back to section 16.6 for some background to help you identify practical behaviours.

4 Explain five barriers to active listening.

5 Why is it important for the project manager to establish a network of contacts within the IS organisation and also within the user organisation? In what circumstances can these networks be useful?

CHAPTER 17

Managing suppliers

17.1 INTRODUCTION

Very often, a project team will have to call upon the services of outside people or organisations to supply specialist services or equipment or to cover a temporary shortfall in the organisation's own resources. Outside suppliers can be used in two situations:

- Where the project team retains direct day-to-day control over the supplier's work. This is the normal situation when, for example, contract programmers are used; aside from the fact that they are paid via invoices rather than through the payroll, they are managed just like any other members of the project team.

- Where a portion of the work is undertaken on a subcontract basis by the supplier, with the project manager exercising control on an 'arm's length' basis.

This chapter is concerned with the second scenario.

The use of subcontractors in a project is very often inevitable. If a software company has offered a 'turnkey' solution to its customer, it will have to deliver a system complete in all its components – hardware, software, communications, training and so on – and will have to buy in the non-software elements from subcontractors. This situation is likely to become more common as projects become more complex and call for the integration of an increasingly diverse blend of skills and resources. Customers, too, are seeking to simplify their own lives by appointing a 'prime contractor' who will take overall responsibility for the whole project and relieve them of the task of trying to manage a number of disparate suppliers. In turn, this arrangement transfers the risks associated with subcontractors onto the prime contractor. It is very important, therefore, that the subcontract arrangements are set up properly, that the risks associated with the subcontracts are addressed and that adequate control is exercised over the work of the subcontractors.

17.2   SETTING UP THE CONTRACT

17.2.1   Subcontractor assessment and selection

Before entering into a contractual relationship with a subcontractor, the project manager should ensure that the subcontractor has been properly researched and assessed. Probably, this investigation should be undertaken by a procurement specialist with assistance from, for example, business information services. The assessment should cover:

● The size, reputation and financial status of the subcontractor. Where the subcontractor is part of a larger grouping, the assessment should include that too.

● The customers and markets served by the subcontractor.

● The relative size of the subcontractor in relation to the prime contractor organisation. The issue here is whether the prime contractor will have the 'clout' – in other words, the experience, resources and influence – to manage the subcontractor effectively and this may not be the case if the business proposed is only an insignificant part of the subcontractor's turnover.

● Reference sites. Particularly where this subcontractor has not been used before, the project manager will want to investigate their 'track record' with other customers.

● A possible inspection at the subcontractor's premises, to check on their methods and standards and possibly on the operation of their quality control procedures.

During the reference visits, an effort should be made to find out what it is like doing business with the subcontractors. Are they co-operative and open or are they secretive and liable to want to argue over everything in strictly contractual terms? There is nothing wrong with being clear about what is included in the contract, but some firms play a form of contractual hard-ball which can make them very hard work, and very unpleasant, to work with.

If there is a choice of subcontractors, a formal tendering process should be followed, with the issue of an invitation to tender supported by a detailed statement of the requirement. Where the customer's requirement is as yet ill-defined, there needs to be a discussion with the potential subcontractors on how the uncertainty is to be handled; are they, for example, prepared to share in the prime contractor's investment of defining and clarifying the requirement before the main development work proceeds?

Once a choice of subcontractor has been made, the project manager must ensure that the requirements on them have been completely covered in the contract, as described in the next section.

17.2.2   The contractual framework

The starting point for a successful subcontract is an adequate definition of the scope of the supply. There must be a complete and unambiguous specification of the equipment and services that are to be provided by the supplier and this specification should cover:

- The functional and technical requirements of the supply.
- The performance specifications, in absolute terms or expressed as a range of acceptable values.
- The budget available.
- A complete and precise list of the deliverables from the supplier.
- The dates on which materials and services must be supplied, and the locations at which they are wanted.
- The method of installation that is required.
- The criteria against which the products and services are to be accepted.
- The project management controls that the purchaser will wish to impose.
- The quality control regimes that will apply to the products and services, including the purchaser's rights to impose their own quality assurance mechanisms.

As purchaser, the project manager needs to ensure that both the developer's and the customer's interests are protected. In particular, it is important to ensure that the contract terms are 'back-to-back'. This means that, if the customer has imposed any terms on the developers, these should be reflected in the terms imposed on the subcontractor. If this does not happen, then the developers will be at risk because of the overlap between the contracts. This situation is represented in Fig 17.1, where the developer has signed up to contract terms that have not been imposed on the subcontractor.

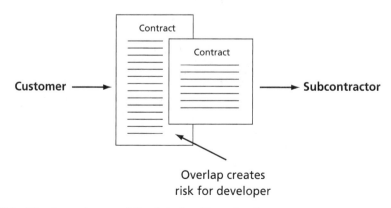

Fig 17.1   The importance of 'back-to-back' contracts

Another important issue to address in the contract is the question of owner-ship of the developed materials. Where the work is being done wholly for and at the expense of the main contractor it is reasonable to expect that the IPR (intellectual property rights) will pass to the main contractor on payment. Where the subcontractor is providing something already owned, perhaps in a modified form, there will have to be some discussion on the ownership of the IPR and the terms on which it will be sold, or licensed, to the end customer. If the subcontractor will only grant a licence for the use of the product, then the contract must include arrangements for the situation that arises if the subcontractor goes out of business. With software, the usual response is to place a copy of the source code in 'escrow', that is lodged with a reliable third party who will release it to the purchaser in certain specified circum-stances, including the bankruptcy of the supplier.

The contract should also cover the arrangements for warranty, support and maintenance of the deliverables after they are handed over to the prime contractor or customer. If the subcontractor cannot, or does not want to, offer continuing support, the project manager must ensure that alternative arrange-ments can be made.

Quite often, the prime contractor will insert penalty clauses into the subcon-tract for late delivery, or 'liquidated damages' clauses to cover various other forms of non-performance; these last set out the amounts that will be paid over in specified circumstances. Although these do give the prime contractor a measure of protection, and may help to offset the operation of similar clauses imposed by the customer, they should be treated with caution. First, even if we are covered financially by penalty clauses and the like, we are still respon-sible for the delivery of the overall system and it will probably prove both difficult and expensive to find a suitable replacement subcontractor. Second, we could incur all sorts of additional costs arising from delays – like staff sitting around with nothing to do – that may not be covered by the liqui-dated damages. Third, the failure of a subcontractor necessarily reflects badly on the reputation and judgement of the prime contractor in using them in the first place. Last, and not least, getting redress through the courts is a lengthy and expensive process with no automatic guarantee of success. The lesson of all this is that it is much better to select the right subcontractor at the outset.

17.3 MONITORING SUPPLIER PERFORMANCE

The subcontractors should be required to produce project and quality plans and to report progress regularly against them. The best idea is to have these plans in a similar format to those used by the prime contractor's team but larger subcontractors will have their own standards and procedures and will wish to follow them. The project manager should, at the least, ensure that these standards and procedures are adequate to give confidence that the work is being properly planned and controlled. The degree to which the project manager will be interested in the detail of the subcontractor's work will depend on its criticality and, for this reason, it is usually desirable to keep subcontracted tasks off the project's critical path. If this cannot be avoided, the amount of project management attention on the subcontractor must be intensified. Once work begins, various methods can be used to keep the progress of the subcontractor's work under review:

Approval of designs, drawings and specifications The project manager should ensure that the project team can inspect and approve the subcontractor's designs as they emerge and time should be built into the project plans to allow for this. Similarly, the subcontractor's plans should be checked to ensure that they have allowed for adequate review time in their own schedule. The subcontractor's documentation should be managed under a proper configuration control regime, ideally the same one as is used by the main contractor.

Progress meetings These should be held regularly and should be aligned with the main supplier's reports to the customer, so that a complete picture of the whole project can be presented. The subcontractor's progress against the agreed plans should be reviewed and any departures investigated. The project manager needs to create an open and co-operative climate so that the subcontractor feels able to raise any issues, problems or concerns and does not hide difficulties until they have turned into real crises.

Witnessing tests The project manager should reserve the right to send observers to witness important tests conducted by the subcontractor. On a large project, with a lot of work being done by a subcontractor, it may well be worth stationing project staff permanently on the subcontractor's premises for this purpose.

Receipt of goods and services from the subcontractor When the subcontractor delivers goods or services, a proper procedure should be followed for checking and receiving them. There should be a check that the acceptance tests have been carried out and signed off and that the items received are of the approved build standard.

Checking invoices All invoices submitted by the subcontractor should be checked to ensure that the work charged for has, in fact, been performed. Particular care should be taken with stage payments that the agreed payment criteria have been met. In general, the main contractor's intention will be to maintain a positive cash flow, that is to pay the subcontractor after payment has been received from the suppliers; but with small subcontractors care must be taken that this process does not force them into financial difficulties that could compromise their ability to complete the contract.

Risk management Risk management is discussed in detail in Chapter 13 but the project manager needs to decide how subcontractor risk is to be handled. One approach is to regard the subcontractor's work as a 'black box' – within it, the subcontractor has complete responsibility for all management issues, including risk management. Another method is to make the operation of risk management processes a contractual requirement, like the operation of quality control, and to carry out audits periodically to ensure that it is being followed. Where there is a high degree of risk associated with the subcontract, however, the best policy is probably to bring the subcontractor within the scope of the main contractor's risk management programme. This will, of course, have to be covered in the contract terms.

Managing the customer interfaces

Quite often, where a subcontractor is working on a discrete or highly specialised part of the overall project, a difficult situation can arise concerning the way in which the subcontractor interacts with the customer. Two undesirable circumstances can develop:

- The main contractor insists that all communication between subcontractor and customer must be channelled through them, even though they have no direct interest in much of the detail being discussed. The result is delay and confusion, with the main contractor being regarded as a nuisance by both the other parties.

- The subcontractor and customer cut out the main contractor and communicate directly, so that the main contractor has no real control over what is going on.

There is no simple answer to this but it needs to be agreed with the other parties the circumstances in which the project manager does and does not want to become involved in their discussions. Certainly, the main contractor should be involved in anything to do with the specification, and perhaps the customer and subcontractor can be asked to copy all correspondence to the main contractor, for review and comment if necessary.

Subcontractor evaluation

At the conclusion of the project, an evaluation should be made of the overall performance of the subcontractor. This should include: the quality of the work performed and of the staff assigned to the project; the subcontractor's ability to meet timescales and deadlines; and an assessment of how easy – or difficult – has been the working relationship. The objective here is to build up data on subcontractors that can be used by later projects when considering using the same suppliers again.

17.4 QUALITY CONTROL AND SUBCONTRACTORS

A major question to be addressed at the outset is whether the subcontractor will work within the main contractor's quality system or not. Ideally, the main contractor's system should apply but this may not be feasible where the subcontractor has a well-developed quality system. Some degree of reassurance will be provided if both main and subcontractor's systems have been approved to an external standard such as ISO 9001.

If the subcontractor does not work to an externally approved standard, but this standard has either been offered by or imposed on the main contractor, then the main contractor will have to seek a 'concession' that the main contractor's standards will not apply to the subcontracted work. This is not, of course, the same as saying that poor quality work will be accepted, just that the subcontractor's system does not have to conform to the same quality system. The project manager should ensure that the subcontractor's quality plan sets out an adequate quality control regime for the subcontracted work.

At each point where the subcontractor hands over completed deliverables to the prime contractor, a set of pre-defined acceptance tests should be performed. The acceptance criteria must be defined and agreed in advance and should cover:

- The test environment.
- The test schedule.
- The responsibility for performing the test – this could either be the prime contractor's, or the subcontractor's, with the prime contractor's staff acting as observers.
- The expected results – as defined in the original specification.
- Any tolerances that are permissible in the results.

In general, the project manager should not authorise acceptance of the deliverables unless they have met the acceptance criteria completely. However, sometimes a tight schedule will dictate that deliverables be accepted subject to certain post-acceptance remedial actions being carried out. Where this happens, an element of risk is clearly involved and the issue should be monitored through the risk management process until the rectification work has been performed and accepted.

17.5 SUMMARY

The use of subcontractors is becoming more widespread as an increasingly diverse range of skills is needed on IS projects and as customers seek to limit their own risk by the appointment of prime contractor to manage and co-ordinate entire IS projects. The main contractor needs to take great care in selecting the subcontractors and in devising contracts that offer 'back-to-back' coverage of the customer's requirements. The work of the subcontractor must be monitored closely, from technical, quality and financial perspectives. At the end of each project, the performance of each subcontractor should be evaluated and the experience documented for the guidance of later projects.

17.6   QUESTIONS

1   Describe three situations in which an IS project may need or wish to use subcontractors.

2   It is important that the contracts between the main contractor and the customer and between the main contractor and subcontractors are *back-to-back*; what is meant by this term?

3   Subcontracts often include penalty clauses to give the main contractor protection in the case of the supplier's poor performance. Why are penalty clauses not the complete answer to safeguarding the main contractor's position?

4   Describe four methods that can be used to monitor supplier performance.

5   Explain how quality control can be applied to a subcontractor's work.

CHAPTER 18

Leadership

18.1 INTRODUCTION

There are almost as many definitions of leadership as there are people who have attempted to define it. Keith Grint of Templeton College, Oxford, writes that between January 1990 and January 1994, 5341 articles about leadership were published across the world in around 800 different English-language management journals. He calculated that the rate of publication was almost five articles every working day. To this total should be added all of the various books dealing with sociology, politics, management, psychology and business that include chapters dealing with leadership. Why do so many people write about leadership, and why is it included here in a book about project management?

There are two kinds of project manager. Let's not categorise them as successes or failures, those who get the job done and those who don't. Any project team member will separate them out; there are those for whom people want to work again and those for whom no one wants to work again. In our lives we work for both and sometimes we have to work on projects for the second kind of project manager, but we don't do it out of choice. Given choice we'd prefer to work again for the first kind. It's leadership that divides project managers into these two categories – the first have it and the second don't. But what is it that they do that turns them into leaders? If we think of the great leaders who have inspired us – Nelson, Churchill, Lincoln, Lawrence of Arabia, or even John Harvey Jones, Margaret Thatcher or Lenin – we might think about the common behaviours or attitudes that bind them together but their activities are all likely to have been fashioned by some great events that thrust them into history. This is unlikely to be the case for a project manager! What we are concerned with is what project managers can do to achieve better results through their people.

Ross Perot, the founder of EDS, said, 'People cannot be managed. Inventories are managed, but people must be led.' Straightaway this brings us to consider the relationship between management and leadership. Some people think that they are the same, some that they are different, some that leadership is part of management and some that management is part of leadership! We want you to hold on to three important concepts:

● Management and leadership are not the same

● You can be competent as a manager and nothing as a leader

● Leadership is an observable, learnable set of practices.

We'll deal with the management v leadership issue now and at the end of the chapter you'll find out how you can be a better leader.

Management is often described as 'getting things done through people' in order to achieve some business or organisational goal. This could be in the public or private sector, in a club, a charity or a church. The emphasis of management is a focus on tasks within a structured, hierarchical environment. Managers are concerned with setting objectives, forecasting, planning, organising, directing, co-ordinating, controlling and communicating. They perform these tasks with different emphasis according to their functional specialism and level in the hierarchy. The emphasis of leadership is more on interpersonal behaviour, on getting people to want to do things, on getting their enthusiastic support. People can operate as leaders without being the department manager or the hierarchical head. They work by influence. In the 1970s there was considerable interest in this difference – more interest than there is now perhaps – and the following differences were suggested:

- Leaders take on a personal commitment and are very active about their goals. Managers on the other hand are rather impersonal about goals: for them goals are organisational and not personal.

- Managers co-ordinate and balance activities so as to meet conflicting schedules. Leaders create excitement and change and enjoy the uncertainty.

- Leaders are emotionally involved with their people, managers maintain a greater distance.

- Managers belong to the organisation and see themselves as conservators, bringing certainty into a disordered environment. Leaders get their identity from their beliefs and ideas and are always looking to change things.

The difference between leadership and management was once summed up in the following way by someone looking out of our office window in Covent Garden in central London:

> 'Imagine there's a sudden power failure on the tube. The system halts and all the lights go out. In the central control room someone is marshalling resources, implementing the standby facilities, rescheduling the trains, calling the emergency services. That's management. Someone else is walking along the darkened platform with a torch bringing a trainload of people to safety. That's leadership.'

As a project manager, you're unlikely to find yourself in either of these circumstances, but you could try out the following example which is adapted from *The Leadership Challenge* by Kouzes and Posner. Assume that everyone working on your project is there because they want to be, not because they've been assigned to it. They are volunteers. What kind of project management would you need to be delivering to make them want to enlist?

A final point in this introduction; we're not saying that leadership is better than management, just that it is different. Projects and organisations in general need both. The opportunity is for project managers to be leaders as well.

18.2   MOTIVATION

Motivation is about what stimulates people to do things. Actors ask directors, 'What's my motivation here' when rehearsing a scene; football teams are 'psyched-up' or 'motivated' by their coach before going on to the pitch; individuals describe their project tasks as 'pretty boring really', meaning that they're not very motivated by their work. There is even a TV keep-fit performer called Mr Motivator! In our context in this book, motivation is about stimulating people to do their job and releasing their energy into their work so that they deliver above-average performance. So what determines an individual's motivation? At first sight, it's a simple process. We have needs or expectations in life which we want to achieve through work. So we bring our needs to a job, and we hope to have them met by what we find when we get there. What might we find? Firstly, there'll be economic rewards, such as pay, pension schemes, health insurance, a company car. These economic rewards might also include the security of having a permanent long-term job. There will also be aspects of the job itself – the job satisfaction – that give us a personal impetus to do the job. Finally there are the social aspects of the job, such as working together – or conversely working alone – belonging to a team or a well-known organisation. The combination of these incentives to work that we choose is of course subjective; your selection is different from the next person's and so on. We also change our preferred combination from time to time. Sometimes we need the money and forgo the social and intrinsic aspects of work; we take on an unpopular assignment because of the premium pay that's offered.

It is useful then for you to understand something about motivation since it will be a foundation to the way your project team works. The problem is that there is no general purpose, useful-in-all-circumstances theory of motivation. Fifty years of research have shown that ideas about motivation have moved from very simple concepts – people work to earn as much as they possibly can, and nothing else matters – to more complex concepts where managers have to understand the different needs and motivations of each member of staff. It seems to us that this is particularly true of highly mobile, expensively recruited and trained specialised professional people who work in IT. There are, however, two general theories that you could carry into work with you and that could give you some models to use when trying to understand 'what makes Frank behave like that?' The two models are those of Abraham Maslow and Frederick Hertzberg. Maslow's was first published in the late 1940s and Hertzberg's in the late 1950s, so both have been examined and criticised over many years, but still have something to tell us today.

Maslow model is called 'the hierarchy of needs' model and in it he suggested that similar needs are grouped together and that we first of all aim to satisfy our needs in one group before turning our attention to needs in another group. He also said that these groups are arranged in a hierarchy that we climb. This hierarchy is shown in Fig 18.1. Beginning at the bottom we aim to meet our physiological needs of hunger, thirst, sleep, exercise and

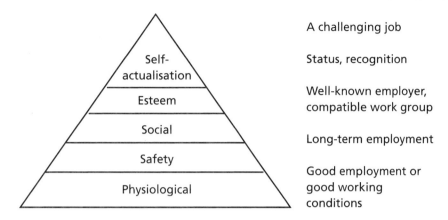

Fig 18.1   Maslow's hierarchy of needs

basic sensory pleasures. Safety needs include safety and security, freedom from pain and physical attack and protection from danger. Social needs include affection, the sense of belonging to a community of some sort and enjoying social activities. The need for esteem includes self-respect as well as the respect of others and can include many work-based issues such as the ability to plan and organise one's own work, status, reputation and recognition by peers and seniors. At the top of the pyramid are what Maslow called 'self-actualisation' needs or being the best you can be – 'becoming everything that one is capable of becoming' as he put it.

Maslow suggests that most people have these needs in roughly this order, but recognised that there would always be occasions when his model didn't fit perfectly. The starving poet writing in his attic bedroom to become 'the best he can be' is dealing with self-actualisation but hardly addressing his physiological or safety needs. Fortunately such cases are rare in project teams and we can use the model with some confidence!

Hertzberg's model is based around answers to two questions asked through a series of interviews.

● When you're satisfied at work, what is it that is making you happy?
● When you're dissatisfied at work, what is making you unhappy?

Responses in the interviews were consistent enough to fall into a pattern and to show two different factors affecting how people were motivated at work. So Hertzberg's two-factor theory of motivation and job satisfaction came to be developed. He called the dissatisfiers *hygiene factors,* and the satisfiers were called *motivators.* Absence of the hygiene factors caused dissatisfaction and their presence meant that people would not be dissatisfied but would still not be motivated. His hygiene factors were company policy and administrative procedures, the level and quality of supervision, salary and benefits, interpersonal relations and physical working conditions. The motivators were achievement, recognition, the nature of the work itself, responsibility and advancement. You will notice a relationship between Maslow's model and Hertzberg's; the first three needs in Maslow's hierarchy equate to Hertzberg's hygiene factors and the top two are Hertzberg's motivators. There are two important outcomes for project managers. Both models show clearly the value of structuring jobs to give emphasis to the motivating factors at work so as to make jobs more interesting and satisfy higher-level needs. Also, the motivators of Hertzberg's model are within the scope of typical project structures and within the authority of project managers.

18.3 LEADERSHIP

In this section we turn our attention to the development of ideas about leadership and we'll examine it under the headings of:

- Leaders are born not made
- Leadership is the functions you perform
- Leadership style

We'll finish in the next section with some practical things that you can do as project managers to improve your leadership and achieve greater results with your people.

Turning first then to the idea that leaders are born and not made, we find the view that leadership consists of inherited traits and characteristics and it is these qualities that distinguish the leaders from the led. World famous authorities were writing as late as the mid-1950s that 'leadership cannot be created or promoted. It cannot be taught or learned' (Peter Drucker in *The Practice of Management* originally published in 1955 but still published in paperback by Heinemann in 1989). This 'traits' theory of leadership was popular in the early part of this century in western democracies and one can see how the great entrepreneurs like Henry Ford, and the officer class of the 1914 to 1918 European war, gave it some credence, but no empirical work has ever isolated these essential traits and characteristics that are passed in a god-like way down the generations. Also the idea that certain people were born to lead and that others were born to be led went contrary to the development of political thought and particularly against the development of democratic ideas in the later twentieth century.

Attention then moved away from 'traits theory' and focused more on what leaders did, not on the personality and characteristics of the leader but on the functions of leadership. Whilst it was recognised that different situations would call for different emphases and that the same leadership position could change with time, the following fourteen functions of leadership were identified.

- *Executive.* The ultimate decision maker, the most senior co-ordinator of policy and its execution.

- *Planner.* Determining how the organisation, department, team or group achieves its goals.

- *Policy maker.* Establishing – with others but in the senior role – the goals and policies for the group being led.

- *Expert.* Here the leader contributes from what he or she knows that others don't. Although using expert advice from others, the leader also has an expert role.

- *Representative.* The leader speaks for the group to the outside world. He or she is the group's official voice and the collector and channel of inward communication.

- *Organiser.* Designer – the leader creates the organisational structure.

- *Reward giver.* The leader controls the led through the power to give rewards and apply punishment.

- *Exemplar.* The leader sets an example of what is expected through personal actions.

- *Arbitrator.* The leader is the final court of appeal for the led and controls the interpersonal relationships within the group.

- *Symbol.* The leader is a focus for the group and gives it some unity, additionally helping to set the team apart from other teams.

- *Backstop.* Individual members of the group can use the leader to take difficult decisions for them.

- *Ideologist.* Groups need beliefs, values and standards of behaviour. The leader creates these.

- *Father figure.* The leader is a focus for the positive emotional feelings of the led.

- *Scapegoat.* The leader is a focus for the negative emotional feelings of the led.

A much more useful approach than this rather functional 'have I done this today' approach is the one associated with John Adair, one of the UK's most influential leadership gurus and the first person to occupy a university chair in leadership in the UK. He held that the effectiveness of a leader is determined by his or her ability to meet three areas of need: the needs of the team, of the task, and of the individual. He represented these by three overlapping circles as shown in Fig 18.2.

The team tasks that an effective leader carries out are:

- building the team and maintaining team spirit;
- developing work methods so that the team functions cohesively;
- setting standards and maintaining discipline;
- setting up systems for communication within the team;
- training the team;
- appointing subordinate leaders.

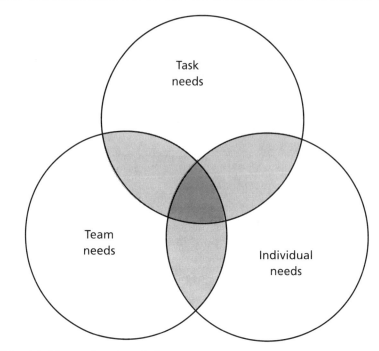

Fig 18.2 Adair's overlapping circles

The leader's task activities are:

- achieving team objectives;
- defining tasks;
- planning work;
- allocating resources;
- assigning responsibilities;
- monitoring progress and checking performance;
- controlling quality.

Meeting people's individual needs includes:

- developing the individual;
- balancing group needs and individual needs;
- rewarding good performance;
- helping with personal problems.

In our view this is a very useful model in a project management context. It connects management and leadership; the task activities and some of the team ones being traditionally regarded as management, whereas satisfying individual needs and building and maintaining the team are leadership activities. The model also works best when there is a clear team focus, as in project activities. It also shows that attention has to be given to each of the three groups of activities although the emphasis will change as the progress of the work develops.

In his book *Great Leaders*, Adair writes:

> 'There are three kinds of need discernible in any human enterprise. First, people need to know where they are going, literally or metaphorically, in terms of their common task. Secondly, they need to be held together as a team. Last but not least, each individual, by virtue of being human and personal, also brings a set of needs that require satisfaction.'

We turn our attention now to issues of leadership style; how the leader carries out his or her leadership functions and relates to the members of the project or group being led. It is increasingly clear that managers can no longer rely solely on using their hierarchical position to discharge their leadership functions. This is particularly true in knowledge-based businesses like computing where individuals develop high skills and where there are many opportunities to use those skills. The importance of considering leadership style is based on the assumption that we are all more likely to work willingly and enthusiastically for leaders who have one particular style of leadership as opposed to another. This is of course a rather simple view since a project team will have many members not all of whom may want the leader to have the same style. No doubt we can all think of people or occasions when 'just tell me what you want and I'll get on with it' is strongly at odds with 'could we discuss this issue and work out together the best way forward?'. Nonetheless, leaders do have a style. Generally it comes from their attitudes and assumptions about human nature and how they would like to see people behave. Their style of leading their people may often mirror how they themselves would like to be led.

We could no doubt list many different leadership styles and identify their main characteristics. People talk of autocratic leaders, charismatic leaders, benevolent leaders and so on, but here we can focus on three general categories that you will probably recognise. The first is the centralist or autocratic or authoritarian leader. Here the centre of power is with 'the boss' who alone makes the decisions, sets policy, allocates work and controls rewards and punishments. No doubt many of the leaders who were 'born and not made' in the industrial revolution operated in this way. At the other end of the scale is the democratic style where more power rests with the group, where leadership functions are shared and where the leader participates more in the group. There is still a clearly identifiable leader but group members have the opportunity to influence and inform decision-making processes and have the authority to take decisions themselves. Off the end of the scale we find the supportive or *laissez-faire* style where the leader consciously decides to let the group have maximum freedom of action and not to intervene. The leader is available to provide support if it's needed but relies on the group members knowing when they need it and feeling comfortable in asking for it. It is, therefore, a very special style requiring considerable maturity and

Increase in subordinate's role

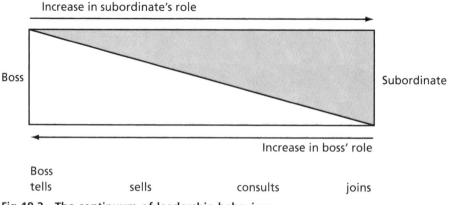

Boss

Subordinate

Increase in boss' role

Boss
tells   sells   consults   joins

Fig 18.3   The continuum of leadership behaviour

skill in the leader and in each individual member of the group. In our view it is unlikely to be useful in typical project management structures. There is no doubt however that there is a resistance to autocratic styles of leadership and this trend looks set to continue. There is even legislation from the European Parliament in areas of employment law which legislates for an increase in the amount of consultation and democracy in industry and commerce.

In the late 1950s two Americans, Tannenbaum and Schmidt, pulled together much of the work on leadership styles when they suggested that leaders have a range of leadership styles open to them from one extreme where the boss exercises maximum control – boss-centred leadership – to the other extreme where subordinates have a great deal of freedom – subordinate-centred or democratic leadership. Their continuum of leadership behaviour which was first published in the *Harvard Business Review* in 1973 is shown in Fig 18.3.

From this model came an identification of four styles of leadership employed by the leader. The leader:

- *Tells.* The leader makes the decision and tells everyone what it is and what they must do.

- *Sells.* The leader still makes the decision but then sells it to the people so that they accept it willingly.

- *Consults.* The leader presents ideas and gets feedback or makes proposals that can be changed. Perhaps at the extreme the leader presents the problem and takes the decision based on the information collected.

- *Joins.* The group make the decision here within the scope of their authority which has previously been described to them. The leader then endorses their decision.

Tannenbaum and Schmidt also suggested that the particular style adopted by the leader depended on three forces: those in the leader, those in the subordinate and those in the situation. For example, a leader who found it difficult dealing with uncertainty, with a subordinate who was inexperienced, in a situation where there was some pressure of time, might well choose to operate at the 'boss-centred' end of the continuum. Conversely, in a relatively non-hierarchical organisation, with subordinates ready to assume some responsibility for decision making and in whom the leader had confidence, then a more appropriate leadership style would be found towards the subordinate-centred end of the continuum. When revisiting this work in the early 1970s they added a commentary emphasising the interdependence of the three forces and they recognised the growing importance of a fourth force: the environment.

In our experience, this is a useful model for project managers to consider since it links into the situational leadership ideas described in the next chapter.

18.4 LEADERSHIP PRACTICES THAT WORK

It will be clear that there is no one best, single style of leadership and that you could usefully use aspects of Maslow and Hertzberg when thinking about motivation and – for leadership – aspects of Adair's three-circle model and the continuum of styles set out by Tannenbaum and Schmidt. With this in mind we want to conclude this chapter with some up-to-date and practical suggestions that result from the work of two American researchers – James Kouzes and Barry Posner. Their work is being carried into business in the UK through the Tom Peters organisation. In the research a sample of leaders were asked what they did when they felt they were at their personal best as leaders, not managers. Over 1300 middle and senior managers provided information based on their own experiences. A further 3000 managers and their subordinates were involved in follow-up work. The findings were dramatic. In their book *The Leadership Challenge* Kouzes and Posner say:

> 'Leaders do exhibit certain distinct practices when they are doing their best. And this behaviour varies little from industry to industry, profession to profession. Good leadership, it seems, is not only understandable but also a universal process.'

To balance this view of leadership, they enquired about the expectations followers have of their leaders. Almost 4000 people contributed to this study. According to this research the majority of us admire leaders who are:

- *Honest.* Followers observe the leader's behaviour and make an assessment about honesty. 'Practice what you preach', 'do what you say', 'let us see your values, where you stand' are what followers say about their leaders. Connected to honesty is trust. Good leaders trust their people and in so doing earn their people's trust.

- *Competent.* Whatever else you are, your people expect you to be competent, capable, effective. Competent at project management certainly – good at setting objectives, planning, scheduling, resourcing, monitoring and controlling – of course. But there's something else. It's something special the leader brings that meets a key need and enables everything else to move forward.

- *Forward looking.* Leaders are expected to have a sense of direction and some concern for the future of the organisation. At first sight this looks like a difficult expectation for a project team to have of their leader. By definition, project teams are formed, complete the project and then break up. There is however a future that project managers can describe. It is the future of the project finished, completed, delivered to the overall satisfaction of the user. It is also a future where members of the project team have developed new skills and had this development recognised, signed off even by the project manager.

- *Inspiring.* We all expect our leaders to be enthusiastic and positive about the future. Followers want to be inspired by their leader. This may be an uncomfortable concept, coming too close to charismatic leadership and touching our emotions, but if our leader displays no commitment, no passion for our goal, why should we?

If this is what followers want, how does it translate into what the leader needs to do? The Kouzes and Posner research identified five leadership practices common to successful leaders. As project leaders you can implement them straightaway. They are:

1 *Challenging the process.* Leaders are not content with what happens now and the way things work now. Leaders want things to be different, better. This is difficult for project managers who work hard to turn uncertainty into certainty. The challenge is to look for a better way of doing this and to be prepared to live with this uncertainty just that little bit longer.

2 *Inspiring a shared vision.* In our own research this was seen as a key characteristic of a leader. There is an urgency to make something happen and to create something that has not been created before. Describing this 'something' in a way that captures the hearts and minds of the team is inspiring a shared vision.

3 *Enabling others to act.* Leaders can't achieve success by themselves. They enlist the support, help and commitment of their followers. A good leader empowers others to move the organisation towards the vision.

4 *Modelling the way.* This is all about behaving as you want your people to behave in achieving the shared vision. This vision can't become a reality without hard work and the leader has to provide the resources to enable the vision to become reality. It is also about practising what you preach. Your people take more notice of what you do than of what you say.

5 *Encouraging the heart.* A timely and honestly meant 'well done' from our boss works wonders. Too often are people called to see the boss because of a failure or a complaint. Not often enough do managers look for opportunities to celebrate a success.

The Kouzes and Posner research shows that good leadership is 'an observable, learnable set of practices.' Like them we commend to you the following behavioural commitments:

- **Challenge the process**
  - Search out opportunities for improvement.
  - Experiment with new ideas and take some risks.

- **Inspire a shared vision**
  - Describe the future for your people and help them to feel what it could mean.
  - Get others to help you to communicate this vision.

- **Enable others to act**
  - Encourage people to work together to solve problems for the group.
  - Develop and coach your people so that they grow in confidence and skills.

- **Model the way**
  - Be the example and behave as you want others to behave.

- **Encourage the heart**
  - Recognise individual accomplishments.
  - Celebrate success.

18.5 SUMMARY

As a project manager you can make a great difference to the success of your team by your leadership. We've seen this so many times that nothing will convince us otherwise. It is not enough to be a good manager even though that is a real achievement in itself.

We discussed the importance of motivating your team and described two useful models: Maslow's hierarchy of needs and Hertzberg's two-factor model. We saw how they fitted together, how they could be used to give us a better understanding about motivation and how project managers could use them to help to motivate their teams.

Finally we looked at aspects of leadership and saw how ideas about it developed over time. We concluded by suggesting that you could make a real difference to the effectiveness of your project teams by adopting the leadership practices described by James Kouzes and Barry Posner.

18.6 QUESTIONS

1 Refer back to the introduction and consider again the leadership challenge at the end of the section.

2 How can Maslow and Hertzberg's theories of motivation help you to organise your project team and the way work is allocated?

3 Think of a situation at home, at work, at university or in a club to which you belong. It's a situation that involves you. You want to change the present circumstances and set a new basis for the future. Using the behavioural commitments at the end of section 18.4, what could you do to change things?

CHAPTER 19

Performance management

19.1 INTRODUCTION

In any project, it is the team who do the work. Their performance is the project's performance; so it is important to be able to get a good performance from everyone. Each person in your team is more complex than all the computer systems you will ever work on. Each of us is an unpredictable mixture of rational thought and emotion, ideas, feelings, ambitions, anxieties, good and bad. The challenge of managing such creatures as ourselves excites many project managers and makes them see this aspect of their job as the most rewarding. The same challenge make other project managers fearful of this aspect of their job. Some of these managers avoid the more risky aspects of managing people by pretending the problems aren't there or aren't important. This is a pity given that the effective management of people is almost always a distinguishing characteristic of a well-run project.

In days gone by, the purpose of a management was to control the workforce: to tell them what to do and keep them at it. These days it is recognised that such an approach will not bring competitive advantage – quite the reverse, in fact. People in our industry today are well educated and expect to be involved in the enterprise to which they commit their time. So while management still needs to co-ordinate the efforts of people and groups, the approach based on power and close control is slowly on the way out. The modern view of management is that it supports the workforce, enables them to do their work and, especially as IT skills change fast and are often in short supply, develops people through coaching and exposure to new skills in their jobs.

Most people carry around in their heads their own private theories of how to deal with people. These develop from personal experience and reflection. Most managers adapt these ideas into private theories of how to manage others and make a team perform. Unfortunately, no one person's experience can tell us the whole story as we are all so different. Some 'private theories' of management are actually harmful and none is good enough by itself. That is why it is important to read about and discuss management methods widely. However, many managers do not bother and the training supplied for this most complex aspect of organisational activity is usually far less than that supplied for more tangible skills such as programming or accounting.

The project manager needs to motivate the team as a whole and motivate each individual separately. Team motivation stems from the personal enthusiasm of the manager, how the work is allocated and structured, a clear vision of the goal and the agreed standards for getting there. The project manager sets an example with his or his own personal organisation and behaviour and creates a climate of progress and acceptance of change. Individual motivation is achieved through personal rapport and the 'unwritten contract' of what the individual and the project manager expect from each other. A crucial ingredient of this motivation is the design of the individual's job, which must have the right amount of challenge and variety and lead towards a visible and significant end product. We all need agreed objectives that tie into goals we understand as well as personal and career development from challenging work, professional standards, feedback and coaching.

You probably already know a great deal about managing performance from your own experience and observations. Your learning will continue as long as you let it and as long as you are prepared to question your current ideas. This chapter will help you.

19.2 SETTING OBJECTIVES

An objective is a statement of something to be achieved. At the minimum, an objective will state the product or result of an activity and a time by when it is to be achieved. The level of challenge presented by an objective should be appropriate to the person who is to achieve it. If it is too low the person has no opportunity for development and may get bored and frustrated. If it is too high the objective may be seen as unachievable and the person will not wish to expend much energy on it. This also means that the achievement of the objective must be in the person's power and not dependent on chance or the actions of others. The objective must also specify a precise outcome so there is no doubt about whether it has been achieved or not. It is useful too if an objective has measurable milestones on the way to completion so you can, if it is appropriate, check on progress.

In fact, it is easy to get bogged down with long lists of criteria for 'what makes a good objective'. Such lists can be helpful if they remind you that your objectives have room for improvement but they can be very unhelpful: setting objectives is hard enough without feeling obliged to work at them until they meet a whole list of qualities. If you feel this is happening when you try to set objectives, step back and remember their purpose: we set objectives to co-ordinate effort across the team and to motivate team members by giving them clear tasks and development opportunities. Objectives lead us towards the overall aim of the project – and towards people's career aims as well – they provide the strategy for getting there by showing each of us the next step we have to take. The purpose is to write objectives which are useful, not necessarily to write objectives that meet any list of qualities.

So let's approach this subject instead by looking at the process of developing objectives. We can imagine a cascade of objectives. At the top is the purpose of the organisation for which you work. Part of that purpose will be the successful completion of your project – that is your project's objective. Part of that will be objectives for particular pieces of work or functions of the system. Contributing to those will be the next level of objectives, those of particular teams. The cascade runs down to personal objectives for each individual on the project and finally to detailed work instructions for each task. This idea is appealing for its logical sense of smaller efforts all combining to achieve combined efforts which come together to meet an overall goal.

However, this neat picture conflicts with one more important attribute of an objective: it must be agreed between the manager and the person accepting it. Simply imposing a set of objectives on someone will very often not work because that person will have no ownership of them and so have little commitment to meeting them. Team members will usually work towards imposed objectives but without much enthusiasm; they will not take so much trouble to solve problems they encounter and their overall level of commitment to your project will be lower. Also, the team members who do the work may have better ideas on how to do it than their managers – some would say they will almost always have better ideas because they are closer to the work. So the idea of a top-down cascade of objectives is complicated by the fact that they must work from the bottom up as well.

This apparent paradox of having a downward cascade of objectives which is agreed and accepted by everyone below can be resolved.

- First, you must communicate a clear vision of what your project is there to achieve. This will enable your team members to appreciate that their objectives must contribute to that purpose.

- Second, you will need to negotiate with subordinates and superiors to achieve a consistent hierarchy of objectives with which all parties are satisfied.

- Third, you must be prepared to reconsider the way you planned to go about things. For example, you may have planned to keep team members on work they are already familiar with in order to get the job done quickly. When you have heard your team members' concerns you may decide to give them work they are less familiar with so they can learn new skills and stay interested in their work.

The negotiations up and down to reach agreement on all sides, the changes in project needs and staffing supply that will happen and the improvements that can always be made to objectives – to make them more specific, measurable and so forth – mean that objectives, like a system design, are never done, finished and correct in one pass. The development of objectives is an iterative process. They will always be subject to change, even after they have been agreed. A set of objectives is a living document.

This means that setting objectives takes a fair, but not huge, amount of work on a more or less continuous basis. Balance that against the benefits: having people working with commitment towards objectives that are truly relevant to the project will mean good productivity. As well as that, the very process of setting and amending objectives with a team member is a perfect opportunity to build your relationship and provide coaching and support.

19.3 REVIEWING PERFORMANCE

Having set objectives, you will be able to review performance against them. Good project managers don't necessarily wait until some project milestone or formal appraisal to review performance: they are constantly alert for any sign that things are not going as they should and will investigate them quickly. They also check team members' work at a frequency which depends on:

- the level of skill or competence of the team member;
- the commitment of the team member;
- the importance of the team member's work to the project.

The frequency of these regular checks will be discussed and agreed with team members. Remember, the purpose of performance reviews, whether it is the annual appraisal or an informal chat in the corridor, is not simply to find instances of poor performance or mistakes and correct them. Better to 'catch people doing something right' and use that as an opportunity to recognise and acknowledge positive contributions.

When you find an aspect of performance that is below the standards you expect or is not contributing to agreed objectives, you have a coaching opportunity. More is said about coaching later in this chapter but for now we shall look at one approach to closing the gap between actual performance and required performance. Your objective is not just to solve the immediately apparent problem but to develop the team member so performance problems like it do not arise again.

Preparation
Gather all the information you can. Clear, indisputable facts are best but feelings are also worth considering in the case of, for example, a team member who has upset another. Be warned that facts which you think are clear and indisputable may not be seen in that way by your team member. If you or the team member's feelings are high at the time have a cooling-off period. Decide on your objective for the performance review. In general it will be to improve performance but you need to work out just what that means in each case.

Establish and agree the performance gap
This involves establishing the standards you expect for your team member's performance and the actual level of performance, to demonstrate that there is a gap between them. Don't get into debates about the facts of the matter. If you have a fact wrong, acknowledge that. If you disagree over what is a fact, listen to the team member then assert the truth as you see it.

It is acceptable to have differing points of view but in the end it is yours that counts. Stay calm and non-threatening and listen carefully to what your team member has to say. Show that you have heard and understood the team member's point of view without necessarily agreeing or disagreeing with it. Do not yet get into discussion of reasons for the gap or mitigating factors; that comes later. You are not trying to apportion blame, just establish the facts.

Explore reasons for the performance gap

As the manager, you are ultimately responsible for any shortfall in performance. Even if it is clearly the fault of the team member, it is no use blaming; you have to find a way forward. So at this stage discuss how the shortfall came about. Some possible causes might be:

- Inadequate job description, work instruction or objectives.
- Lack of training or on-the-job coaching from you.
- Personal problems such as a medical condition or problems outside work.
- The team member did not understand or accept the performance standards.
- The team member has a grievance against the organisation and is taking private industrial action.

Focus on behaviour – what the team member did or didn't do – rather than personality. This is the time to discuss mitigating factors but the key skill is listening. Ask open questions and concentrate on the responses without making judgements about them to make sure you get a good picture of the team member's point of view. You can give your point of view only when you have done this so avoid questions like, 'Surely you must have thought that . . .', as these carry your judgements. You may find the performance problem is a result of a deeper problem such as dissatisfaction with career progress. Only patient listening will uncover such underlying issues. It takes time, so make sure you have allowed enough.

Agree steps to eliminate the gap

The possible reasons for poor performance listed in the paragraph above could be overcome in many ways. It is better if the team member suggests solutions as the member will be more committed to personal ideas for eliminating the performance gap. You may have to accept that the member's performance shortfall was a result of a shortfall in your own performance: perhaps you had not given enough time to coaching or support or objective setting. You were never meant to be perfect and you can use cases like these for your personal development and as a means for building trust between you and the team. If the performance problem does turn out to be the result of a more personal problem, you must refer the team member to someone qualified to deal with it. You may also decide to lower the performance you expect of that team member until the problem is resolved. If so, you must explain this allowance to other team members without, of course, breaching confidence.

Summarise   Go over the main points of your discussion again to make sure you both have the same understanding. Make sure the steps for eliminating the performance gap are clear, with precise dates and actions to be taken. Inform the team member whether you are keeping a written record of the interview, and if so, for how long. Inform the team member what will happen if the agreed steps are not taken. Finish with an assurance that there is nothing to worry about if the team member does what you have agreed.

Follow up   You need to fix a follow-up date to review progress towards the agreed actions soon after the first interview. You will also need to agree other review dates to monitor progress all the way back to the required performance standard. Recognise progress but do not hesitate to take the matter further if progress is unacceptable.

This model can be applied to all sorts of performance problems. For most problems, in the first case it will be applied very informally – just a chat in a quiet corner which the team member will not think of as anything more than helpful concern on your part. For more serious problems, and lesser problems that are not resolved by the informal chat, you will need to increase the level of formality. This may make you feel uncomfortable. If so, talk it over with someone first. If you ever come close to invoking formal discipline procedures always discuss it with a qualified person such as a Personnel Manager.

19.4 PERFORMANCE APPRAISAL SYSTEMS

Most organisations have some form of formal performance appraisal system. They vary a great deal in purpose, depth, style and degree of bureaucracy. The also vary in the benefits they bring to an organisation and the degree of respect they attract from the workforce.

You need to ask: 'What is the purpose of my organisation's appraisal system?' The answer may be: 'To assist the management in the determination of pay rises – and perhaps promotions within a grade or job title system.' In this case the key feature of the appraisal must be fairness. Find out how the pay system works in your organisation so you can make it work for the staff. No pay system is ever totally objective. You need to make sure the subjective element is understood by your team members. It helps if you have clear objectives against which you can measure performance. The situation you are aiming for is that everyone understands why they got the pay rise they did.

The answer may be: 'To develop staff.' In this case the formal appraisal system is just one component of your continuing effort to develop a flexible workforce, able to work in a variety of situations, to contribute in many ways and with a range of skills that spans the whole of software development. Fairness is not really an issue in this case as the appraisal focuses on one person at a time.

Most likely, the answer to the question is: 'A bit of both.' The appraisal system exists to develop staff and to assist with decisions about pay. Even if it is said to be only about pay or promotion, you will want to use it as an opportunity to develop your staff. Even if it is said to be only about development, your staff probably believe, rightly or wrongly, that what goes on at the formal appraisal will affect their pay levels in the future.

This leads to a problem. If your boss asks you: 'In what areas of your work do you need to improve?', then you'll probably be prepared to discuss some if you think the purpose of the meeting is to help you develop. But if you think your boss is gathering information for the next pay review, you may be tempted to brush over your weaknesses.

The way around this problem is to tie good pay awards with proven development. After all, why should an employer give you more than a basic rise if you are no more skilled than you were last year? Now, when your boss asks you about your weaknesses, you are doubly keen to discuss them, both to have them resolved and to be rewarded for this development at the next pay review. The importance of setting objectives for a team member's development is now clear.

Preparation for an appraisal

The best way to prepare for an appraisal is to practise day-to-day developmental management: regularly revisit the objectives you agreed with a team member, review performance at appropriate times and provide coaching whenever an opportunity arises. You may find it helpful to keep a log of these ongoing interactions, so when the time comes for the formal appraisal, your preparation is mostly done. But you will still need to review all that has happened in the previous period and decide what you want to achieve in the appraisal. The team member also needs to prepare. Fix the meeting far enough ahead to allow sufficient time. Remind the member of the purpose of appraisal and the type of preparation you think they should do. If it is the first appraisal you should sit down and talk the process through. Remember, people are often frightened of their appraisal.

During the appraisal meeting

You and your team member need to review past performance, if only to set the scene for looking to the future. You will find many books give you formulae for how many good points are needed for each bad point or rules such as to start and finish with good points and sandwich the bad points between. These hints are useful but what matters more is how you go about raising bad points – or improvement areas, or development opportunities, or whatever you wish to call them. One approach is not to raise them at all but to ask the team member to assess personal performance using a technique called drawing out. This means asking neutral, not loaded, questions about how they think they have performed, particularly strong points and areas in which they would like to improve. Most people are very modest about their performance. You will find you have many opportunities to praise the team member for contributions they have overlooked or downplayed. They are likely to come up with more areas for improvement than you could identify and will be more keen to work on them than if you had pointed them out. Drawing out avoids the risks associated with criticising a colleague, and it usually leads to greater improvement than criticism would have done.

But there are problems with drawing out. First, you must make sure your questions are entirely neutral. You will have your ideas about areas in which the team member should improve and, when the member does not identify them, it is tempting to turn neutral drawing out into a form of forced confession. This is a serious mistake as it will undermine your credibility as a genuine listener and therefore as a good manager. If your team member comes up with several valid areas for improvement but not a minor one which you had thought of, you may wish to abandon your minor point in favour of the ones identified by the team member. Do not abandon your idea if it is important or simply to avoid any awkwardness in bringing it up. If you decide not to abandon it, don't dress it up as drawing out. Say: 'I've thought of an area I think you should work on . . .' It might seem a crucially important problem to you but the team member may not think so or may genuinely have not noticed it. A second problem with drawing out is that you can overdo it. Most team members will want to know what you think of their performance. So give them your views on what they have said even if it is a simple agreement.

The most important activity during the appraisal interview is listening. If you find you are doing most of the talking you are doing it wrong. Second most important is a 'future orientation': however the areas for improvement have been identified, you and your team member need to devise a plan for making the improvement happen.

Recording the appraisal interview

You may have to complete a form summarising the discussion. An example of an appraisal form is included here (Fig 19.1). If the contents of the form are going to be used for decisions about pay or career development you need to get the form right. But very often the main benefit of appraisal is the private discussion between the two of you, building your relationship, reflecting and learning from the past, planning developments in the future. In that case, don't let the form get in the way. It might be useful in setting an agenda for your discussion and recording the main points, or you may decide to set your own agenda and complete the form in the sequence that seems best. If the team member has any problems that you think might lead to disciplinary action it is essential you record these. It is also only fair to record other significant problems or else you are giving the team member leave to ignore something which may slow their career progress for years to come. Opinion is divided over whether to complete the form during the interview, and so avoid any dispute over wording later, or write it up alone while the team member is back at work. Decide for yourself but be consistent and don't be one of those people who writes it up the next day, the next week, never. Your team member should get a copy of the completed form.

STAFF-IN-CONFIDENCE *when completed*

APPRAISAL FORM

Staff member's name: *Luke Igoe*
Location: *Kent*
Appraiser's name: *Harish Mistry*
Date of this appraisal: *8 Jan 96*
Date of the start of the period covered by this appraisal: *2 Jan 95*

Department: *Software systems*
Roll number: *21894*

Date of last appraisal: *4 Jan 95*

OUR POLICY

The company aims to develop its people; to realise their potential and maximise their contribution to the business. Personal appraisal is key to this policy: an opportunity for staff to discuss their performance and development needs to the mutual benefit of both the business and the individual.

- Staff are recommended to have an appraisal at least once a year. Management may insist on an appraisal taking place if it is felt necessary but otherwise the onus and ownership is with the member of staff.

- The purpose of appraisal is staff development. There is no direct link between appraisal and pay or promotion, except that appraisal is often the most direct and visible way to achieve development, which may then be rewarded.

- Appraisal achieves this development through providing an opportunity for a member of staff and an appraiser to stand back from day-to-day activity and review what has happened, discuss problems and opportunities, and plan development through the setting of objectives.

- This form is an aid to and a record of the discussion. It may not always be necessary to complete every part of the form and additional pages may need to be added.

- The process begins with the staff member completing the self-assessment parts of the form. The use of self-assessment stems from the company's belief that the best development occurs in areas identified by the individual concerned. The self-assessment will require careful preparation and consideration. Staff members may ask advice of anyone they choose before completing these sections and written advice is available from the central personnel office.

- The process continues with an appraisal interview. The appraiser is usually the staff member's immediate line manager and must have received appraisal training: the minimum training acceptable is coached completion of the appraisal workbook. The appraiser provides feedback on the self-assessment in order to point out any blind spots the staff member may have about his or her contribution. This then leads into a discussion on future development, including specific plans for the future.

- The process ends with a review of this document. The reviewer is usually the appraiser's line manager. The purpose of the review is to check the value and correct conduct of the appraisal.

- After review, this form is logged and filed. It can then be read only by the staff member, personnel officers and managers at or senior to business director level.

Version 5, November 1995. Page 1.

Fig 19.1 Appraisal form

STAFF-IN-CONFIDENCE when completed

SELF-ASSESSMENT

1) Describe the job(s) you have done over the period of this appraisal. Mention tasks and deliverables.

- Detailed design, coding and unit testing of modules from the 'customer' subsystem.

- Unit Test planning and approval.

- Integration of 'customer' modules into prototype subsystem

- Running tests; removing defects

2) Describe the new knowledge and skills you have gained over this period. This can be done by listing the codes of competences you have gained from the company's job competence manual.

- Detailed design from level 2 documents.

- Use of configuration management toolset.

- Removing defects from own work and that of others.

3) List all training courses you have completed since your last appraisal, including open learning and workbook-based courses.

- Open learning course 'teamworking' 10–11 July 1995

- CM toolset workbook — April 95

Fig 19.1 Appraisal form (*continued*)

STAFF-IN-CONFIDENCE when completed

SELF-ASSESSMENT

Assess yourself according to the criteria listed below. The 'zero' column reflects the high average standard of our company.

CRITERIA	≡	=	–	0	+	‡	‡	Comments
1. Job and professional knowledge				✓				
2. Work to time and budget				✓				
3. Quality				✓				
4. Relationships/interpersonal skills					✓			I get on with most people
5. Written communication			✓					Improving
6. Spoken communication				✓				
7. Organisation and planning				✓				
8. Motivation and commitment				✓				
9. Problem solving and initiative					✓			Developing this as I solve problems*
10. Flexibility				✓				
11. Decision making				✓				
12. Development of others					.	✓		Helped new colleague
13. Commercial awareness		✓						Little experience yet
14. Internal/external client focus			✓					Little experience yet

* With system tests.

The 'comments' column should include comments on the relevance of the criteria to your job, any significant changes to your performance in that area, special circumstances, etc.

What do you consider to be your particular strengths?

- Getting along with other people; helping them and co-operating.
- Attention to detail.
- Personal organisation.

What aspects of your performance do you particularly wish to develop?
- I get frustrated when things hold us up.
- I want & need more commercial/financial & external client experience.
- Written work – I'll always want to improve in this area.

Page 3

Fig 19.1   Appraisal form (*continued*)

STAFF-IN-CONFIDENCE *when completed*

FEEDBACK

This section is completed by the appraiser.

1) Having read the self-assessment, what parts do you particularly agree with?

> Luke's views on his ability to deal with others
>
> and his need to develop commercial skills.

2) What parts of the self-assessment do you particularly disagree with?

> Luke's written work is already better than average.
>
> While attention to detail is a commendable quality,
> Luke must take care not to get bogged down in detail.
>
> Luke has not mentioned his knowledge of the operating
> systems, on which many of us depend!

3) What are your overall comments on the staff member's performance?

> Luke has become a competent software engineer.
>
> He needs to start planning his career further than
> just the next set of skills.

Page 4

Fig 19.1 Appraisal form (*continued*)

STAFF-IN-CONFIDENCE when completed

THE FUTURE

What work can be foreseen for the staff member at the moment?

Delivery of 'customer' subsystem. I intend Luke to spend more

time with the external client during this stage of the project.

possibly move on to installation work, which will mean spending

time at external client sites.

Staff member's longer-term career aspirations.

Luke has not given this matter sufficient consideration beyond

identifying a need for commercial skills. where does he intend

this to lead?

Learning and development needs resulting from the above sections.

Luke needs to spend time discussing his long-term career

aspirations and thinking about how to achieve them.

More commercial skills will develop with his planned future

work. We need to arrange formal coaching to help this happen. It

will also bring a wider perspective, which will help overcome his

occasional frustration.

Page 5

Fig 19.1   Appraisal form (*continued*)

OBJECTIVES

Objective	Success criteria	Target date
Meeting with Phil Lindsey to discuss long-term career	Meeting held and actions planned.	1st March 1996
Luke & Harish to plan time for coaching into delivery schedule	Coaching occurs & learning logged	Sept. 1996
Open Learning Course	'Career planning'	1st May 1996

Appraiser's signature: *H. Mistry*   Date: *10 Jan 1996*

Reviewer's name: Caroline Stephen

Reviewer's comments on this appraisal:

This is a useful document with clear and practical objectives. Luke and Harish have done this appraisal with the thoroughness they bring to other tasks.

Reviewer's signature: C. Stephen   Date: 10 Jan 1996

Staff member's closing comments on this appraisal:

This appraisal was a useful opportunity to stop and reflect. I agree I need to do this more. Thanks to Harish for arranging for Phil Lindsey to be my Mentor.

Staff member's signature: Luke Igoe   Date: 11 Jan 1996

Page 6

Fig 19.1 Appraisal form (*continued*)

The secret of successful appraisal is to make it an ongoing process, part of your regular contact with team members, just as you regularly review objectives and progress towards them. The formal appraisal then becomes just a summary of all that has happened, with no surprises on either side, and an opportunity to step back, reflect on it all and plan for the future.

19.5   REPRIMANDS

The previous two sections dealt with the continuous process of developing staff. There are occasions, however, when a single event requires a quick response. For example, an outburst of anger or an excessive lunch break require an immediate reprimand or you will be seen to be condoning the action. Like some other aspects of management, giving a reprimand fills some managers with dread because they are fearful of the consequences. But there is nothing to fear if you approach the reprimand from the point of view that it is not a telling off, like parents give to naughty children, but another opportunity to build the relationship with your team member and provide coaching. The purpose of the reprimand is to improve performance. The process of delivering a reprimand described below is a tailored version of the general performance improvement process described in section 19.3.

Fact-finding and diagnosis

If you have witnessed the event in question personally you need to make sure your feelings about it are controlled before taking action. If you have had the event reported to you, remember such reports are often interpretations of the facts. Keep an open mind until you have heard the other side of the story. This means the fact-finding continues into the interview with the individual concerned. You could start with a question like: 'I've heard there was an altercation of some kind in the tea room this morning. Can you talk me through events as you saw them?' Reflect back the content of what you are told as well as the feelings behind it to get a clear understanding. Summarise this to make sure you have a correct understanding.

Communicating the reprimand

If, having heard all sides of the story, you decide a reprimand is in order, here are a few guidelines for communicating it:

- Do it in private and keep the discussion confidential.
- Stick with the facts of what the person said or did at the specific instance or instances you are discussing. Do not make generalisations such as, 'You're always upsetting people' – this cannot be literally true and so is easily attacked. Also avoid comments about character such as, 'You're difficult to work with' – this may be your view but you need to justify it with examples.
- Do not get into an argument – as soon as you do, you've lost. When the team member responds, listen and reflect back what you have heard to check and show you have understood. Be prepared to change your mind

but if not, stick with your view on the matter while also acknowledging the team member's view.

- Explain the consequences of a repetition of the behaviour, such as a formal warning.

- Disclose your personal disappointment over the incident.

- Finish with a statement like, 'Aside from this one aspect, your work is going really well and I'm especially impressed with the way you . . . so it's important that this present issue doesn't recur.'

Follow up
When you next have a chat about progress as part of your general supervision, bring up the issue that led to the reprimand. If appropriate, acknowledge any improvements and congratulate the team member over the way they took it. You could ask for feedback on how you handled it: the team member may have things to off-load and talking these through will help. Reaffirm the value you place on having that person in your team. All this will help commitment, performance and motivation. If feelings have calmed down you can use the event to progress your relationship. Discussing what led to the event and how the reprimand went may lead you both to agree a new coaching style or that more challenging work is needed. If things are no better you will need to take it further using the performance improvement process described in section 19.3 or your organisation's formal discipline procedure.

19.6 PERFORMANCE IMPROVEMENT THROUGH COACHING

So far, much of this chapter has dealt with situations in which there is a performance problem. But if you wait until there is a problem before helping someone develop you will soon earn a poor reputation. The development of team members is now seen by many people as one of the main reasons for having managers at all so you need to be doing it all of the time. One of the first questions to tackle is: who needs coaching? The simple answer is everyone but it is possible to spread your coaching effort too thinly. It may be better to concentrate your efforts on just one or two team members for a few months, then review the situation. Don't forget you can sometimes delegate the coaching of more junior team members to senior team members. This will help them both but you need to keep an eye on things.

There are three matters to consider when deciding where to focus your coaching effort:

- *Motivation.* How much does each team member want to develop at this stage in their career? What sort of skills or work are they interested in? Do they bring enthusiasm to their work? If not then the new skills you help develop may be put to little use.

- *Potential.* Is the team member capable of learning the new skills at the moment? Consider long- and short-term potential.

- *Benefits the coaching would bring.* If a person is already good at their job and happy in it, coaching will bring less benefit than if it were applied to someone with room to improve.

Having identified that a team member needs coaching, how do you go about it? There can be no doubt that the prime means of helping someone to develop a new skill is to give them a job that requires use of that skill. If you divide up your project's work so everyone works with just a narrow set of skills, not only will they become frustrated, they will develop only their narrow set of skills and so be a less flexible workforce.

Once the work has been divided in a way that exposes the team member to new skills, you can take them through a process of learning and development. The process outlined below is based on *Situational Leadership*, developed by Kenneth Blanchard and others.

Situational Leadership uses two sets of management behaviours: direction, which is one-way communication consisting of giving specific instructions and close supervision; and support, which is two-way communication, consisting of listening, supporting, encouraging and talking around problems.

1   The model suggests that people new to a job or unfamiliar with a task tend to be very keen but not very competent. This is sometimes called 'unconscious incompetence' as they may not be aware of their lack of ability. They need some support and a great deal of direction.

2   As time moves on, they start to acquire skills but the initial enthusiasm wears off. They have had a few setbacks but, with your help, have learned from them. They still need direction as they have more to learn, but you must increase the level of support.

3   Later still, they reach a stage of competence at the job, but enthusiasm and commitment waver up and down from day to day. This is the stage most of us are at for much of the time. They need less direction now. More than a little direction will probably irritate as they know the job now. They still need a good level of support to keep them emotionally tied to the work.

4   If the three earlier stages have been done well, new team members will probably make it to the fourth stage. They are very skilled at the job and it has become part of them, so that they always tackle it with energy. They require only infrequent direction from you and the level of support can be cut down, though never removed entirely. Such a team member takes up very little of your time now and is probably ready for a new challenge. What can you delegate next?

This model suggests that your management style needs to change as team members change. That sounds obvious and it is, but managers don't always do it. The model is simple but there are some important things to remember when using it. First, people do not move through the four stages at a smooth rate. People move at different speeds depending on their ability and

Table 19.1 Summary of appropriate coaching styles at changing stages of development

Stage	1	2	3	4
Level of skill	Low	Fairly low	High	Very high
Level of commitment	High	Moderate	Variable	High
Direction needed	High	High	Low	Low
Support needed	Low	High	High	Low

the work involved. People also move backwards through the stages: someone once very committed to the job becomes weary of it; someone once highly skilled gets sloppy. You need to adjust your coaching style appropriately (see Table 19.1).

It is not for you alone to decide on a team member's stage of development and the style it requires. This is best done in partnership. You need to agree any changes in coaching style with the team member or they will wonder what is going on! Every change in style will feel like a risk to you because it is a risk to delegate important work to someone else. You may feel you want to be in control more, doing the most important work yourself, giving precise instructions for how to get a job done and supervising closely. This won't work. Your staff will become demoralised and you will overwork. Effective managers take risks – but they limit them by planning and managing the risk.

They can design exposure to new skills into a team member's job and then coach them – or have someone else do the coaching – even though the acquisition of those skills forms the main process by which technical skills are developed in your team and the industry as a whole. A well-thought-out appraisal system and appropriate monitoring of performance play their part. There are other ways of developing skills that work well alongside these primary means. The first is training courses – often the first solution thought of when a skills deficit is noticed. Courses make a big difference when a good one is used at about the right time but are of limited use unless tied into coaching on the job. As well as traditional courses, consider courses delivered by technology such as computer-based training. There are correspondence courses, videos and – often overlooked – books. You can also consider conferences, lending a team member to another team and promoting internally as an alternative to recruiting in from outside. Our industry often complains of skills shortages. You can help avoid this problem by developing your staff through coaching.

19.7 PERFORMANCE MANAGEMENT TOOLS

This section presents an overview of methodical approaches to skill development and to the assessment of and reward for skill acquisition. The traditional approach most often taken in analysing an area of skill is to break it down into its component parts, often in great detail. This approach has had great success in the design of industrial processes. In recent years, however, the concept of the 'competence' has become accepted in the service industries and many professions. A competence is a detailed statement of what a skilled worker will do to achieve a task within the job and the standards by which the activity will be done. A competence is a basic unit of skill. On the positive side, this approach to the analysis of skill enables jobs to be defined in great detail, training to be targeted at the identified skill elements and the assessment of people against the required skills. Other

Table 19.2 Example of a competence: from a systems company

OPERATION OF A SUPPORT SERVICE COMPETENCE
Description: the participant must be able to provide a centrally-supported service
for a development project.

Condition	Activity	Criteria
Given maintenance requirements	(a) Monitor performance against agreed service levels	Performance statistics, activity logs and fault logs are regularly collected and analysed. Performance degradation of the system is recognised and possible solutions researched and actioned. Unreliable or outdated components are replaced. Need to enhance or upgrade the system is recognised and reported to management.
Given agreed service levels	(b) Monitor customer satisfaction	Regular reviews of service performance are conducted with users. Users are informed of problems and consulted as to solutions.
Given changes to required service	(c) Establish changes required	Changes in requirements are documented. Plans for changes in capacity to meet changed requirements are researched fully. Plans for changes in maintenance requirements are researched fully. Alternative plans and costs are presented clearly and discussed with management and users.
Given requirement to change configuration	(d) Initiate changes to configuration	Instructions to users are given clearly and checked to have been understood. Changes initiated are in accordance with manufacturer's and organisation's procedures. Documentation requirements are specified.

potential benefits are the identification of best practice and accurate recruitment based on selecting candidates with a defined skill profile.

On the negative side, this approach can become bureaucratic and inflexible: large documents are written describing the identified skills which can be out of date before they are published. The focus sometimes shifts so far towards analysing a skill that the question of developing it is overlooked. If pay is linked to the acquisition of competences the issue becomes contentious and a great deal of resentment can be generated over what counts as a competence, what it takes to be accredited as having one and their relative value. Skilled engineers may resent the apparent reduction of their skill to small elements and may be right in thinking that this reductionist approach loses a great deal of what the job as a whole entails.

In the face of these potential advantages and dangerous pitfalls, many organisations and some professional bodies are devising their own system of methodical skill definition, designed to suit their own purpose and circumstances. Your organisation may well have such a system in place, perhaps as part of a professional development scheme. If so, it is important that you understand what it is trying to achieve – and what it is not trying to achieve – as well as how to operate it on behalf of the staff of your project.

The system will be documented. Like a quality system, it is there to help you, but it will not always help if you want instant answers. If the system has been devised thoroughly there will be a considerable volume of documents but structured in such a way that the section you need at any time can be found quickly. Like a quality system, it should have a means for you to challenge it if you find it unhelpful so that it can be continually improved. Such improvement processes will be built into the system so it can keep up with changes in technology and working practices. No job is the same as it was a year ago.

In the same way, no one job is the same as any other so it is usually not worth trying to define every aspect of a job and including them all in the job definition. There are certain skills that everyone needs. These are the core competences and include skills such as writing a progress report, positive meeting contributions, telephone skills and health and safety awareness. Then

Table 19.3 Example of a competence: from a civil service organisation

EQUAL OPPORTUNITIES COMPETENCE

Performance criteria	Outcome
Is committed to equal treatment for all staff.	People help and support each other and there is a good team spirit.
Ensures equal opportunities and fairness for all staff so that no member of the team is unfairly discriminated against.	Team readily co-operates to achieve team goals.

there are skills which are part of some jobs but not all and yet are still common enough for it to be worth analysing them. These are the job competences and could include skills such as writing a unit test plan, conducting an analysis interview and presenting a training event. Every job will also require its special skills which are not a part of the formal skills system – for example, the skill of determining which skill to use in a given situation or some technical skill related to a project application. Just because these skills are not listed in the list of competences, do not forget to coach people in them or recognise their effective use.

A job profile is a list of all the competences a person requires to perform a job. Ideally, the job holder will have enough of these competences to do the job but not have them all, and so can develop these competences through doing the job. A job holder who has all the required competences may or may not be able to do the job as a whole well but will probably become bored by the lack of new skill challenge.

Systems such as these can help you in your performance management activities by defining the standards of the job and identifying the learning needed by each member of your team. Acquisition of competences can by itself be a useful reward and motivator. Staff may be able to earn a professional or vocational qualification through the acquisition of competences although our industry does not, at the moment, have any such qualifications which have much value in the labour market. If your organisation has such a system it should provide a useful framework for many of your performance management activities. Even if your organisation does not have such a system you can involve your team in their own management and development by discussing the core competences with them as a group and discussing job competences with them individually.

But always remember, a framework such as this is meant to help and is not an end in itself. Also remember that skill is in many ways a political commodity: skills have value and people who have a skill may resist attempts to analyse what they do for fear it may result in their skill having less value either by being over-simplified or by being passed on to many other people and thus losing its scarcity.

19.8   SUMMARY

Managers who are uncomfortable with the human side of projects sometimes dismiss it as 'soft stuff' of little relevance. This may help them feel better but they are underrating what many other managers see as the most challenging and rewarding part of their job. It is also the aspect that makes perhaps the biggest difference in the success or failure of a project.

The project manager can make an immense difference to productivity, morale and the quality of working life by paying attention to performance development, through designing the project so staff get to use a wide range of skills and seeing they receive the necessary coaching and support to master these skills. This in turn can help our industry overcome problems of skill shortage and damage to our reputation from the regular stories in the news of expensive, even catastrophic, project failures.

Effective performance management takes time, but the effort required from you is spread, so you rarely spend a long period on it. Performance management becomes a natural part of every day.

19.9 QUESTIONS

1 You are dissatisfied with the general level of performance of one of your team. The quality of work is below your expectations. How will you deal with this?

2 A member of your team exhibits disruptive behaviour. Her work is good but she is not a team player. The consequences are that she does not contribute to team effort and her colleagues find her difficult to work with; the project team secretary has refused to work with her at all. How could this serious problem have arisen? What can be done now?

3 Describe the process of setting objectives. What might be three objectives for a newly-appointed junior programmer?

CHAPTER 20

Project teams

20.1 INTRODUCTION

The previous chapter dealt with the management and development of your individual team members. This chapter deals with the selection, management and development of your team as a unit.

You will not usually be in a position to select all the members of your team from everyone available on the external labour market. More often you will find yourself taking on an intact team or that team members are supplied by an internal resourcing function. However, you are very likely to be involved in selecting team members at regular intervals, either from inside or outside your organisation, to cover a growing need for staff or to replace people who leave. That is why the recruitment process is covered in this chapter. Whether you select, inherit or simply receive the members of your team you will need to work at developing them from a group of individuals, each with his or her own interests, goals, style and ambitions, into a team that works together to achieve common goals, using each other's strengths to best advantage. You can make an enormous impact on the extent to which the people on your project build into a team. This chapter covers the induction of new team members, theories on team development and team work and practical advice on what you can do to encourage the people who work for you to work together. The sequence of this chapter is designed to take you through the recruitment process, the induction of new people into your project and the building of teams.

20.2 JOB DESCRIPTIONS AND PERSON SPECIFICATIONS

The recruitment process starts with the identification of a vacancy to be filled. Recruitment is an expensive and risky process so it is worth spending time on each stage including this one. Unfortunately, this stage is sometimes done with little thought: when a person leaves a team, it is assumed a vacancy is left, and then that recruitment is the means of filling the vacancy. Let us examine these two assumptions and consider alternative actions.

First, when someone leaves the team it does not always mean a vacancy results. Project teams grow and shrink: is a person's departure a timely opportunity to start reducing the number of people working on a project that is approaching its goal? If not, can the work be subcontracted to another team or organisation? Can it be automated? If the answer to all these questions is 'No' you can still consider whether the job that has been vacated could be spread between other members of your team who may appreciate an additional challenge, especially if the new work gives them opportunities to develop new skills.

If, after considering the questions above, you still decide that a person's departure leaves a vacancy to be filled, consider the second assumption: do you need to recruit someone to fill it? It might be a better option to promote a more junior member of your team into the vacated job and then consider recruiting to fill the more junior job. This has many advantages: the job is filled by someone you know, which takes much of the risk out of recruiting (you still have to recruit for the more junior position but a mistake here is likely to be less costly), your promoted team member knows much about your work already and the message to all your team members is that there are opportunities for promotion while they work for you, which is very likely to have a positive effect on their motivation and commitment. So do not assume that a departure always creates a vacancy. It may instead be an opportunity for you to do something creative with your team.

The other side of the coin is that vacancies do not arise only from people leaving; they come about as projects grow and as the level of work expands beyond the capacity of a team. The generation of vacancies as a project grows will have been included in the planning of the project. As with other aspects of project planning, you need to monitor actual events against the plan and act accordingly. It may be that the project requires staff earlier or later, or more or fewer than was estimated at the planning stage.

The generation of vacancies as the amount of work exceeds what your team can deal with requires attention. You can reach the stage where your team is overloaded, losing its commitment and starting to make mistakes without you even realising it, perhaps because you are working very hard yourself. So monitor the level of effort your team is having to provide and, if it gets high, take steps before they all resign! The steps could be the recruitment of more staff, a reduction in the amount of work your team has to do, a change in procedures to make the work flow faster, better equipment or any other number of possibilities.

Let us assume now, that having considered the present state of your project and the future demands expected, you have decided there is a vacancy to be filled. The next activity required is job analysis. This involves defining the tasks which comprise the job: what is to be done, what is provided to the job holder and what the job holder is expected to deliver. At this stage, the attention is on the job itself and not the person who will fill it. In other words, job analysis is an impersonal description of tasks, inputs and outputs with no consideration yet of what it will take to do the job. This separation is deliberate and is intended to avoid unconscious assumptions being made about the required job holder. Job analysis is done in a similar way to system analysis: you talk to the people who will need to work with the job holder and perhaps people who have held similar (or even the same) jobs in the

---

JOB DESCRIPTION

Job Title: Software Development Engineer
Job Grade: Professional Engineer/Manager
Reports to: Software Release Development/Manager
Job Purpose: The Software Development Engineer is responsible for the development of the software which will provide an identified functional thread of an IT system. This responsibility starts with the analysis of the client requirement for the functional thread and concludes with the acceptance by the client authority of the delivered software.

Specific duties:
* Production of an analysis document which specifies the functionality of the system thread. This will be done using SSADM version 4 and must be formally accepted by the client authority and the release manager responsible for the overall software release.
* Production of a subsystem design document using SSADM version 4. This must be accepted by the system design co-ordinator.
* Leading a team of contractors who will write and test the software.
* Leading a team of contractors who will produce system test documentation.
* Ensuring the system tests are conducted and all remedial work done until all HP systems tests can be shown to work correctly.
* Taking all steps required to enable the client authority to accept the software for the functional thread.
* Managing the above work to ensure as far as possible that it is completed within budget and by the required deadline.
* Monitoring progress and reporting it accurately to management. This will be done using the 'Multiskill' project management toolset.

General duties:
* To work with colleagues to achieve overall success of the project and profitability.
* To respond to changing needs, changing jobs and new technical skills.

Available resources:
* The Software Release Development Manager will be 20% available to the Software Development Engineer for coaching, support, advice and other assistance.
* The contractors will be supplied by the Resourcing Department in accordance with their Service Level Agreement.
* The Software Development Engineer will have access to the internal consultants whose job is to assist production staff with their specialist advice. Currently the available internal consultants cover analysis, design, project toolsets, quality, training and testing.

Other details:
* Terms of employment are as specified in the company's Staff Handbook.
* Internal and client confidentiality must be maintained.
* The job is based at the company's Maidstone office.

Fig 20.1 Example of a job description

past. As project manager you will have your own ideas about the design of the job. Find out what is required of the job holder and write this in a document which is called a job description.

The job description says nothing about qualifications or experience levels – these come at a later stage. Job descriptions are used to write job advertisements for the press and for specifying vacancies to recruitment agencies. Anyone can write a job advertisement if they have a complete job description but to write them well requires the specialist skills of a personnel professional. An example of a job description is shown in Fig 20.1.

Job descriptions are also used in the next stage of the recruitment process: the derivation of the person specification. This uses the information in the job description and any general company standards to describe the characteristics of a person who could do the job satisfactorily. It is important to derive the person specification from the job description and general company standards, rather than write it independently, in order to avoid any unconscious assumptions about the type of person required to do the job. For example, if all previous holders of similar jobs have been university graduates it might be natural to assume all future holders of such jobs must be graduates. This might not be necessary. Working from the job description makes it more likely that such assumptions will be avoided. It also helps avoid the unfair or even illegal elimination of some candidates from the job because of unfounded assumptions about age or gender.

Examination of each element of the job description identifies required characteristics for the person specification. General company requirements, which are also included, might include a willingness to work on defence projects or a preparedness to work away from home for extended periods. But take care: a requirement for mobility might unfairly put off or exclude a good candidate who has young children in school or a partner with a fixed job. So make sure all general requirements really do apply in the case of the job you are filling.

Person specifications usually list the required characteristics in two categories: essential characteristics and desirable characteristics. Essential characteristics are those that the job requires and which cannot be learned or trained easily. Desirable characteristics are those which either are not essential for the job but would help or which are essential but which the job holder can learn, either on the job or through training, without it causing serious delays or problems. A common and regrettable mistake is the selection of a person who already has all the skills and knowledge required. Searching for such a person is arduous and sometimes impossible. Even if such a perfect candidate is found, the job will be unchallenging because he or she knows it already. It is often better, cheaper and easier to recruit someone who has most of the required skills and knowledge but has an opportunity to grow into the job through learning the remaining skills and knowledge. It also demonstrates your commitment to training staff in the skills they need, which makes your organisation more attractive to potential recruits.

PERSON SPECIFICATION

Physical Attributes:

Essential: Good attendance record. Tidy appearance.

Desirable: Excellent health record. Smart appearance. Positive impact upon others. Able to work extended hours under pressure.

Note: This job would suit someone with a mobility disability but is not suitable for job sharing.

Attainments:

Essential: Qualified practitioner in SSADM version 4. Knowledge of project management tools and techniques. Some supervision experience.

Desirable: Knowledge of 'Multiskill' project management toolset. Experience of leading a team in a commercial environment. Management qualification.

Intelligence:

Essential: Demonstrated ability to understand software, systems development and IT in general.

Desirable: Demonstrated understanding of commercial pressures in an organisation with clear financial targets.

Aptitudes:

Essential: Excellent written communication skills. Good use of spoken language. Programming skills. Able to learn new technical skills fast.

Desirable: C++ programming skills

Interests:

Essential: Computing as an industry and a career.

Desirable: An interest in industrial applications of IT. Interests which involve interaction or communication with other people.

Evidence of Character:

Essential: Works well in a team, especially when the pressure is on. Able to listen to and accept others' points of view. Willing to accept customer changes.

Desirable: Influence skills. Has led a team to success when significant obstacles had to be overcome. Has experience of dealing with customers who show excessive concern for their own needs over supplier's needs

Personal Circumstances:

Essential: Willing to work beyond contracted hours on occasion. Willing to adapt to organisational changes.

Desirable: Already has all permits required for work in this country.

Fig 20.2 Example of a person specification

Person specifications usually list the required characteristics under a set of general headings such as those shown in Fig 20.2. Do not be too concerned about which heading a characteristic should be under; the important question is whether the characteristics are derived from a genuine need of the job or not.

The job description has been used to identify potential candidates through the use of an agent or an advertisement. With the person specification complete you can begin the process of selection.

20.3 RECRUITING THE TEAM

Your agent or advertisement should result in a number of applications arriving. If not, you need to reconsider: are you asking for too much or offering too little? Assuming you have a good number of applications you can now shortlist those you will invite for interview.

Shortlisting means working through the applications, removing those that clearly fail to meet the essential requirements for the job. Not all the characteristics on the person specification can be assessed from the written application alone or no further selection would be necessary but some important ones can. Using as an example the person specification above, the application will tell whether the candidate is qualified in SSADM, has the particular experience mentioned and it demonstrates the candidate's level of written communication skills. By removing the applications that fail to meet the minimum standards you identified earlier, you produce your shortlist. If the process leaves you with too many candidates for interview, use the desirable characteristics on the person specification to eliminate more. If there are still too many, consider sending out a form which requires more detail or talking to candidates by telephone to gain more information. The important point is to stick with the characteristics you identified in advance of reading the applications, and not to be swayed by anything else. We all have our prejudices and unless the process sticks closely to the identified characteristics it is easy to be influenced by factors such as similar background or interests to your own.

Invite the shortlisted candidates to visit your office to find out more about the job and attend an interview. The letter should contain a note of thanks for and interest in the candidate's application, more information about your organisation and the job on offer, a choice of dates, details of what will take place during the visit and information about how to find the office.

We are all influenced by first impressions. Sometimes, the ability to make a good first impression is an important job characteristic, for example when recruiting a salesperson. For many more jobs it is not. The other point about first impressions is to remember that the candidate is considering you and your firm just as much as you are considering the candidate. So make sure the first impressions your candidates get of your firm are positive. Many organisations make costly mistakes over simple matters like informing Reception that the candidate is expected. Other 'obvious' requirements, such as refreshments being available, travel expenses being refunded, the availability of existing team members to meet and a quiet interview room being booked are sometimes overlooked. A smart presentation about your organisation and its work and a sociable lunch can make a positive impact as well.

You need to prepare yourself by being thoroughly familiar with the written application and the job documents and by shutting out of your mind all the other matters that require your attention, such as work, home and so on. You need to prepare the interview room with an appropriate layout: comfortable chairs around a coffee table, or two chairs at ninety degrees by the corner of a desk will relax you and the candidate more than if you face each other across a desk. Finally, you need to prepare your interview plan and interview notes form.

The interview plan consists of the sequence you intend for the interview. The main element of your plan will be to work through the key components of your candidate's history as outlined in the written application. The plan is a straightforward document. As explained later, you cannot plan all the questions you will ask because most questions are a response to things the candidate says. What you can do, in addition to the simple interview plan, is mark up the candidate's written job application with ideas for areas you may be able to probe. You can also plan how you will use each interview to develop your interviewing skills as is shown at the bottom of the example in Fig 20.3.

The interview notes form (Fig 20.4) consists of a list of those characteristics, taken from the person specification, that you will assess in the interview, a column to indicate whether the candidate has demonstrated each of these characteristics and space for a few words to remind you what the evidence was. There is also space at the bottom for you to note key words to remind you of areas you wish to probe some more.

Interview Plan

1. Welcome; introductions; agenda. Establish rapport.
2. Open questions on educational history.
3. Open questions on previous jobs.
4. Open questions on interests and circumstances.
5. The company: history, business, opportunities.
6. The job: requirements, good aspects, not so good aspects.
7. Anything you want to ask me? Anything else you want to say?
8. What happens next – you should hear from us in one week.
9. Thank you, goodbye – escort candidate back to Personnel Department.

Fig 20.3 Example of an interview plan

Interview Notes Form		
Characteristic	**Y or N?**	**Evidence**
Good appearance		
Adequate health		
Impact upon others		
Has worked under pressure		
SSADM version 4		
Project management tools and techniques		
Supervision experience		
Commercial environment		
Management qualification		
Ability to understand IT		
Financial targets		
Spoken communication skills		
Programming skills (C++?)		
Able to learn fast		
Computing as an industry and a career		
Interest in industrial applications of IT		
Interests with other people		
Works well in a team under pressure		
Listens to and accepts others' points of view		
Customer experience		
Influence skills		
Has overcome significant obstacles		
Willing to work beyond contracted hours		
Willing to adapt to organisational changes		
Has required permits		

Areas to probe ...

Fig 20.4 **Example of an interview notes form**

As suggested in the plan above, the interview begins with friendly chat to build rapport and put the candidate at ease. You will be able to make the most accurate judgements about a candidate if he or she is as relaxed as possible. Many amateur interviewers like to do the opposite: they put the candidate under deliberate pressure. This is unhelpful because few jobs require the ability to cope well with deliberate interview pressure and it is not a reliable predictor of how the candidate will cope with ordinary work pressure.

With the opening small talk done, you can begin with the main business of interviewing. Taking each of the candidate's main areas of experience in turn, including work experience, education and interests, begin with an introduction such as: 'I see from your application that you worked for Megacorp for two years.' This allows the candidate to focus on this aspect of the past before you move on to the first open question: 'Tell me about your time there.'

Open questions are questions which invite the candidate to talk at length. Closed questions invite a shorter answer. So begin discussing an area of experience with a question which is open but not so open that it leaves the candidate with no idea of where to start; for example, 'Tell me about your main achievements' gives the candidate little idea of what sort of answer is wanted. Perhaps the interviewer asking such a question has little idea either.

As the candidate answers your open question, make a note of keywords to remind you of areas which you want to probe further. When the candidate finishes talking you can start to probe these areas, first with an introductory question like: 'You mentioned you had to deal with clients. Did any of them ever cause you problems?' Then, if the candidate answers yes, follow this with, 'Tell me about one example.' This gives you information about the candidate's experience of dealing with customers, which is one of the characteristics wanted in the example above.

Other methods of probing an area for more information are:

- Requesting more information: 'Tell me more about the system testing you did.'

- Reflecting back key words from the previous answer. This encourages the candidate to say more about the words you picked on. For example, if the candidate said, 'We did the design using Merise' you could respond: 'Merise?' The candidate will then tell you about this method.

- Just staying quiet and waiting for the candidate to say more. Candidates often need time to think or to find the right words. Give them that time. Poor interviewers fill even tiny pauses with a rephrased question which may only confuse the candidate, or possible answers, which make the whole process simply a multiple choice test.

The most precise form of probe question is the closed question, which invites a short answer on the specific information you require: 'What design method did you use?' 'How much money were you responsible for?'

In order to be able to probe you need to spot things the candidate says which can be probed. *The key skill in selection interviewing is being alert for areas you can probe which will give you evidence that your candidate has or has not in the past demonstrated one of your required characteristics.* To an extent you can prepare for this in advance. For example, if your candidate has worked in a fast food restaurant it is likely to mean having had to deal with awkward customers. But you need to listen carefully to all your candidate says in order to spot things to probe further for the evidence you require. If you are listening properly you will always have another question to hand.

When you have finished probing an area or period from the candidate's application, reflect back a summary of your understanding of what you have been told. Begin with, 'Let me just check that I have got all this right . . .' Summaries are useful as they allow the candidate to correct misinterpretations, which are common, and to add more information which may help. They show you have listened and they tie up the area you have been talking about, laying the ground for the introduction of the next area. Although they do so much, summaries are often omitted from interviews, perhaps because interviewers are not used to doing them as part of everyday conversation.

The 'funnel' diagram in Fig 20.5 illustrates the process you go through with each area of the application form or curriculum vitae; in other words each previous job, education course and other sections from the form. You start with an introduction and an open question, then probe, staying alert for anything which gives you the evidence you need.

The diagram shows how probing a candidate about a summer job at a warehouse can provide evidence of a candidate's experience of procedures. By asking what the candidate actually did at this job, the interviewer can determine how precisely the candidate stuck to procedures, and whether the candidate showed initiative in challenging them and was given responsibility for changing them. Probing for such evidence, on what the candidate has done in the past, is a much better determinant of what the candidate is likely to do in the future than any other interview technique. Having achieved this, the interviewer could lead on to other aspects of the warehouse job to find evidence of customer contact, team problems, reliability and many other characteristics. Then the interviewer can open a new 'funnel' by introducing the next period of the candidate's history.

Just as there are useful kinds of question to ask, there are some types to avoid. In particular, try to avoid:

✗ *Leading questions* – these indicate the answer you expect. For example, 'I imagine you had to go through a formal process to get the changes agreed?'

✗ *Hypothetical questions* – these ask how a candidate would respond in an imaginary situation, for example, 'How would you go about selecting a team member?' The reply is a best guess at what the candidate thinks you would like to hear. It is much better to stick with what the candidate actually has and has not done.

Introduction of next area	*'I'd like to talk about your summer job at Barker's warehouse.'*
Open question	*'Tell me about the work there.'*
Probes	*'Say some more about the control system.'* *'What did you do when it went wrong?'* *'What happened next?'*
Closed question	*'How often did this happen?'* *'Were you responsible for these changes?'*
Summary	*'Let me see if I've got all this correct ...'*

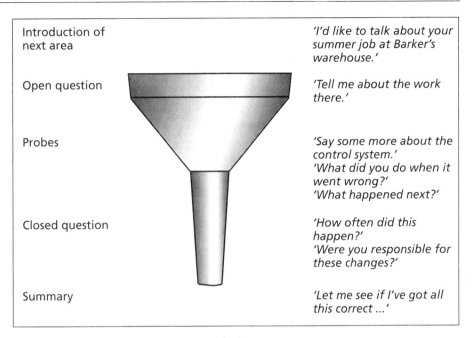

Fig 20.5   The 'funnel' questioning technique

✗ *Multiple questions* – these are rambling questions, frequently asked by inter-viewers who are not sure what they want to ask or who find silence so awkward they fill the candidate's thinking time with rephrased versions of the question: 'How was the work organised? I mean, was there a formal procedure or did you have to respond as things arose – not that there's anything wrong with that? And did you work alone or with the others? As a team, I mean?'

✗ *Aimless questions* – many interviewers have 'pet' questions which they always ask without any real idea of what they are looking for. Questions like: 'Where do you see yourself in five years' time?' and 'What are your strengths and weaknesses?' may be designed to extract evidence for a job characteristic, but more often are used to fill time by interviewers who will make their selection decision on subjective feelings about the candi-date.

✗ *Riddles* – silly questions such as 'How would you estimate the number of fish in a pond?' Candidates may have heard these before and, even if not, the replies to such questions can never be as reliable as evidence of the candidate's behaviour in real situations.

By the end of the interview, you will have one or many pieces of evidence that the candidate has or lacks the characteristics, including technical skills and interpersonal abilities, you have listed on the person specification. If you have no evidence for a characteristic you could try to find it by some other means or you must highlight this as an uncertainty and therefore a risk. All candidates who lack essential characteristics can be eliminated. Others can be ordered by the number of the desirable characteristics they have and the strength of the evidence. The candidate at the top of your list can be recommended for the job. If no candidates have the essential characteristics, you have to go back to the start and reconsider your vacancy.

As soon as you have said goodbye to the candidate, write up a formal report of the interview. Do not delay it for any reason. Your notes and jottings on the interview notes form are not sufficient, and writing them out will help clarify your thoughts. By sticking to evidence for or against the characteristics you have determined you need, you are far less likely to be influenced by subjective judgements and the unfair prejudices we all have.

The interview is not your only means of assessing whether a candidate has the characteristics you require. Some of the others are described below but only in outline; you need to consult a recruitment specialist for greater detail.

- Examination of the written application, as already mentioned.
- Get the candidate to do some technical work. This is particularly appropriate when recruiting contractors for a particular technical skill. For example, when recruiting C programmers, give them a short but typical specification of one of your programs. They then write the C code and you can assess its quality.
- Simulations, such as group exercises. For example, a group of candidates are given a problem which they have to solve together. Trained observers watch for evidence of particular interpersonal skills. One example is that the group of candidates is the board of a company and they have to elect one of their number as the new managing director. Observers look for evidence of listening, building on other people's ideas, asking opinions and other desirable behaviours.
- Selection tests. There are many of these on the market and they appeal to many recruiters because they make the selection decision less personal. This does not make the decisions better. Used with caution by trained professionals, selection tests have their place as part of the process. They are not acceptable as a means of avoiding the responsibility of making a selection decision.
- Bring potential recruits in on short-term contracts to begin with. Those who perform well over a period of a few weeks can be offered a permanent position.

Once a successful candidate has been identified, a contract and other formalities are needed but this book assumes these matters are dealt with by a central personnel department. You may wish to contact the successful candidate to sell your job more and invite them to visit again.

When it has been confirmed that a new person is to join your team you need to devote some time to planning the new member's induction. Even a person transferring from another team in your organisation needs a planned

INDUCTION PLAN

Name:
Position being taken:
Start date:

Day One
Introductions to team colleagues
Overview of project:
- Customer
- Deliverables
- Technology
- Progress to date – planning & monitoring
- Organisational structure – where you fit in
Demonstration of system
Health & Safety – a legal requirement in many countries
- Fire drill, fire exits, fire extinguishers
- First aid
- Office hazards
- Dangers of working with computers (eye strain, muscle strain, etc.)
Senior team member to demonstrate development environment
Lunch with team
Company culture – level of formality; social scene; how things work here
New person's aspirations
Our expectations
Read top-level documentation

Day Two
Introductions to management
Detailed working of our part of the system:
- Purpose of subsystem
- Interfaces
- Database
- Algorithms
- Input and Output
Local environment:
- Shops
- Banks
- Post Office
- Transport
- Facilities
Read functional specification of our subsystem

Day Three

Fig 20.6   Part of an induction plan

induction as the impact the first days make on a team member has a profound and long-term effect.

Do not assume that you will think of all the new things you need to cover with a new person on the first day. Matters which seem simple and obvious to you may get overlooked. The other danger is overloading the new person on day one. So spend time listing everything a new person needs and then planning it out over days or even weeks, as suggested in the sample from an induction plan in Fig 20.6.

20.4 THE LIFECYCLE OF TEAMS

Thorough inductions help new team members to settle in quickly and begin adjusting to and developing within the team. But just as individuals mature and develop, given the right circumstances, so too groups move through stages of development. Charles Handy suggests that four stages of a group's development can be identified. They are described below and in his book, listed at the end of this book. This model is particularly applicable to new teams.

1 **Forming.** At first the team is a group of individuals. On the surface, the group discusses its purpose, methods, problems to overcome and so forth. Beneath the surface, members are trying to decide the extent to which they are accepted by the group, the extent to which they accept the group and its members, who has power and will take charge, who will challenge this leadership, what roles others will take and what sorts of relationships are going to form.

2 **Storming.** The forming stage usually leads to the storming stage. This conflict can be about goals, leadership, work methods, relationships, hierarchy and so forth. Agreements will be reached, then broken. Sometimes these matters are dealt with peacefully. Often they are suppressed only to reveal themselves, perhaps in another form, later. Otherwise, a certain amount of disagreement has to be aired and resolved before the group can move on.

3 **Norming.** The resolution of conflict requires the agreement of group norms and practices. The storming process results in agreed approaches to decision making, work sharing, meetings and work processes as well as generally accepted styles of interpersonal relationships such as the level of trust and openness.

4 **Performing.** Once the norms have been agreed the group can use them to achieve its task.

In practice, these four stages overlap. A group may be at several stages with different aspects of its work at the same time. Groups revert from a later stage to an earlier one, especially when a new or suppressed conflict causes a team to revert from performing back to storming. While an interesting model, what matters is how a project manager can use it to help move teams to the 'performing' stage as quickly as possible.

At the forming stage, you can assist by encouraging open communication. Do this by being open yourself about your personal goals and the concerns you have about the project. Spend time with your team members allowing and encouraging them to speak their minds. Team-building activities such as training and social events will help.

When your team is in storming mode, as it will be on occasions, you may feel disappointed or upset by what may appear to be childish, obstructive or counter-productive behaviour. Suspend these judgements, remembering that real people have a child-like component and personal and social needs. The behaviour you are observing is a natural part of the team development process. So do not clamp down on storming, although there will be times when 'enough's enough' – you can intervene if you judge that the storming is getting out of hand. Try to guide the energy liberated by storming into problem solving rather than personal antagonism. Finally, remember that people can feel hurt by the storming process, so give these people time to express their upset and help them forgive their colleagues. They may also have to forgive you: although you will have tried hard to be fair, people have different ideas of what fairness means.

The norming stage is an opportunity to demonstrate your management skills by acting as a chair or co-ordinator for the process. As norms and work styles emerge, you can explicitly identify them and get everyone's clear agreement. If you don't, your team may believe they are all agreeing to something but have differing ideas on what that something is.

The performing stage is what all managers strive for. Once reached it requires effort to maintain it. The agreed norms and procedures will need to be changed as circumstances change, and it will help if these agreements are done in an overt way. But while the 'impersonal' aspects of teamwork, such as agreed ground rules and work methods, do help a team to work together, they are not by themselves sufficient for teamworking. A person will only commit to the team as long as the team is meeting personal, social and career needs. So do what you can to stay aware of the more personal needs of your team members and then find ways of meeting them.

20.5   BELBIN ON TEAMS

One of the most original and useful studies of team effectiveness is the work of Dr Meredith Belbin and his colleagues. This section gives a brief summary of their findings. More detail can be found in Belbin's own books. One of them is listed at the end of this book.

Belbin made a study of teams of managers in business simulation games and compared a team's degree of success with the results of psychometric instruments (questionnaires which attempt to measure aspects of personality) completed by the team's members. The key finding was that there is no one type of person who makes an ideal 'team player;' what matters is that the team contains a mix of various types. Even teams deliberately formed entirely of, for example, very intelligent people did not fare well. Further work enabled Belbin to identify eight 'team roles'. If all the team roles are filled, a team stands a very good chance of success. If key team roles are missing it weakens the team and can lead to failure. The eight team roles are described below with their key strengths and allowable weaknesses. The roles are given current names; Belbin's original names for some of the roles, which you may have heard before, are in brackets.

- **Co-ordinator** (Chair): this role can be taken by any member of the team, not necessarily the appointed leader. The role provides consensual leadership, co-ordinating the team's efforts but somewhat lacking in originality.

- **Shaper**: an alternative form of leadership, the shaper leads 'from the front,' pushing activities forward and bringing 'shape' to the team. The Shaper is dynamic and can be inspiring but can also be abrasive.

- **Innovator** (Plant): a source of original, even inspired ideas, the Innovator is creative but sometimes forms a personal attachment to impractical ideas.

- **Resource Investigator**: the type of person who is never in the office except when on the 'phone. The Resource Investigator is the team's link to the outside world, and as such is another source of ideas, though not such original ones. The Resource Investigator knows people who can help the team, but once a problem is solved can lose interest with its implementation.

- **Monitor/Evaluator**: this is the person who sifts the group's ideas and separates those that are practicable from those that are not, keeps the group on the right track but is often insensitive to people's feelings.

- **Team Worker**: this person is very concerned with feelings, is sensitive to personal needs and upsets, works hard to keep people happy and maintains a positive atmosphere within the team but is indecisive in a crisis.

- **Implementer** (Company Worker): the practical organiser who takes an idea and produces a schedule. The implementer works well with milestones and plans but can be inflexible when things have to change.

- **Completer** (Completer/Finisher): the progress chaser. This person worries about what can go wrong with a project, checks up on detail and focuses the team on its deadlines, but can be too fussy.

When a team is balanced, the strengths of each role counter-balance the weaknesses of others. Most teams require this balance at all stages of a project. Innovators and Resource Investigators may be most useful at early stages but they are needed later too.

Most of us have one or two of these roles which we fill easily, and perhaps a couple more secondary roles which we can take on if our primary roles are being filled by others.

Project managers are not advised to select their teams on the basis of Belbin's team roles but to use this knowledge to help avoid the common problem of recruiting or promoting only people like themselves, which leads to convivial but unproductive teams. Belbin's work is most useful for developing existing teams: helping people to understand the strengths their colleagues bring and helping a team to identify which roles they lack, so they can compensate or seek external assistance.

20.6   THE EFFECTIVE TEAM

This chapter has shown that there is much the project manager can do to create and maintain an effective team. This is important because once a team has fallen apart and become disillusioned it is a very tough job to change things back. Prevention is much easier than cure. You can develop your team quickly by selecting people who can do their job to a large extent but find scope for challenge and personal development within it, then giving them a thorough induction, then allowing the team to develop through finding its own ways of doing things. You can encourage the process by providing a clear vision of the team's purpose and objectives, being open and encouraging openness in others and taking steps to find ways of compensating for missing 'team roles' within your team.

It is natural for many people to see their team as an extension of themselves, just as many people see their work as part of themselves. In the latter case, this close identification with work can make people reluctant to see faults in their work. In the former case, managers can become reluctant to see problems in their team. So it is worth making an active effort to identify potential problems before they develop. The points below describe some warning signs and give some suggestions on what to do about them. But every case is unique and there are no guaranteed formulae for dealing with people.

- *Productivity slips.* You may notice this from productivity figures or by less direct observations: people coming in late, more absenteeism, complaints from other teams which depend on yours or a general atmosphere of going slow. Possible causes are a lack of identification with the work – you need to establish a clearer vision and purpose for your project; lack of a personal sense of direction – you need to spend time with team members on career and personal development planning; a belief that effort is unrewarded – ensure your team have the tools and support they need so that their effort results in better performance, and then reward that better performance, especially with personal recognition such as praise.

- *Discord within the team.* There are two sorts of discord to watch out for: those caused by cliques and those caused by bogeymen. Cliques differ from innocent friendships within your team in that cliques are more deliberately exclusive of those outside and they often have a political purpose, such as the monopolisation of high status or highly skilled aspects of the team's work. If you perceive a clique forming, explore the political purpose of it and find some better means of meeting this need for all your team. The bogeyman is a common feature of work units. What happens is that one individual becomes the focus for all the team's discontent – everything is seen to be his or her fault. If you believe the 'bogeyman' to be an innocent victim, show your support and lead the team into finding the real causes of its problems.

- *Blame*. Cliques and bogeymen are forms of passing blame within your team. Your team may also start blaming another team for its problems; for example, a project team blames its problems on suppliers of hardware, desks or whatever. This can put you in an awkward spot. Support your team in their fair and considerate demands on others but if blame is becoming a habit it may be that your team is seeing its work as more important than the wider purpose of the organisation. Does your stated vision for the team ignore its context? Is your team becoming isolated? Are you empire building?

Finally, when discussing the development and maintenance of your team, it is worth considering the matter of termination. It is right and natural that team members reach a stage when the best course of action is to leave the team. The first case is a team member who knows the job thoroughly and performs well. You will want to retain this person in your team as long as you can but after a time the person will want more challenge. You will often be able to provide this challenge within your team, but if not, do not try to hold on to this person too long. It may breed resentment. The second case to consider is a team member who is not performing or who is behaving in some difficult manner. Other chapters in this book give advice for developing such people but there will be times when you wish to end their membership of your team. Do not shirk this uncomfortable aspect of your job but do seek advice from a personnel professional first.

20.7   SUMMARY

There is a great deal project managers can do to forge the members of their project into an effective team. There is much scope for managers to choose and express their own style; for example, you can choose the extent to which you share social activities and discuss out-of-work matters with your team. Any choice here can be effective, depending on your team and your circumstances. The only choice that is ineffective is to ignore this aspect of project management – some managers find it awkward or risky and so prefer to hide behind their terminals, focusing their attention on spreadsheets and planning tools. But, although this option appears safe, it is the path of real risk. If your team wants your project to succeed, the chances are it will.

20.8   QUESTIONS

1   Using the example of a job description in Fig 20.1, develop a job description for a project manager.

2   From the job description, prepare a person specification. Think about how this would need to reflect the different environments of (*a*) a big financial institution, (*b*) a computer services company and (*c*) a government department.

3   When you first assemble your project team, what can you do to build team spirit? What behaviours are the different individuals likely to exhibit during this team-building process? How do you demonstrate your leadership?

CHAPTER 21

The working environment

21.1 INTRODUCTION

The working environment means more than just the physical environment of your workplace; it means the emotional environment as well. You could call it the climate or the atmosphere. It is not tangible and cannot be controlled in the way an electric heater can but you can control it to an extent in more subtle ways. The lack of direct control over the emotional environment makes some project managers uneasy, so they ignore it or hope it will fix itself. Some may believe that the team climate just happens and that there is nothing they can do to influence it. But there are actions you can take to influence the climate and ensure it does not just 'happen'. It is essential that you do this as a positive climate brings fulfilment and satisfaction for your team and productivity and quality results for your project. A poor climate means your project will always be struggling uphill.

We all know from Chapter 18 that people do not work just for the money. People come to work to fulfil a need for achievement or advancement, or to occupy their time, or to have social interaction, or all of these and more. Work is now one of the main means of meeting new people and even partners for life. While most of us can observe and relate to these other reasons for coming to work, few realise the extent to which people use work and the other people there to meet their personal, social and psychological needs. Larry Hirschhorn calls this other aspect of organisational life 'The Workplace Within', while Gerard Egan calls it 'The Shadow Side'. This chapter offers you a short insight to this other aspect of the world of work and concentrates on the skills you need for dealing with some of its main manifestations: conflict, stress, grievances and problems which require counselling.

This 'shadow side' of work offers a new range of problems for you to deal with. It also offers you tremendous opportunities to tap and channel the fundamental motivations which different people have.

21.2 CREATING THE WORKING ENVIRONMENT

Although the working environment is more than just the physical environment, there is a relationship between them. If people are happy with the nature of their work and with factors such as recognition, responsibility and opportunities for development, they are likely to be committed to their jobs and not especially concerned about the physical environment. You may have come across teams that worked well and cheerfully in less than comfortable surroundings. You may remember the earlier example of the artist starving in a cold attic room, but content because he can do the work he loves. But when people are dissatisfied with their jobs, for whatever reason, they complain about the physical environment, the organisational environment – such as company policy and supervision style – and salary. You may have come across examples such as people who work in luxurious modern offices but complain because the subsidised canteen only offers two choices of hot meals.

This does not mean that you can ignore complaints about tangible issues such as the physical environment; dealing with such matters may not create satisfaction but it will reduce dissatisfaction, and taking such grievances seriously is a good opportunity to demonstrate that you care. But it does mean that, as well as doing what you can about the overt source of dissatisfaction, you should look for the deeper causes as well. A method for doing this is given later in this chapter. It also means that simply trying to brighten up the physical environment, for example with a new coat of paint or a few potted plants, will not improve the climate of your team if there are more fundamental problems to be resolved.

A physical feature of the workplace which does have a direct impact on the team climate is the physical layout of your building. First of all, where are you? A project manager who sits overlooking the team members gives an impression of very close supervision which will be interpreted as a lack of trust. On the other hand, a project manager who stays in a separate office with the door closed will be seen as out of touch, whose judgements of people and problems will not be given credibility. Secondly, where are the team in relation to each other? If team members sit facing away from each other they will feel isolated and will not communicate as effectively as they would if they were able to see each other easily. On the other hand, this may be desirable if too much communication is getting in the way of work!

Moving away from physical factors, there is much more that you can do to influence the working environment. Several have already been mentioned in this book: encouragement, praise, a clear vision or objectives and career development for all staff who want it. These factors seem obvious and are but it is often the obvious factors which get overlooked. Perhaps the most powerful means of influencing the working climate is to demonstrate the working style you want your team to adopt. This is more than simply setting a good example; it means modelling the style of interpersonal relationships you would like to see. You can model trust by delegating new work to people and giving your permission for people to try new ways of doing things, being willing to take the risk that they may not get it right at first. You can model openness and learning from mistakes by disclosing errors you have made in the past and how you have gained from them. Managers, like parents, do not have to be perfect. You will need to consider how close you want to get to your team: how well do you know them? On what do you base your assessments of them? Other small things you can try are the little social rituals such as doughnuts on Fridays, drinks after work on birthdays, tea and talk at eleven o'clock and monthly awards for the greatest achievement and the greatest foul-up – celebrating the opportunity to learn from it. You will be able to think of other factors influencing a positive climate which you have come across. Try them. Better still, get your team to come up with ideas.

21.3   HANDLING CONFLICT

Earlier chapters have shown that conflict is a normal part of a team's development. Conflict often spawns creativity. Conflict shows people care. But raw conflict can be destructive if it is uncontrolled. It can mutate into personal animosity, with grudges being held and sides being taken. If you take a back seat and let things take their natural course you may find it leads to intractable problems such as these. The solution is to channel the creative energy generated by conflict into joint problem solving. This is especially true when the conflict is between you and someone else. Specific actions you can take are to give both parties an opportunity to present their case without interruption, ask probing questions and invite the other party to give full consideration. Stay neutral yourself and show neutrality in what you say and how you say it. At the very end of the discussion you may choose to abandon your neutral stance and make a decision yourself or you may leave it to your team. Very often you will find that, if you manage the process of debate well, the conflict will have evaporated and been replaced by mutually agreed progress. Don't imagine that you can keep out of conflict within your team – it is your business even if you would rather it were not.

The previous chapter also discussed the particular forms of conflict that arise when some members of your team collude to form an exclusive clique or to identify a bogeyman onto whom they project their dissatisfactions and anxieties. Both of these are really forms of psychological defence mechanisms: people form exclusive cliques when they feel threatened, as cliques give them a fantasy of being safe and special. People outside the clique can see it clearly but those within invariably deny it exists. People blame all their problems on a bogeyman to protect them from feeling responsible for any of their problems themselves. The problem is that those excluded from the clique or picked out as a bogeyman suffer unfairly and the divisions in your team can have long-term negative consequences on your project. Negative consequences include direct obstruction of work and communication and less direct obstruction of career development opportunities, which has an impact on productivity and morale. A section in this chapter deals with counselling and some counselling techniques can help people identify the real cause of their insecurity and so take responsibility for their problems. In particular, you should be prepared to challenge any statement or behaviour which appears to arise from one of these defence mechanisms.

One form of conflict that is often identified is the personality clash. There is such a thing as a personality clash: it occurs when two people have strong and opposite psychological traits and they are not sufficiently mature to recognise the strengths of the opposite type. Using Belbin's team roles identified in the previous chapter, we can say that Innovators and Monitor Evaluators are likely to conflict over the value of an idea and Shapers and Implementers might argue over the pace of work. Two Shapers in a team may clash unless one is happy to take a secondary role. These conflicts reduce when all concerned can recognise that each brings a valuable contribution to the team. Education and training on team dynamics can therefore help as will a focus on a shared objective. Separation is sometimes the only solution. If one individual frequently has clashes with several different people it implies he or she is the source of the problem. Some people seek out conflict as they crave little victories over other people. Such behaviour needs to be confronted. If you can help a team member realise why he or she is seeking out conflict, not only will you have removed a source of strife from your team, you will also have improved their quality of life.

However, many conflicts are blamed on a personality clash when this is not the real cause. Managers may prefer to dismiss conflict as a personality clash because that implies it is no one's fault and the manager could do nothing about it. In reality, the conflict may be one of the types already described or it may have structural origins. Some organisations have conflict designed into them, making destructive confrontation inevitable. A typical error is the splitting of dependent activities into separate functional groups. For example, analysis and programming are both parts of the software development process. Splitting the project into an analysis team and a programming team is a recipe for mutual antagonism. Look at your organisation chart and think about how you share out the work of your organisation: is conflict 'designed in'? If so, consider restructuring your project so that teams are all focused on some ultimate deliverable.

21.4 MANAGING STRESS

The problem of stress at work is starting to receive more and more attention in the medical and management press. It has been related to the greater pressure exerted on enterprises from global competition and to the isolation we feel as a result of communicating by remote rather than intimate means. Because the issue of stress is receiving more attention you probably know a great deal about it already. You may be aware that stress has been linked to diet: a balanced diet without too many additives helps relieve stress. Stress has been linked to drugs: if you are used to more than a small intake of tobacco, alcohol or caffeine you will experience stress as a result, so cut down on tea and coffee. Stress has been linked to lifestyle: a moderate amount of exercise helps reduce stress and it is important to make time for activities outside work such as hobbies and meeting friends and family. This section is not intended to replace such commonly available advice on managing stress that can be obtained from health books and medical professionals; it aims instead to examine certain aspects of stress that relate to a project-based work environment.

We all need some level of stress. Without some pressure there would be less motivation to work and many of us would become bored. The amount of pressure which is comfortable varies from person to person. What this means is that some people take steps to avoid pressure: some look for less stressful jobs while others cope with their pressure by planning their work in order to avoid crises. But many other people like a crisis and, sub-consciously, create them. Work is left until the last minute and so has to be done in a rush; activities are invented which 'have to get done' although they may in fact be of little significance; items are left unorganised so a big show can be made of frantic searches; little problems are exaggerated; there are many sighs, groans and other indications of a person making heroic efforts for the good of the company. This style of hasty activity is sometimes given the noble title of 'fire-fighting' but it has been said that most 'fire-fighters' in this sense are also arsonists! By creating pressure, people get the excitement they want from work. It can also generate a feeling of importance: 'Look how hard I am working – this organisation really depends on me!' 'Look at all the papers on my desk – I have a really heavy workload!' This type of reasoning may be implied in the behaviour of an apparently very busy person with the hope that his or her 'hard work' will be noticed, leading to promo-tion or to the avoidance of redundancy. In many cases, it works. But an effective manager takes a cautious view of people who appear to be constantly busy and knows that effective people have occasional busy periods but most of the time are quietly efficient.

But however effective a project team is and however well planned the project is, the approach of a deadline for delivery can cause a period of high pressure if unforeseen events mean there is a great deal of work to do in a short time. If these circumstances are infrequent and not too long they will do no great harm but you should ensure that your staff have time to relax and at least one day off work every week. Indeed, short bursts of pressure can build team spirit and generate loyalty but only if they are short and not too frequent.

You need to look out for signs of stress in yourself and members of your team. Typical signs are working long hours, irritability, sickness, excess reliance on tobacco or alcohol, creating drama out of minor incidents, destruc-tive criticism of colleagues, a change in behaviour, fatigue and expressions of hopelessness, worthlessness or their opposite: extreme confidence or arrogance. Stress is not simply caused by too much work; too little work, or work that is insufficiently challenging, can be just as stressful. Stress can also be caused by conflict, especially if it becomes harassment or bullying, which must never be tolerated in your team. Lack of a clear job description or job goals can be stressful as can problems outside work. Most project managers are aware that life events such as marriage, divorce, bereavement and the arrival of a baby – especially the sleep deprivation which often comes with it – all bring stress, and allowance for members of their team in these situations must be made. Sensitive project managers are aware that smaller events away from work such as an argument at home, a move and financial problems all bring stress as well. You may be able to provide some help, refer your team member to someone who can give expert advice or simply provide some counselling as described later in this chapter. Even if you cannot help directly, you could temporarily adjust the standards you expect from a team member with stressful problems at home by, for example, allowing some extra time off. Finally, remember that one common source of stress at work is management. The type of problems you could be causing include an inappropriate leadership or coaching style, taking decisions too late or without the involvement of the people affected by them, restricting access to challenging or attractive work or simply demanding too much of your team.

When signs of undue stress have been detected you can select from the great many solutions that are available. A change of diet, more exercise, less exercise, some time off work, counselling, improved job design, training, greater or less delegation, help with planning finances or careers or improved resources at work are all possible means of reducing stress, depending on what is causing it. But very often, the cause and so the solution of stress problems relate to personal organisation and time management. Many people, especially managers, spend more time looking for things than they imagine. They also waste time doing work that should be delegated, supervising too closely, switching between activities and being at formal meetings and informal encounters which they do not need to attend. So attention to the basic personal skills of time management and self-organisation, as well as a recognition that such problems are often a subconscious choice, is often a means for a less stressful life. Some things to do right now: schedule in some time, say one hour a week, to devote to your personal organisation. Clear out drawers, files and cupboards. Throw out old documents. Then devise a better filing system for organising what you have left. When this is done you can reduce the time spent on personal organisation to as little as twenty minutes every week. Next, schedule in some time, perhaps another hour once a week, to devote to planning. This does not mean project planning, which you are no doubt doing already, but personal planning. You might, for example, decide to fix regular slots for dealing with mail and administration. You could spend the time planning how working on your project could be made better for you and your team. You could reconsider your goals or think of new ways of approaching the problems which face you. It is perfectly acceptable to arrange regular slots when you tell everyone you are not available, giving you uninterrupted time to work on these tasks, provided that you agree an equal amount of time when you guarantee you will be available for them. Finally, don't forget to find time to relax. Just a few moments every now and then will help you get through the day without feeling so exhausted at the end.

21.5 HANDLING GRIEVANCES

The handling of grievances is an excellent example of how espoused management practice frequently differs from actual management practice. Ask a manager how he or she deals with grievances and a typical answer might be: 'If someone came to me with a grievance, I'd listen carefully and make sure I had understood. We'd talk the matter over in order to get to the bottom of it. Then I'd consider carefully and, where I thought the grievance was fair and I could do something about it, I would. If there were any aspects of the grievance which I disagreed with, or which I felt I could do nothing about, I would explain my reasoning and hopefully we could come to some compromise.' All very sensible, but far removed from what happens in most cases. Many organisations have a code for the management of grievances but, except where there is a strong trade union presence, would be hard pressed to find a recent instance of it being followed.

First of all, most grievances are never raised with management because the management are not trusted to deal with them fairly. Instead, grievances get expressed between employees in whispered conversations or out of work. This griping lowers morale and does nothing to resolve the grievance, but for the employee it often seems to be the only outlet for complaints. Secondly, this lack of trust is generally quite appropriate. For when grievances are expressed to management, most are ignored, trivialised or generate a defensive reaction. These are all means of avoiding having to recognise that a grievance exists. The grievance is ignored by putting it down as just some 'difficult' person moaning or simply choosing not to notice it at all. It is trivialised by dismissing the complaint as being of no consequence and therefore requiring no management attention. The third approach, the defensive reaction, is worst. It occurs when a member of staff raises a grievance and subsequently receives some form of rebuke or disciplinary interview. These forms of response to a grievance happen because management often cannot bear to believe that anyone in their team might have cause to complain. Just as we often hold idealised images of ourselves, so managers, seeing their project or organisation as an extension of themselves, hold an idealised image of it. Grievances are then seen as a personal attack.

Because people feel their grievances are not being addressed, the problem tends to 'brew up' in their minds. It occupies more and more attention and, probably, discussion time at the coffee machine. Unless the grievance is dealt with effectively, people start to leave, protest in some silent way such as pilfering or arriving late, or the grievance may burst out of its containment in a dramatic row.

How should you handle grievances then? Simply in the manner that everyone knows they should be handled, more or less as outlined at the start of this section. Listen, discuss, then plan. Grievances need not be confrontational; they can be an opportunity for you to improve conditions on your project and attract loyalty. The paragraphs below give some tips for achieving this.

First, reflect on how you have handled grievances recently. If you manage more than a tiny number of people, it is very likely that at least one of them will have had a grievance in the past year. If no grievances were raised, why not? It could be that you are not trusted to deal with them. Find an opportunity to show that you can and, instead of showing outrage, show gratitude that the employee trusted you and gave you an opportunity to improve their conditions of work. If grievances were raised, how did you handle them? Did you take offence and show it, or has the problem been resolved to everyone's satisfaction?

Second, encourage people to raise their grievances so they can be addressed, in the same way that some businesses encourage complaints, as they are an opportunity for improvement. For example, you could regularly include an item in team or individual meetings on 'What's irritating me.' Everyone, including you, uses this as an opportunity to air and discuss grievances.

Third, turn grievances into joint problem-solving sessions. To do this you need to see the grievance as separate from you, your team and your management style. Explore the problem. What does the person with the grievance want? If you can find out what the fundamental problem is you can often delegate its resolution to the person who raised it in the first place.

When people have a personal grievance, such as anxiety over career progress, they will often come to you with a less personal grievance, such as a complaint over a lack of car parking facilities. The reason for this is that problems with career progress are rarely simply other people's fault. The individual probably believes, or fears, that he or she is partially responsible for a slower rate of career progress than that desired. Rather than face this unpleasant possibility, the grievance is subconsciously transferred onto an issue over which the individual cannot possibly have any responsibility, such as some physical feature of the workplace. While the presented problem of car parking should be considered, you also need to explore such grievances to see if there is a deeper, more personal source of dissatisfaction. This requires the use of counselling skills.

21.6 COUNSELLING

Counselling is traditionally seen as a specialist service provided by trained experts to people with some serious problem such as a marital crisis or a bereavement. While these traditional domains of counselling are flourishing, the concept of workplace counselling has recently been receiving much attention. Workplace counselling is provided by people with a lower level of training than professional counsellors but with enough skills and a willingness to help people with everyday problems, such as those which commonly arise at work. This section introduces the concept of workplace counselling and the key skills and attitudes required to do it adequately. No book can

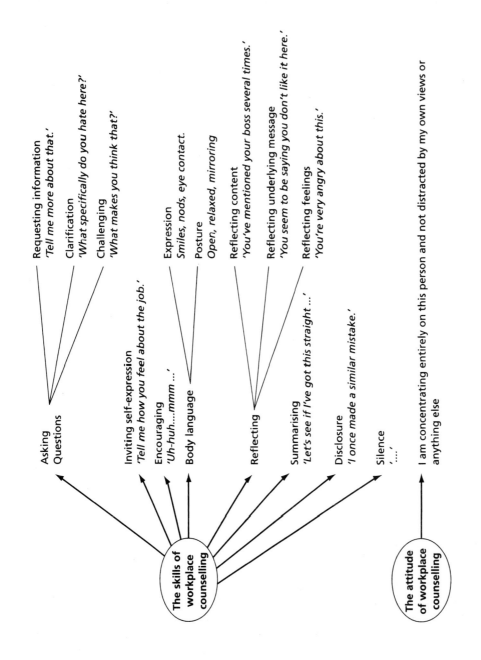

Fig 21.1 Key skills and attitude of workplace counselling

substitute for effective training when it comes to interpersonal skills such as counselling. Fortunately, such training is readily available. Counselling is *not* giving advice, telling people what to do or indeed solving other people's problems at all. Counselling is helping other people to solve their own problems.

This sounds fine but it's not as easy as it sounds. Figure 21.1 shows the key skills, which are described in the paragraphs which follow. Most of us are better at some than others, perhaps because we use them in normal conversation. Other skills feel awkward and new. Therefore it may seem natural to help a person using the sorts of skills that you have always used, the ones that most people tend to use when talking to a person with a problem. Typically, the 'natural' approach is to give advice, as other people's problems always seem easy to solve. Advice giving starts with a statement like: 'What you should do is . . .' or 'If I were you . . .' While giving advice is sometimes the right thing to do, for example when someone comes to you with a straightforward technical question which they cannot answer themselves, very often advice is not only unhelpful, it can be counter-productive. If you always solve your team members' technical problems they will grow dependent on you rather than willing to try their own solutions. When it comes to less technical problems, again advice is occasionally the answer, but you can never fully understand another person's problem and, even if you could, the solution which might work for you might not work for the other person in their circumstances. Your advice might then show your lack of understanding, which can be interpreted as a lack of care. Your advice may simply not be workable in the situation the other person faces which can lead to a state of helplessness: 'No one can solve my problems!' As the other person will have been thinking about the problem much more than you, it is almost certain that any solutions you offer as advice will have been thought of before. Your suggestion of obvious answers will then appear as an insult to their intelligence.

So cast aside your previous approaches to helping people with problems and consider the skills of workplace counselling presented here. The first one is asking questions. Questions can be used to encourage a person to talk about an aspect of their problem and to clarify some of the details. For example, if the person says, 'I hate it here,' you can probe by asking, 'What specifically do you hate?' The other person may not have thought about exactly what the source of their unhappiness is. Your probing with gentle questions like these can help identify the real source. Questions can also be used to challenge implied assumptions and personal perspectives presented as facts. For example, if someone expresses a worry such as, 'I don't know what I should do to help my cousin,' you could challenge the implied assumption with: 'Why do you feel you have to help your cousin?' If someone expresses a fixed perspective by saying: 'Noel is really difficult – he keeps interfering with my work,' you could challenge with: 'Are you sure the problem is entirely Noel's?' Complaints and criticisms about other people always need to be challenged but that does not mean they are always unjustified – you need to probe to find out. Questions can also be used as a more gentle way of suggesting possible solutions if you feel you really have to do this. For example, 'Have you thought of asking him to leave you alone?'

Inviting self-expression is a particularly useful form of question. You can use it to encourage people to consider their feelings about a situation instead of just the facts. Feelings are often at the root of problems and conflict while 'facts' are not as objective as we might imagine.

Encouraging means all those little noises we make which encourage a person to continue. You can also say things like 'Yes ... go on.' Take care in using words like 'Right' and 'OK' as the tone of voice you use can make these words sound like a request for the other person to stop talking rather than continue.

Body language is a big topic and one for which the saying 'A little knowledge is a dangerous thing' is apt. Be very cautious about interpreting another person's body language unless you have had considerable training. But *your* body language can be used to encourage a person to open up, which is what you are trying to achieve when counselling. A relaxed posture, a comfortable amount of eye contact and appropriate responses such as a smile or a raised eyebrow all encourage a person to continue. You may also have noticed that, when two people are in rapport, they tend to adopt similar body postures. This means that, by subtly following the other person's movements, without copying them directly, you can encourage a state of rapport to develop between you.

Reflecting means repeating back a key word or phrase, commenting on what the other person has said or picking up on some unspoken message or feeling you suspect is there from 'reading between the lines'. Simply repeating back a key word or two, as a question, from what the other person has just said will encourage them to say more about it. For example, if the person says 'There seems to be some tension between him and me,' you could respond 'Some tension?' and they will then expand on what is meant. This repeating is something we often do as part of everyday conversation but without realising it. As it is done subconsciously, it may seem a strange thing to do which will not get a good response. Try it – reflecting is one of the best ways to lead a person to disclose what is really on their mind.

Summarising what the other person has said shows you have listened and gives the other person a chance to add to or correct what you have heard. In any work interview or meeting, summarising has a very positive effect. Unfortunately it is not used much, probably because we do not use it with our friends in ordinary conversation. If you want to pick just one new interpersonal skill to work on, you would probably improve your communications skills the most by working on doing more summaries. A summary is a statement like this: 'Right, can I just see if I'm with you so far? You are upset by what you see as Noel's interference; you have acknowledged that from his point of view he is probably just trying to help;

but all the same it irritates you because it makes you feel he doesn't trust your competence. Is that right?'

Making a disclosure about yourself may seem risky, especially if you need to feel in control. But in fact it builds trust; it opens a door for the other person to come through. Making a disclosure does not mean saying, 'I had a similar problem once and this is what I did . . .' as that is the same as giving advice. It means disclosing that you too have problems, have anxieties and have made mistakes. If you do need to feel in control, you could reflect on why that is. Such a feeling can be unhelpful in counselling and many other situations.

Perhaps the most powerful workplace counselling technique is silence. It can feel very awkward to sit in silence even for just a few moments but it gives the other person time to find the words or the courage to say them. Too many managers fill their employees' air time with what they want to say. So be prepared for a silence to hang for a fair while and only fill it when you are sure the other person needs you to break it. Finally, it can be helpful to have a box of tissues nearby. If the other person needs them, just hand them over and give time for recovery without saying anything.

But workplace counselling is more than just a matter of skills. If you simply act out these listening skills without genuinely being interested in the other person your insincerity will show. So forget that car repair bill, ignore your worry over the leaking radiator and suspend all judgements. You are fully available for the other person's problems, views and solutions. This is the attitude of workplace counselling, without which use of the skills is just a hollow sham. This attitude will also help you avoid some of those destructive behaviours that people do without realising it, such as interrupting and making judgements. Only attempt workplace counselling if you have the time and the will to help in this way. Assure the other person that everything they say will be kept confidential and then keep this promise.

The basic idea of counselling is that if you can encourage people to talk their problem through with you, they will have to put vague thoughts into words, answer questions they may not have asked themselves and consider their problem from new points of view. This process helps them to reconsider their problem and come up with their own solutions, to which they will be more committed than any you might have suggested.

Your counselling skills will improve with practice, training and further reading on the subject. You will then be able to use workplace counselling for team-building, coaching, discipline, development and for helping people facing conflict, retirement, redundancy, change and personal problems.

The skills and attitude of workplace counselling are much more effective at helping people to develop than simply telling them how they should change. But it is not always the approach to take. There will be times when there is a problem with an employee's work or behaviour and all your counselling has not led to the person identifying and resolving it. In these cases, use the coaching or reprimand approaches described in Chapter 19. There are occasions when giving advice is appropriate, as described at the start of this section. There may also be occasions when you are out of your depth with basic workplace counselling skills. If a fellow employee has a serious problem, such as one involving drink or gambling, you have to refer them to a counsellor who is better qualified to deal with such issues. You can find such people through your personnel manager, medical professionals or the telephone directory.

21.7 SUMMARY

The last three chapters have examined the human side of project management. People are far more complex and varied than money, yet the training and attention given to people who specialise in the human aspect of work is considerably less than that given to people who specialise in the financial aspect. The human side of project management is fraught with dangers and risks such as conflict, lower morale and even sabotage. On the other hand, managing this aspect of your project presents you with your greatest opportunities for making a real difference and for bringing commitment, motivation, satisfaction and success.

You probably reached the position of project manager through your competence at technical skills, including skills such as planning and monitoring. It is likely that managing people is a new discipline for you. Many project managers choose to ignore it, because deep down they lack confidence in dealing with people problems and even perhaps because they are afraid of getting hurt in the process. You have probably seen such managers and may even have suffered under one. As well as being a key ingredient to the success of a project, the human side of management is a discipline that offers life-long learning opportunities for you. Ignore it at your peril.

21.8 QUESTIONS

1 Consider a project manager with a team of 15 to 20 people: a mixture of analysts, designers, programmers and support staff. The project also uses some specialist staff on a part-time basis. How could the project manager influence the working environment of such a team so as to get the best out of them? What are the behaviours that he or she could exhibit that would have an effect on the working style of the project team?

2 Conflict and stress arise naturally in IS project teams. Some people argue that a little of both is useful, but everyone agrees that too much is destructive. How could you organise your project team to minimise the destructive effect of conflict and stress?

CHAPTER 22

The project manager

22.1 INTRODUCTION

You should by now have a clear idea of the job of the project manager, and you may be asking yourself, 'What sort of person makes a good project manager?' This chapter considers just that question. We've looked at it in a number of ways and set out some ideas for you to consider. We've included:

- One company's vision of the role of the project manager.
- An outside perspective showing what the IS project manager can learn from management in other fields.
- A developmental approach used in one company we have studied.
- How psychometrics can help in the selection of the right person for the job and with the development of the right person once they are in post.
- One company's research into how psychometrics helped.

Together, such an approach to the topic should give you a clear outline of what it's like to be a project manager in an IS environment. And it should also help you to clarify your own idea about your development as a project manager.

22.2 THE VISION

One major international systems company has a vision statement that, for them, sums up what they want every one of their project managers to commit to. They accept that not all of it will be true for all of their project managers all of the time, but they have defined the feeling of the role in a way that everyone who starts managing projects for them knows what is expected of them in terms of attitude and final goal. As you read it, ask yourself if you would want to be seen like this by your manager, your peers, your customers and your team. If the answer is 'yes', then maybe it could be a vision for you as well as for others.

'As a project manager, you are determined to succeed and to bring your project to a successful conclusion – on time, within budget and to the customer's satisfaction. This isn't easy but it is rewarding.

'It's not easy. You have to meet the client's requirements and bring together equipment, software and people to deliver a solution to a problem that hasn't been solved before. You know that equipment will be late, that software will give you problems and that you won't always get the people you need when you need them.

'You accept this. It's no use crying over spilt milk, you have to get on with the job: replan, reorganise, reschedule, reallocate and remotivate. You said that you didn't want a boring job and that you wanted a challenge, an opportunity to shape events, the chance to build your reputation and your company's – well, you got it. Overcoming problems and winning through to the end is part of what turns you on. It feels good to manage a complex issue through to a successful conclusion.

'But you don't have to do this on your own. You are the leader, but it's a team task and a team success. Team spirit, helping people grow and harnessing their skills and enthusiasm is important to you. You have a personal commitment to their development. You manage people well as individuals and as a team. They respond to you and trust your judgement. You enable them to perform.

'Managing projects is what you do best. People know you and you are valued. Each project is different, each a new challenge. You welcome this challenge: it gives you new opportunities to learn. Your contribution is consistently above average, beyond the norm – even in a goal-orientated, customer service industry like ours. You wouldn't have it any other way.'

For us this sums up the essence of being a project manager. Whilst all of the obstacles are perhaps not present in every project, the spirit of this vision statement is uplifting and motivational.

22.3 AN OUTSIDE PERSPECTIVE

Many project managers feel that their role is very different from that of the traditional manager and thus that they can learn very little from old-style management textbooks. Let us examine this in more detail. If we define a project as something with a clear start and finish, as something that brings about change and that has a clearly stated objective, then humanity has been managing projects since the dawn of time. Hunting a woolly mammoth or raising a crop are both projects that conform to this description. Given that, are there many differences between the relatively new discipline of project management and that of older traditional management? Traditional management priorities often centre on control: controlling the team, the task and the individual. Classic texts tell us that the traditional manager has the functions of control, co-ordination, communication and the setting of performance standards. Are these so different from what today's project manager does?

There are some major differences. For example, there are differences in timing:

● Traditional management is continuous while a project is finite.

● Traditional managers expect to stay in post for a considerable length of time while project managers expect to manage a project for a finite length of time.

As well as this, the role of the IS project manager is to create a product – usually a new IS system incorporating hardware and software. The primary tool in this task is the brainpower of the project team. In this the project manager is different from traditional managers whose primary task is often to keep the status quo operational, whether this is to keep the assembly line moving or the office department functioning at full efficiency. Essentially, traditional management is often seen as being repetitive while project management is mostly non-repetitive.

If project managers want to make best use of the skills and abilities of their highly able workforce, they must be willing to give them information so that they can develop a rational understanding of the tasks assigned to them. A skilled software engineer will function much better if he or she knows not just what is required but why it is required. In this way, the software engineer is not only doing the required job but is also quality checking the analysis and design work that was done previously. Again, this is different from traditional management.

While traditional management often looks in great detail at how the workforce should be supervised – with close supervision often being recommended – many, if not all, professional engineers will look for an absence of detailed supervision, freedom from administrative routine where feasible and a working environment which sets him or her free to perform at their best. Naturally, in such an environment, the project manager has to trust the team to go a good job. The degree of control and supervision given so that they can do this good job will be different from many earlier management disciplines.

This shows that there is greater possibility for failure in project management than in traditional management. In traditional management, a manager will establish a closed loop in which staff performance is noted and measured, compared with performance standards and then any necessary corrective action is taken.

Particularly during the initial stages of an IS project, the analysis and design phases, the project manager is often flying blind. The degree of risk and uncertainty will vary from project to project, but all projects will contain some risk, and many are highly risky. Nothing exactly the same as this piece of work has been attempted before, so the project manager often faces real difficulty – in spite of all the tools and techniques – in predicting the outcomes of the work being done, and has the additional problem of knowing that any mistakes will have profound and perhaps costly consequences later in the project.

If there are differences between traditional management and IS project management, are there similarities between general project management, which has been a recognised discipline for over 50 years, and IS project management? Consider the following extract from an article published in the *Harvard Business Review* in 1959. It is by Paul Gaddis and is a classic early discussion of the emerging role of project management in hi-tech industries:

> 'Generally speaking, the project manager's business is to create a product – a piece of advanced-technology hardware. The primary tool available to him is the brain-power of men who are professional specialists in diverse fields. He uses this tool in all the phases of the creation of his product, from concept through the initial test operation and manufacturing stages.'

The article then goes on to address many of the issues current today: what does the project manager do, what kind of person is he, what training is required? So, in almost 40 years of examination we're still puzzling over the same issues. Like leadership, perhaps project management isn't the simplest job in the world! As an illustration of how the world keeps on reinventing the same old wheel, we came across a definition of project management and a list of the skills of a project manager produced quite recently by a well-respected international body.

A project was defined as 'a set of interrelated activities, with an agreed start and finish time, that is undertaken by an organisation in order to meet defined objectives within the constraints of time, cost and resources at specified quality requirements' and a project manager as 'the individual to whom authority, responsibility and accountability have been assigned for the overall management of resources – including the technical, time and cost aspects – of a project, and the motivation of all of those involved'.

When looking at the project manager in this context, those skills that will make a good project manager together with the attributes and skills which the project manager should develop to ensure the effectiveness of the team and the individuals in that team were described. There is much here that reflects the work of Gaddis all those years ago, much that reflects the engineering disciplines and the contractual nature of the project manager's role, and much that is currently occupying present-day thinking about the development of project managers. These skills are:

- *Leadership:* project managers should be able to stimulate action, progress and change.
- *Technological understanding:* project managers need too have an accurate perception of the technical requirements of the project so that business needs are addressed and satisfied.
- *Evaluation and decision making:* project managers should have the ability to evaluate alternatives and to make informed decisions.
- *People management:* project managers should be able to motivate and enthuse their teams and have a constant personal drive towards achieving the project's goals.
- *Systems design and maintenance:* project managers should be able to demonstrate their individual competence and have a complete working knowledge of the internal administration of their project.

- *Planning and control:* project managers should be constantly monitoring progress against the plan and taking any necessary corrective action using modern planning and monitoring methods.

- *Financial awareness:* project managers should be proficient in risk management and have a broad financial knowledge.

- *Procurement:* project managers should understand the basics of procurement and be able to develop the procurement strategy for their project.

- *Communication:* project managers should be able to express themselves clearly and unambiguously in speaking and writing and be able to do this in a wide range of situations and with a wide range of people.

- *Negotiating:* project managers should be skilful in managing their clients and should be able to plan a negotiation strategy and then carry it out.

- *Contractual skills:* project managers must be able to understand the contract that defines their project and should be able to manage subcontractors to ensure that the contractual terms are met.

- *Legal awareness:* the project manager should have an awareness of any legal issues that could affect the project.

22.4   A DEVELOPMENTAL APPROACH

It is clear that in any project team the project manager is the key figure. However, as we have seen, although there is no standard project in our industry, there are, however, certain skills and qualities of project managers which can contribute materially to the success of any project with which they are associated. These are increasingly called competences, but they are often little more than the list above: groups of abilities and talents which shape the way the project manager does the job and so have an impact on the whole project. We can get a better grasp of these skills, abilities or competences if we break them down into four key areas. The skills and qualities that project managers use to manage:

- Themselves, such as time management.

- Their one-to-one interactions, such as negotiation skills.

- Their one-to-many interactions, such as with their team.

- The task, such as monitoring.

Let's look at them one by one, staring with self-management. Anyone setting out to manage the complexity of a project must be able to manage their own self. Many of the key qualities and skills for self-management are identified in Fig 22.1.

In addition, it is expected that a project manager provides the strength of character and the vision to keep the project on course. Along with this would go the ability to be seen as a respected and commanding figure within the team, the company and the customer's organisation. This won't come out of

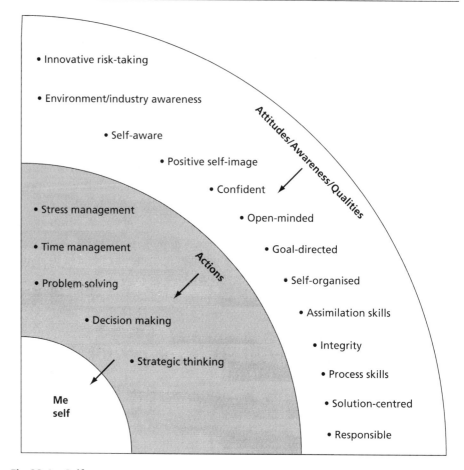

Fig 22.1 Self-management

thin air, but it is often something that can be fostered in new project managers by their seniors. Without role-models, it is unlikely any aspiring project manager will ever learn what leadership looks like in their organisation. The project manager will set the tone for all of the interactions on the project. In every interaction, those who are involved learn the way the project manager does things – and this then becomes the project way of doing things.

Dealing with people on a one-to-one basis is a major part of the project manager's job. Sometimes these interactions will be with customers, sometimes with subcontractors, sometimes with project members; sometimes they will be with more senior staff, sometimes with junior staff. Regardless of who they interact with, project managers must be seen to be professional and competent by all who watch them. Many of the key qualities and skills are shown in Fig 22.2.

Project managers frequently need to deal with large groups of people, for example in meetings or when giving presentations. Many feel anxious at the thought of presenting to a potentially critical audience, but the skills involved

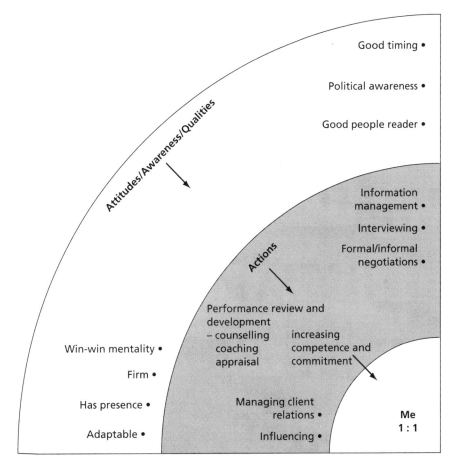

Fig 22.2   One-to-one interactions

in doing so are an important part of the role. Also, the project manager will want to support the team wherever possible, but must be able to be authoritarian and critical where necessary. A judicious mixture of praise and control will be appreciated by all the team. As the leader of the project, it is the project manager who will drive, guide and motivate the team and gives it direction. Doing this well will enable the project manager to command the respect of the team. Figure 22.3 shows many of these key qualities and skills.

Everything described so far is of no use at all if the project manager does not manage the task adequately. Good communication and excellent self-organisation are no substitute for the planning, monitoring and control processes that the project manager will create. The effectiveness of these areas will be the key to the outcome of the project. So the project manager must be a capable planner, with the ability to identify the work to be done as well as the checks and balances needed to manage and control it. These key tasks are shown in Figure 22.4.

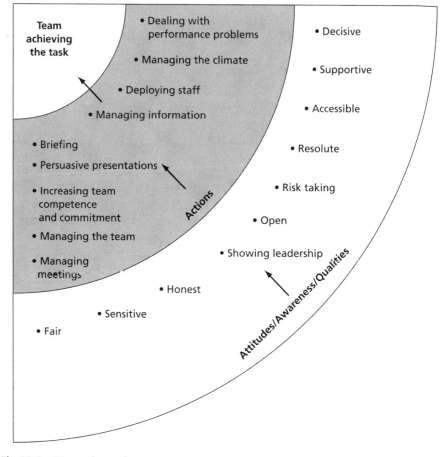

Team
achieving
the task

• Dealing with
  performance problems

• Managing the climate

• Deploying staff

• Managing information

• Briefing

• Persuasive presentations

• Increasing team
  competence
  and commitment

• Managing the team

• Managing
  meetings

• Honest

• Sensitive

• Fair

• Decisive

• Supportive

• Accessible

• Resolute

• Risk taking

• Open

• Showing leadership

Actions

Attitudes/Awareness/Qualities

Fig 22.3 Managing others

22.5 USING PSYCHOMETRIC ASSESSMENT

There is a truism: projects don't fail – people do. And in companies that are project-led, nowhere is this more evident than in the selection and development of project managers. As will be obvious by now, a good project manager, well-supported by more senior management, can mean the difference between the success and failure of the whole project. You will know for yourself that when you are most committed to the work you are doing and when you are most productive, there will be a number of factors at play. One of the most significant factors for most people is that intangible one known as job satisfaction. For most of us this means a feeling of being challenged and of meeting the challenge; of working with others and helping them to give of their best as they help us give of our best; of feeling positive about the work we are doing and the way we are doing that work.

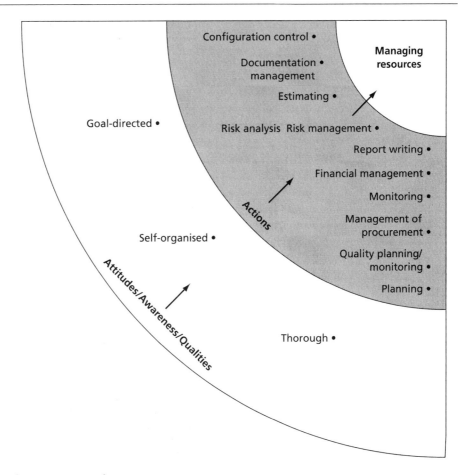

Fig 22.4   Managing resources

The Institute of Personnel and Development published in early 1996 a study of staffing in UK companies. Their data gave turnover figures indicating that, on average, organisations can expect to replace the equivalent of their entire part-time staff every three to four years and to replace their full-time staff every six to seven years. If staff are unhappy, they will leave – if they can – more quickly than this. For each person who leaves, another has to be recruited, selected, trained, and so on. How much will this cost your company each year? The Institute's data also demonstrated that the loss of just one professional – like an experienced IS specialist – costs, on average, £23 000. So it can be a costly business to replace staff, and there are other, hidden costs. The wrong person in the job will make mistakes while in post, is likely to miss opportunities or perhaps foolhardily commit the company to supplying something they cannot deliver.

From this it is clear that we need to ensure that:

● Companies must get the right people in the job as project manager.

- Companies must support, train and develop them on the job so that they perform well and have a satisfying job, ensuring that they want to stay with the company.

How can this be done easily and economically? Psychometrics can help, especially with selection and recruitment.

Psychometrics is often thought of as a buzzword, with many people using the results being unclear about what it really means. But with over 80 per cent of Britain's companies claiming to use them for recruitment, it is a good idea to outline their usefulness. Psychometrics are often called psychometric tests, as if somehow they could tell who were 'good' candidates for a job and who were 'poor'. It's more accurate to talk of psychometric measures or psychometric instruments, as many of them do not have 'passes' or 'failures'. They cannot distinguish between good and bad candidates – only a person can do that – but what we get from a reputable psychometric instrument is objectivity: correctly administered, there will be standardised conditions for carrying out the psychometric, standardised instructions, time, content, scoring and interpretation. This objectivity means that direct comparisons can be accurately made, both with other candidates for a job and with an appropriate comparison group. And this means a greater likelihood of selecting the best candidate for the job.

There are three main types of psychometrics: tests of maximum performance or ability tests, measures of typical performance such as personality questionnaires, and interest inventories. Together these three can tell us a great deal about someone, and provide information that it would be almost impossible to gain through interviews. Let's look at them one by one and consider how they could be used to help in the selection and development of project managers.

Ability tests

There are two main types of ability tests (note that these are true tests, because it is possible to set a pass mark), attainment tests and aptitude tests. Attainment tests measure the results of formal training and are little used. Many employers simply check that a person has a particular educational qualification, and that can be done much more easily than by a test. Aptitude tests measure the ability of the person to acquire further knowledge or skills in a particular area. These are much more widely used. They are very good at measuring how good someone is in a particular skill area, such as verbal critical reasoning. If it is essential that the successful candidate is good at drawing inferences quickly and accurately from written text, then this is a good test to use. Ability tests are not all paper-and-pencil tests. Simulations such as in-tray exercises are becoming increasingly popular, especially at senior management levels. Here the candidates are presented with a pile of letters, memos and items of background information. They are required to deal with this in a specified time and are awarded scores on abilities such as organising, forecasting, decision-making and written communication.

Interest inventories

Interest inventories contain a wide sample of questions which might cover hobbies, school or university work, previous work experience or general life experiences and measure the direction in which an individual may want their career to go. Interest inventories are particularly used in career counselling, and as such are particularly useful when someone is thinking of changing career – after all, that person may be able to do the job but would they enjoy doing it and would they stay in post? In both sales and management, for example, research evidence suggests that potentially effective managers may be identified by a specific pattern of likes and dislikes.

Personality questionnaires

In many cases, the most important and useful type of psychometric measure is the personality questionnaire. Since personality is defined as 'a person's typical or preferred ways of behaving, thinking and feeling', you can see how important personality is in determining how well or badly someone might do their job. If you were drawing up a list of the characteristics you would want in a good project manager, you may well use something like this list which is used by a major airline:

- *Influence/Leadership.* Able to take charge and control a group towards an objective. Makes their presence felt in groups. Motivates subordinates, delegates effectively and monitors performance.
- *Communication skills.* Able to comprehend and express ideas accurately and persuasively both orally and in writing.
- *Organising/Planning.* Able to think ahead, prioritise and organise work. Is able to structure activities and meet targets within appropriate budgets.
- *Motivation/Energy.* Shows energy, drive and enthusiasm. Maintains a high output. Proactive and ambitious.
- *Creativity.* Generates and is receptive to new ideas. Seeks to innovate rather than necessarily accept the established solution.
- *Analytical.* Reasons objectively and critically with both verbal and numerical problems. Comprehends and processes information at a high level of complexity.
- *Empathy.* Able to understand the strengths, weaknesses, views and feelings of others. Supports others and is a good team member.
- *Emotional maturity.* Responds well to criticism. Frank and open. Able to take pressure.
- *Decision making.* Having the confidence to take own decisions. Being prepared to take a balanced risk and be held accountable for the outcome.
- *Commercial awareness.* An interest in, and understanding of, the financial and profit implications of actions taken. A hard-headed concern for the bottom line.

Look closely at each characteristic described here. How many of the qualities asked for are aspects of personality? Just in case you were wondering, every characteristic asked for in this list could be measured accurately by psychometric measures, leaving it up to the skilled interviewer to determine who would be the best for the job from a range of people who could all do it well. Research conducted with companies has established that up to 70 per cent of attributes associated with success at work are dimensions of personality rather than ability. Looked at in this way, it becomes vitally important to be able to measure these attributes in an objective and accurate way. From the point of view of the would-be project manager, the same considerations apply. Few people would want to pin their hopes of a successful career on something which would be unsuitable, so the earlier a person can find out a career which best suits their strengths, the better.

One company we worked with has used psychometrics to test out the profiles of its project managers. Firstly those managing project managers were asked to list the qualities that they greatly valued in the most effective of their project managers. The project managers were then 'tested' to see whether they exhibited what was sought after by their bosses. The qualities that were most important to their managers were:

political awareness

being a good people reader

being good at negotiations

giving persuasive presentations

being good at influence

having a positive presence and confidence.

Next in order of importance were:

responsible leadership

risk-taking

innovative, problem-solving

strategic thinking

self-organised

goal-directed thoroughness.

Least important, though still of above average importance, were:

assimilation skills

good decision-making

a win-win mentality

being supportive

being tough

being good at time management

being open-minded

sensitive.

The following list shows what was actually found. Each quality has a number beside it, between one and ten. Five is an average score for a group of managers, so we would expect all of the good project managers to be scoring five or more in each of the qualities their managers value.

In the first group were:

political awareness	5
being a good people reader	5
being good at negotiations	5
giving persuasive presentations	5
being good at influence	5
having a positive presence and confidence	5

Interestingly, for all that these were the most important to their managers, the project managers were no better than average.

Next on the list were:

responsible leadership	8
risk-taking	3
innovative, problem-solving	6
strategic thinking	7
self-organised	7
goal-directed thoroughness	7

In this group, our project managers were mostly above average. The exception is in risk-taking. Further research indicated that the group of managers actually wanted what they called 'a safe pair of hands', someone who could be trusted with a major project. When they were initially talking about risk, what they really wanted was intellectual risk – innovation, in other words.

The least important list showed:

assimilation skills	9
good decision-making	6
a win-win mentality	6
being supportive	7
being tough	5
being good at time-management	4
being open-minded	6
sensitive	5

Here again, we have almost the same picture. In many of these areas, the project managers were above average. Two attributes are particularly worthy of mention. In assimilation skills, we found that verbal skills were higher than mathematical skills, reflecting the fact that managing a project often involves having to read and understand long, complex documents.

In time management, what came to light was that many of the project managers – enough to skew the average score considerably – were highly involved in the detail of their projects. This frequently meant that they were unable to carry out all of their own work in the allotted time. Those who were asked about this all admitted that it was a failing, but felt that the project could be at risk if they did not devote their attention to this level of detail.

What does this research actually tell us? Well, it validates the perceptions of those who select, train and manage project managers in the company where the research was done. There was a company feeling that they knew what a good project manager was, and this tested out: looking at the 20 key competencies, the project managers came out below average in only three. In addition, this tells us that psychometrics measure what good project managers actually do, and can give us a yardstick to help establish whether someone new to the job would find it a satisfying career.

22.6 SUMMARY

We've looked here at the role of the project manager in a number of ways, and in each way the results have led to a similar conclusion. In one sense, we have gone full circle from the vision of the project manager at the start of this chapter to the list of qualities with numeric scales beside them which also describe a good project manager.

In each part of the chapter there is another important message: some things about the job can be learned – like learning how to negotiate effectively, learning how to motivate the team or learning how to understand a contract, while other things are inbuilt. Anyone can learn the basic skills of managing a project, a few people, the right people, can go much further. And this is not just because they have the skills, it is also because they have the aptitude for career project management.

22.7 QUESTIONS

1 How does the 'vision of the project manager' in this chapter relate to the way you see the job? Are there aspects of the job that don't appear in the vision? Why might that be?

2 Consider the skills and qualities of project managers described in 'the developmental approach'. Can you add to these? How far do you see yourself being proficient in these skills? How could you develop further?

GLOSSARY OF PRINCE TERMS

Acceptance Letters Acceptance letters are written during the final stages of a project. It is possible to have a maximum of five letters but there must always be at least two. The two essential letters are the *User Acceptance Letter* and the *Business Acceptance Letter*. The User Acceptance Letter is written by the project manager or the stage manager on behalf of the Project Board and records that the system meets the user acceptance criteria. The Business Acceptance Letter is written by the Executive (see Fig 3.1) on the Project Board after reviewing the delivered project at the end of the final stage.

Other letters are the *System Acceptance Letter*, the *Operations Acceptance Letter* and the *Security Acceptance Letter*. The first of these, the System Acceptance Letter, is produced at the end of systems testing to show that the system has successfully met the system test requirements and is ready for user acceptance testing. It is prepared by the stage manager or by the project manager on behalf of the senior technical member of the Project Board. The Operations Acceptance Letter confirms that the system complies with the operations acceptance criteria. In a distributed system or a system that is to be run at many locations, the operations manager at each site will prepare it. In some circumstances a Security Acceptance Letter will also be required. It confirms that the system complies with the security acceptance criteria, and is prepared by the Executive on the Project Board.

Activity Network A diagram showing the various project activities, put into a logical sequence, taking into account the *dependences* between activities.

BAC See *Business Assurance Co-ordinator*.

Baseline Baseline is a term used in *configuration management* (see glossary item below). It is a snapshot of the current stage of a *configuration item*. The very first baseline will therefore be established by the specification of the item. Subsequent baselines will occur when there is an important change in how the item is represented as it is transformed in the design and coding process.

Business Assurance Co-ordinator The Business Assurance Co-ordinator is one of the roles on the Project Assurance Team. It is the focal role for all administrative controls and is responsible for planning, monitoring and reporting on all of the business assurance aspects of the project. More information about this role is in Section 3.4.

Checkpoint A checkpoint is one of the regular control points in PRINCE. Control is exercised through the checkpoint meeting which is conducted by the Project Assurance Team. The meeting provides the information used to measure actual performance against plan. The output from a checkpoint meeting is a *Checkpoint Report*.

Configuration A configuration is a description of something. It was first used to describe the collection of hardware devices that made up a hardware system. The PRINCE definition of a configuration however is that it is the complete technical description of everything that is required to 'build, test, accept, install, operate, maintain and support a system.' It includes all the documentation about the system as well as the system itself.

Configuration Control This is the process of evaluating, approving and co-ordinating all of the changes proposed to configuration items. Configuration management and configuration control on a large project may warrant the need for a *configuration librarian*.

Configuration Item A configuration item is a component of a configuration. It could be something quite small such as a piece of code shared by several programs (the formula for a tax calculation, for example), or something larger such as the hardware and software for a local area network. Whatever its size, however, it is of sufficient importance to be subject to *configuration management*.

Configuration Management Configuration management is the process of identifying and controlling changes to configuration items.

Control points There are four control points that are found within all stages of a PRINCE project:

- *End-Stage Assessment*
- *Mid-Stage Assessment*
- *Quality Review*
- *Checkpoint*.

Dependency A relationship between two activities whereby one activity cannot start until the other has been completed. Dependences therefore constrain the sequence in which a project may be executed.

End Stage Assessment An End Stage Assessment is made at the end of every stage of a project and is a mandatory control point. There is a formal presentation to the Project Board of the current status of the project and of the plans for the next stage.

ESA See *End-Stage Assessment*.

Exception Plan An exception plan is produced by the Project Manager whenever it is apparent that the *tolerances* assigned to the project are likely to be exceeded. The exception plan is considered by the Project Board and, if approved, will take the place of the original Stage Plan for the remainder of that stage.

Executive The Executive is a member of the *Project Board* and normally chairs the Board. The Executive reports to the *IT Executive Committee* and is responsible for ensuring that the project meets its defined business objectives within the set constraints of budget and timescale.

Highlight Report Highlight Reports are produced at the end of each reporting period by the project manager. These reports record progress to date and highlight any problems encountered during the period and any problems anticipated.

Impact Analysis Impact analysis is connected with the process of *configuration management*. It is the name given to the process of assessing the impact of making a change to the existing system.

Individual Work Plan Individual Work Plans are created by team leaders for the individual members of their teams. They are the lowest level of technical plan.

IS Steering Committee This body is responsible for setting the IS strategy for a department or organisation. It therefore identifies opportunities to use information technology to further the organisation's business objectives.

IT Executive Committee This group is responsible for initiating individual projects that support the IS strategy. For each project, it appoints the *Project Board* and sets the project's Terms of Reference.

MSA See *Mid-Stage Assessment*.

Mid-Stage Assessment This is an optional control point. A Mid-Stage Assessment can be called at any time during a stage by the Project Board. The PRINCE standard guides suggest that typical reasons might be the need to authorise work to begin on a subsequent stage before the completion of the present stage, to make decisions about unplanned situations, or to have a review part-way through a long stage.

Off Specification Report This documents all circumstances where the delivered system fails to meet its specification. They are often also prepared after a Quality Review to note errors that have been detected but not corrected during the immediate follow-up period.

PAT See *Project Assurance Team*.

PBS See *Product Breakdown Structure*.

PFD See *Product Flow Diagram*.

PRINCE **PR**ojects **IN** **C**ontrolled **E**nvironments. A structured method for the management and control of IS projects; it is being developed further for the management of projects in other disciplines.

Product Activities in PRINCE focus on the planning and control of project products. A product is any item of hardware, software or documentation produced at any time during the lifetime of the project. PRINCE identifies three kinds of products: *management products* that are produced as part of the management of the project; *technical products* that actually make up the system; and *quality products* that are produced for the quality system or by it.

Product Breakdown Structure All *products* are identified in a Product Breakdown Structure that shows their relationship in an hierarchical way. This is described in more detail in Section 4.4.

Product Description A definition of a *product*, including its purpose and composition and the quality criteria that will be applied to it.

Product Flow Diagram Project This shows how the products are produced. It is produced from the *Product Breakdown Structure* and is described in more detail in Chapter 4. It may seem strange to offer a definition of a 'project' in a book about the project management of information systems, but as much of the book uses the PRINCE methodology as an example, it would be incomplete not to give the PRINCE view of a project. Projects have five characteristics. They are concerned with the *production of products*, and there is a *set of activities* to produce these products. To produce these products, *resources will be consumed* within the *finite lifespan* of the project and under the *control of the organisation structure* set up for the project.

Project Assurance Team The Project Assurance Team helps the project manager to preserve the continuity of project development activities and the integrity of the products being produced.

Project Board Most computer system development projects are run by project leaders or project managers under the overall supervision of some kind of co-ordinating committee. Generically these are often referred to as Steering Committees. With the PRINCE project management methodology however this overall supervisory role is very clearly defined, and is exercised by the Project Board. The Project Board has three roles: an executive role which is filled by a senior manager and which chairs the Board, a senior user role that represents the user interests, and a technical role that represents those parts of the organisation that are responsible for the technical implementation of the system. The term 'Steering Committee' is usually reserved for the IS Steering Committee which is a top management group responsible for the overall direction of an organisation's information systems strategy.

Project Closure At the end of the whole project, it is formally approved and signed off by the *Project Board*. The Project Closure Meeting is usually combined with the *End-Stage Assessment* for the final project stage.

Project Evaluation Review This document is produced as input to the *Project Closure* process. It records the lessons learned from the project and thus contains valuable guidance that can be used when planning future projects.

PID See *Project Initiation Document*.

Project Initiation Document This document is prepared by the Project Manager and the Project Assurance Team and is approved by the *Project Board* at the start of the project. It sets the boundaries and objectives for the project, and typically includes:

- Terms of reference
- Acceptance criteria
- Project organisation and responsibilities
- Project plans
- Plans for the first stage of the project
- A statement of the business case
- An assessment of the business risks associated with the project
- Product descriptions
- Project issue report.

Quality Review Quality Reviews check that products meet an agreed set of quality criteria. The reviews are run by a chairman, and have a presenter and several reviewers.

RFC See *Request for Change*.

Request for Change This is a formal proposal to change the specification of the system. It is prepared by the Project Manager based upon a *Project Issue Report*. If the proposed change may be accommodated within the tolerances assigned to the project, the change may be approved by the Project Manager; otherwise, it may give rise to an *Exception Plan* and has to be approved by the Project Board.

Senior Technical A member of the *Project Board*, the Senior Technical Member represents the interests of the developers of the proposed information system.

Senior User A member of the *Project Board*, the Senior User represents the interests of the users of the proposed information system.

Stage PRINCE requires that all projects be subdivided into stages. A Stage has a defined set of *products* and is a defined piece of work that can be managed. A stage is managed by a stage manager.

TAC See *Technical Assurance Co-ordinator*.

Technical Assurance Co-ordinator A member of the *Project Assurance Team*, the Technical Assurance Co-ordinator is responsible for defining the technical standards to be used in developing the project's products and also for planning, monitoring and reporting on the technical conduct of the project.

Technical Exception This is an unplanned event which may affect one or more of the project's products. In the first instance, the Technical Exception is dealt with by raising a *Project Issue Report*. This may then lead to a *Request for Change* or to an *Off-Specification Report*.

Technical Plan A plan showing the technical and quality activities that will be completed against a timescale. Technical Plans may be created at Project, Stage or Detailed levels.

Tolerance Tolerances are set by the IT Executive Committee or by the Project Board for the project as a whole or for a stage within a project. They describe the variations from plan that can be permitted without further reference to the setting body. The project manager and the stage manager then manage the project within these tolerances.

UAC See *User Assurance Co-ordinator*.

User Assurance Co-ordinator This is a role in the project assurance team and represents the user role in the development of the project.

BIBLIOGRAPHY

Introduction

The following is a selective list of the books and other documents that the authors have found useful over the years in their own practice of project management and to which they have returned in preparing the current book. We have classified the publications into a number of headings but this is, to some extent, arbitrary and an individual book will often contain valuable insights that could equally well appear under other headings.

Change, business strategy and information systems

Corporate Culture, Charles Hampton Turner (Piatkus)

Understanding your organisation's character, Roger Harrison in *Harvard Business Review*, May/June 1972

The Gods of Management, Charles Handy (Souvenir Press)

Managing at the Speed of Change, Darryl Conner (Villard Books)

Managing IT at Board Level, Kit Grindley (Pitman Publishing)

Strategic Management, Gordon E Greenley (Prentice-Hall)

Strategic Management and Information Systems, Wendy Robson (Pitman Publishing)

Five Ps for strategy, Henry Mintzberg, in *California Management Review*, 1987

How competitive forces shape strategy, Michael E Porter, in *Harvard Business Review*, 1979

The 7-S framework, Robert Waterman, Thomas Peters and Julian Philips, in *Business Horizons*, 1980

General project management

Managing High Technology Programs and Projects, Russell D Archibald (Wiley Interscience)

The Management of Projects, Peter W G Morris (Thomas Telford Ltd)

Project Management, Dennis Lock (Gower)

Successful Project Management, Milton D Rosenau, Jr (Van Nostrand Reinhold)

IS project management

Principles of Software Engineering Management, Tom Gilb (Addison-Wesley)

The Mythical Man-Month: Essays in Software Engineering, Frederick P Brooks Jr (Addison-Wesley)

PRINCE manuals, NCC Blackwell

Introducing PRINCE, Colin Bentley, NCC Blackwell

Practical PRINCE, Colin Bentley, NCC Blackwell

Project planning, scheduling and estimating

Software Engineering Economics, Barry W Boehm (Prentice-Hall)

Controlling Software Projects, Tom De Marco (Prentice-Hall)

Cost Estimation for Software Development, Bernard Londeix (Addison-Wesley)

Sizing and Estimating Software in Practice: Making Mk II Function Points Work, Stephen Treble and Neil Douglas (McGraw-Hill)

Estimating with Mk II Function Point Analysis, Ian Drummond (HMSO)

Quality

Quality is Free, Philip B Crosby (McGraw-Hill)

Software Quality Assurance & Management, Michael J Evans and John J Marcinak (Wiley-Interscience)

Design and code inspections to reduce errors in program development, Michael Fagan, in *IBM Systems Journal* No 3, 1976

Risk management

Risk Analysis for Large Projects, Dale Cooper and Chris Chapman (Wiley)

Software Engineering Risk Analysis and Management, Robert N Charette (McGraw-Hill)

Software Risk Management, Barry W Boehm (Computer Society Press)

Value engineering and value management

Value Engineering: the Organised Search for Value, L W Crum (Longman)

Techniques of Value Analysis and Engineering, L D Miles (McGraw-Hill)

Beyond value engineering: SMART value management for building projects, Stuart D Green, in *International Journal of Project Management*, February 1994

Sales, negotiation and customer management

Strategic Selling, Robert Miller and Stephen E Heiman, (Kogan Page)

Account Strategy for Major Sales, Neal Rackham (Gower)

Making Major Sales, Neil Rackham (Gower)

Getting to Yes, Roger Fisher and William Ury (Hutchinson)

Everything is Negotiable, Gavin Kennedy (Arrow)

The Skills of Negotiating, Bill Scott (Wildwood House)

Professional Service Firm Management, David Maister, in *Journal of Management Consulting*, 1989

Negotiation Skills, Fenman Training, Clive House, The Business Park, Ely, Cambridgeshire, CB7 4EH

For more information about the Buyer's Cycle: Huthwaite Research Group, Hooker House, Wentworth, Rotherham, S62 7SA

Leadership, performance and teamworking

Working in Organisations, Andrew Kakabadse, Ron Ludlow and Susan Vinnicombe (Penguin)

Great Leaders, John Adair (Talbot Adair Press)

Management and Organisational Behaviour, Laurie J Mullins (Pitman Publishing)

The Leadership Challenge, James Kouzes and Barry Posner (Jossey-Bass)

The Alchemy of Leadership, Keith Grint

How do you motivate employees?, Frederick Hertzberg, in *Harvard Business Review*, January–February 1968

How to choose a leadership pattern, Robert Tannenbaum and Warren Schmidt, in *Harvard Business Review*, May–June 1973

Management Teams: Why They Succeed or Fail, R Meredith Belbin (Butterworth-Heinemann)

Understanding Organizations, 4th edn, Charles Handy (Penguin)

Leadership and the One Minute Manager, Blanchard, Zigarmi and Zigarmi (Fontana)

The working environment

Working the Shadow Side, Gerard Egan (Jossey-Bass)

The Workplace Within, Larry Hirschhorn (MIT Press)

Journals

Project, magazine of the Association of Project Managers, APM

International Journal of Project Management, Butterworth-Heinemann

INDEX